Lesson Plans

# Physical Education
for
# Elementary
# School Children

eighth edition

## Glenn Kirchner
Simon Fraser University

## Christine Tipps
University of Wisconsin-Oshkosh

 **WCB** Wm. C. Brown Publishers

ISBN 0-697-12639-0

Printed in the United States of America by Wm. C. Brown Publishers
2460 Kerper Boulevard, Dubuque, IA 52001

10 9 8 7 6 5 4 3 2

# Contents

# Introduction

This guide has been written to assist classroom teachers of grades kindergarten through six in sequentially planning their own physical education programs. Part 1 explains how to develop a yearly instructional program and how to adapt the sequential units in this resource manual to a variety of local teaching conditions.

Parts 2, 3, and 4 are resource sections for three different instructional units in the elementary school. Part 2, "Game Activities," contains a sequential series of detailed lessons for each of the developmental levels (I, II, and III). Developmental Level III utilizes separate units for each of the major team game activities. Part 3, "Gymnastic Activities," and Part 4, "Dance Activities," contain sequential lessons for each of the developmental levels as well. All lessons are written to meet the developmental levels of student ability and interest.

On the right-hand side of each lesson are specific references to Kirchner, *Physical Education for Elementary School Children,* eighth edition, Wm. C. Brown Publishers, Dubuque, Iowa, 1992. These references will provide clarification, illustrations, and descriptions of skills and related activities.

# Designing Yearly Programs, Units, and Daily Lesson Plans

**Part** 1

This section describes how to plan and develop a physical education program by completing the following sequence of steps.

Step 1:  Establish the Basic Purpose and Objectives of Physical Education
Step 2:  Select General Activity Areas and Appropriate Units
Step 3:  Adapt Units to Individual Teaching Conditions
Step 4:  Adapt Lesson Plans of Each Unit to Your Own Teaching Situation

The steps in this process explain how to select activity areas and units of instruction from this guide, how to adapt each unit to local teaching conditions, and how to expand or modify the lesson plans of each unit to meet the unique instructional requirements of each teacher. Complete the suggested tasks for each step before progressing to the next step in the process.

## Step 1:  Establish the Basic Purpose and Objectives of Physical Education

The philosophy of a physical education program is normally expressed in a general statement such as the one presented in the accompanying chart. Most school districts will provide this type of statement in their curriculum guides or will accept statements issued by state or national physical education organizations. To complete the first part of step 1, copy the appropriate statement or write your own purpose of physical education in the space provided.

**Purpose of Physical Education**

_____
_____
_____
_____
_____
_____
_____
_____
_____
_____
_____
_____
_____
_____
_____
_____
_____

## Stating Purposes, Objectives, and Learning Outcomes

General statement explaining the **Purpose** of physical education

expressed in terms of statements of the basic **Objectives** of physical education

translated into **Learning Outcomes** for each unit of instruction

**Example Statements**

**Purpose**
"The basic purpose of physical education is to assist each child to develop his or her optimum level of health and well-being and to acquire the attitudes, knowledge, and movement skills that will lead to lifelong participation in enjoyable and wholesome physical activities."
*Kirchner, 8th ed., ch. 1*

**Objectives**
1. To enhance physical growth and development.
2. To develop and maintain optimum physical fitness.
3. To develop body management and useful physical skills.
4. To develop positive personal and social development.
5. To develop wholesome recreational skills.
6. To foster intellectual growth.
7. To develop creative talents.
8. To develop a positive self-image.
9. To provide enjoyment through play experiences.
10. To develop an understanding and appreciation of human movement.
*Kirchner, 8th ed., ch. 1*

The second part of step 1 is to state the *basic objectives* you wish to accomplish in your full year's physical education program. The objectives listed in the chart are similar to those stated by most national, state, and local physical education associations. These objectives, however, should be carefully analyzed and, wherever necessary, modified or expanded to clearly reflect the nature and unique emphasis of your own instructional program. The objectives you state in the space provided should be used as the criteria for the development of your yearly program, units, and daily lesson plans.

**Objectives of the Instructional Program**

1. _____
2. _____
3. _____
4. _____
5. _____
6. _____
7. _____
8. _____
9. _____
10. _____

These objectives should also be used as guidelines for all other aspects of your program, such as selection and emphasis of teaching strategies, organizational procedures, and evaluative techniques.

## Step 2: Select General Activity Areas and Appropriate Units

This guide contains three general activities of games, dance, and gymnastics. Under each of the three developmental levels (I, II, III) shown in the accompanying chart, there are two or more units for each activity. Each unit contains a series of detailed lesson plans. Any lesson within each unit may be expanded to two or more lessons according to the ability of the class or the specific interest of each classroom teacher.

To complete step 2, choose the activities that you will teach during the year and estimate the approximate amount of time you will devote to each unit of instruction. A blank Yearly Program Planning Sheet is provided on page 11 of this guide. A sample teaching situation is also provided to illustrate how a third-grade teacher completed this task. Teachers need only insert their own information on the blank Yearly Program Planning Sheet as they follow Ms. Brown's model (p. 10).

## How to Complete the Yearly Program Planning Sheet

There are three closely related parts of the Yearly Program Planning Sheet that *must* be completed according to the following sequence.

### Complete A. Time and Space Allotment (p. 11).

According to our example, Ms. Brown (see page 10) has—

    a. three, thirty-minute P.E. periods each week in the gymnasium throughout the year (36 teaching weeks × 3 or 108 P.E. lessons);

    b. one or two *possible* thirty-minute lessons outside (36 or 72 possible lessons outside);

    c. one or two *definite* fifteen-minute classroom lessons (36 or 72 definite lessons in classroom).

According to your teaching situation, fill in the appropriate figures below and the space provided on the top of your Yearly Program Planning Sheet (p. 11).

    a. P.E. periods in gymnasium per week

_____ × _____ = _____

_____

| number of available periods in the gymnasium per week | number of teaching weeks in year (to calculate teaching weeks divide total number of school days in year by five) |
|---|---|

    b. P.E. periods outside

_____ × _____ = _____

_____

| number of available periods outside per week | number of teaching weeks |
|---|---|

    c. P.E. periods in classroom

_____ × _____ = _____

_____

| number of available periods in classroom | number of teaching weeks |
|---|---|

Total number of physical education    _____

periods in the school year    _____

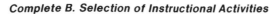

***Complete B. Selection of Instructional Activities***

To complete this section, review each of the teaching units containing the appropriate developmental levels. As soon as you have a general idea of each unit, begin filling in the required information under each column of the Yearly Program Planning Sheet.

According to Ms. Brown's checks (p. 10) under each column and written comments, she has reviewed each chosen unit of instruction and indicated where some problems may arise. For example, she is concerned about the high risk of gymnastic activities and her generally low level of teaching competence in this activity. This will require more preparation and perhaps the elimination of the more high-risk gymnastic skills that she feels unsure of teaching. She sees the importance of creative dance activities, but also notes the low interest on the part of her class. The latter will require a review of more creative and appropriate teaching strategies when teaching this activity.

***Determine C. Length of Units***

On the basis of the information contained under "Teacher-Learner and Administrative Considerations," choose the appropriate number of lessons you wish to devote to each unit. As a general guideline, begin this process by first allocating equal time to game, dance, and gymnastic activities. This is accomplished by giving 30 percent of *all* available instructional time to each of the game, gymnastic, and dance activities and holding 10 percent of the total time as a reserve block of available time.

In Ms. Brown's situation, as shown on page 10, she has scheduled six teaching units. Under "Game Activities" she decides to allocate fifteen gymnasium classes and five outdoor classes to unit 1. At this stage she has not used the available periods for gymnastic and dance activities. As each unit develops, she may add one or more lessons or, depending on the needs and interests of her class, develop new units.

## Summary of Step 2

Step 2 is one of the most important steps in the development of a yearly program. During this part of the planning period, each teacher is required to immediately translate her or his stated goals into meaningful units of instruction. This process requires the teacher to almost simultaneously review each unit suggested for his or her grade level, plus the appropriate chapters in the textbook. The main point is *review* each section (not remember every lesson or section in the text) to make a tentative selection of units as well as determine their approximate length. The Yearly Program Planning Sheet provides the basic structure of the teacher's yearly program. Modification of each respective unit plus the addition of new material can be done during the instructional year. Step 3 will explain how each unit can be organized and taught to meet a variety of unique teaching, learning, and administrative considerations.

## Ms. Brown's Yearly Program Planning Sheet (Sample Teaching Situation)

**A. Time and Space Allotment**

| | No. of P.E. Periods | (a) In Gym—3 | (b) Outside—1 | (c) Classroom—1 | Total Periods |
|---|---|---|---|---|---|
| **Teacher** Ms. Brown | **Length of Period** | 30 minutes | 30 minutes | 36 classroom | = 108 + 36 + 36 |
| **Grade** 3 | **Number of P.E. Lessons** | 36 teaching | 36 periods | periods | = <u>180 periods</u> |
| **No. of Children** 26 | (School weeks in year: | weeks × 3 periods | outside | | |
| | 180 ÷ 5 = 36) | per week = 108 | | | |

### Teacher-Learner and Administrative Considerations

| B. Selection of Instructional Activities | Page In Guide | Value | | Student Interest | | Safety Risk | | Teacher Competence | | Facilities (comments) | Equipment | C. Length of Unit No. of Lessons | |
|---|---|---|---|---|---|---|---|---|---|---|---|---|---|
| | | High | Low | High | Low | High | Low | High | Low | | | | |
| **Game Activities** | | | | | | | | | | | | | |
| Unit 1: Ball Skills (hand-eye) | 00 | x | | x | | | x | x | | adequate | class sets of balls | 20 | |
| Unit 2: Ball Skills (foot-eye) | 00 | x | | x | | | x | x | | adequate | class sets of balls | 20 | 40 lessons |
| **Gymnastic Activities** | | | | | | | | | | | | | |
| Unit 1: Gymnastics (Level 1) | 00 | x | | x | | x | | | x | adequate | small equipment sufficient | 15 | |
| Unit 2: Gymnastics (Level 2) | 00 | x | | x | | x | | | x | | large equipment limited | 15 | 30 lessons |
| **Dance Activities** | | | | | | | | | | | | | |
| Unit 1: Folk Dance | 00 | x | | x | x | | x | | x | adequate | need music tapes | 9 | 24 |
| Unit 2: Creative Dance | 000 | x | | | | | x | | x | adequate | need tapes | 15 | lessons |

Review and choose units from developmental level II.

In terms of your stated goals.

In terms of their needs and interests.

Consider their age, in relation to nature and activity.

Consider your teaching skills and experiences in each activity area.

Consider quality and quantity of facilities and equipment: Describe situation for each unit.

Attempt to provide a balanced program of activities.

| Work Sheet | | % | Number of Days | Calculations | |
|---|---|---|---|---|---|
| 180 periods | Games | 30 | 54 days | 180 | |
| 30-minute lessons | Gymnastics | 30 | 54 days | × .3 | |
| 5 lessons/week | Dance | 30 | 54 days | 54 | |
| | Not Scheduled | 10 | 18 days | | 180 |
| | | 100% | 180 days | | .10 |
| | | | | | 18 |

## Yearly Program Planning Sheet

**A. Time and Space Allotment**

Teacher _____

Grade _____

No. of Children _____

No. of P.E. Periods

Length of Period

No. of P.E. Lessons

(a) In Gym _____  _____  _____

(b) Outside _____  _____  _____

(c) Classroom _____  _____  _____

Total Periods _____

Duplicate or modify this sheet to meet individual needs

| B. Selection of Instructional Activities | Page In Guide | Teacher-Learner and Administrative Considerations | | | | | | | | | C. Length of Unit |
|---|---|---|---|---|---|---|---|---|---|---|---|
| | | Value | | Student Interest | | Safety Risk | | Teacher Competence | | Facilities (comments) | Equipment | No. of Lessons |
| | | High | Low | High | Low | High | Low | High | Low | | | |
| **Game Activities** | | | | | | | | | | | | |
| Unit 1: | | | | | | | | | | | | |
| Unit 2: | | | | | | | | | | | | |
| Unit 3: | | | | | | | | | | | | |
| Unit 4: | | | | | | | | | | | | |
| **Gymnastic Activities** | | | | | | | | | | | | |
| Unit 1: | | | | | | | | | | | | |
| Unit 2: | | | | | | | | | | | | |
| Unit 3: | | | | | | | | | | | | |
| **Dance Activities** | | | | | | | | | | | | |
| Unit 1: | | | | | | | | | | | | |
| Unit 2: | | | | | | | | | | | | |
| Unit 3: | | | | | | | | | | | | |
| Unit 4: | | | | | | | | | | | | |
| **Other Activities** | | | | | | | | | | | | |
| Unit 1: | | | | | | | | | | | | |
| Unit 2: | | | | | | | | | | | | |
| Unit 3: | | | | | | | | | | | | |

| Work Sheet | Activities | % | Number of Days | Calculations |
|---|---|---|---|---|
| _____ periods | 1. _____ | | | |
| _____ -minute lessons | 2. _____ | | | |
| _____ lessons/week | 3. _____ | | | |
| | 4. _____ | | | |
| | 5. _____ | | | |

## Step 3: Adapt Units to Individual Teaching Conditions

The completed Yearly Program Planning Sheet (see p. 11) indicates the types of activities to be taught and the assigned number of lessons for each respective unit. Step 3 explains three different ways to schedule units in a one-year physical education program.

There are three basic ways to organize and schedule the units of instruction provided in this manual. The Solid Unit, shown in the accompanying chart, is the most commonly used unit in the upper elementary grades. The length of this unit may vary from one to six weeks depending on the nature of the activity, available facilities, and other related factors. Next, the Modified Unit provides for a major emphasis on one activity and a minor time allotted to one or more other activities. This type of unit provides enough flexibility for teachers of any grade level to cope with virtually all learning or administrative considerations. Finally, the Multiple Unit is perhaps the most adaptable to early primary children. This type of unit, however, requires a lot of preparation, constant shifting of apparatus and, all too often, a loss of continuity within each activity area (8th edition, p. 104).

### Types of Units

| Solid Unit | Modified Unit | Multiple Unit |
|---|---|---|
| Teach one type of activity for *all* of the lessons in a unit—<br>1. to provide continuity;<br>2. when facilities and equipment are only available in large blocks of time;<br>3. when teacher and student interest is high;<br>4. when large apparatus is involved (example: setting up gymnastic apparatus in gym for three solid weeks to allow for maximum use during each period);<br>5. when weather permits. | Teach one activity for the *majority* of lessons in a unit—<br>1. to provide continuity with periodic breaks for variety;<br>2. to cope with weather conditions by allowing one or two "floating" optional outside lessons in another activity. | Teach *two or more* activities concurrently—<br>1. to allow a variety of activities to be taught within a single lesson or from day to day;<br>2. for flexibility—inside on wet days and outside on dry days;<br>3. to adjust to the short attention span of primary children. |

Step 3 will continue the same process as shown in the previous step. Each teacher should complete one of the accompanying Unit Scheduling Sheets (pp. 15–19) using the solid, modified, or multiple method of scheduling units of instruction. The following illustration will assist in scheduling your own program.

*Example: Ms. Brown's Grade 3: Three periods per week.* (Note: In the following example no physical education is scheduled for Tuesday and Thursday of each week.)

In Ms. Brown's Unit Scheduling Sheet (p. 14) we have illustrated how her selected units from the Yearly Program Sheet (p. 10) can be scheduled in three different ways. For example, the first solid unit of games begins in week two of September and continues until the end of the second week in October. With three scheduled physical education periods per week, it will take her five teaching weeks to complete this unit. If you refer to the game unit 1, developmental level II, on page 42, you will note there are only seven lessons in this unit. However, *each* lesson may be expanded to two or more lessons as illustrated at the side of each lesson. Ms. Brown's understanding of the class's level of ability was the basis of the estimated fifteen lessons to complete this unit. The "extra" eight lessons (unit 2—developmental level II) were used to expand any one of the successive detailed lessons according to the needs or unique interests of her class.

A variation of this unit is shown immediately below the illustrated solid unit. The only difference in the second example is that the first three units of games, gymnastics, and dance are taught alternately for one-week blocks of time. Some teachers may elect to follow this approach to provide variation, yet keep a major emphasis on one type of activity for a full week.

The modified unit (p. 16) is quite similar to the solid unit with the exception of *interspersing* other types of activities throughout this unit. Other activities may be lessons from different units or special activities such as orienteering, new games, or hash running. The latter activities may be just for fun and variety or as a means of testing the interests of the class.

The last type of unit shown on the Unit Schedule Sheet is the multiple unit. This involves concurrently teaching three different units of instruction. As illustrated in the chart on page 18, the first lesson of games unit 1 (developmental level II) is taught on Monday, followed by lesson one of dance unit 1 (developmental level II) and lesson one of gymnastics unit 1 (developmental level II). A similar pattern should be followed in each succeeding class until each unit is completed.

## Complete Step 3

These three basic ways of organizing units of instruction have respective strengths and weaknesses. Duplicate sufficient copies of the appropriate unit worksheet provided on pages 15 to 19 in order to plan a full year's instructional program.

## Ms. Brown's Unit Scheduling Sheet

Example: Ms. Brown, grade 3, three P.E. periods (30 minutes) per week. *Note:* This illustration does not include any other scheduled time.

**Ms. Brown's units selected from developmental level II.**

| | September October | November | December | January | February March | April | May | June |
|---|---|---|---|---|---|---|---|---|
| | 1 2 3 4 1 2 3 4 | 1 2 3 4 | 1 2 3 4 | 1 2 3 4 | 1 2 3 4 1 2 3 4 | 1 2 3 4 | 1 2 3 | 4 |
| **Solid Unit** Complete all lessons in each unit before starting a new activity. | Games Unit 1 (15 Lessons) | Gymnastics Unit 1 (15 Lessons) | Dance Unit 1 (9 Lessons) | Xmas Holi-days / Games Unit 2 (15 Lessons) | Gymnastics Unit 2 (15 Lessons) | Dance Unit (15 Lessons) | Swim Unit 1 (9 Lessons) | Games Unit 3 (15 Lessons) |

**Solid Unit**

Example: 3 physical education lessons per week

| **or Variation of Solid Unit** |
|---|
| Complete lessons 1–3 of games unit during week two of September. Follow with lesson 1–3 of gymnastic unit 1 during week three and lessons 1–3 of dance unit 1 during week four. Repeat rotation until first three units are completed. |

1 2 3 4 1 2 3 4 1 2 3 4 1 2 3 4 1 2 3 4 1 2 3 4 1 2 3 4 1 2 3 4 1 2 3 4 1 2 3 4

Games Unit 1, 3 Lessons / Gymnastics Unit 1, 3 Lessons / Dance Unit 1, 3 Lessons / Games Unit 1, 3 Lessons / Gymnastics Unit 1, 3 Lessons / Dance Unit 1, 3 Lessons / Games Unit 1, 3 Lessons / Gymnastics Unit 1, 3 Lessons / Dance Unit 1, 3 Lessons / Games Unit 1, 3 Lessons / Gymnastics Unit 1, 3 Lessons / Games Unit 1, 3 Lessons / Gymnastics Unit 1, 3 Lessons

Continue alternating games, gymnastics, and dance for one-week blocks of time to the end of the school year.

---

**Modified Unit**

Example: 4 physical education lessons per week

| | September October | November | |
|---|---|---|---|
| | 1 2 3 4 1 2 3 4 | 1 2 3 4 | 1 2 3 4 ... |
| **or Modified Unit** Teach 80 to 90 percent games and remaining percentage to gymnastics or dance activities. | Games Unit 1: 15 lessons for games interspersed with 2 gymnastics and 3 dance lessons. | Gymnastic Unit 1: 15 lessons for gymnastics interspersed with 2 dance lessons. | |

**Modified Unit 1: Example Week 1**

| Monday | Tuesday | Wednesday | Thursday | Friday |
|---|---|---|---|---|
| Games Unit 1 Lesson 1 | Gymnastics Unit 1 Lesson 9 | Games Unit 1 Lesson 2 | No P.E Scheduled | Games Unit 1 Lesson 2 |

---

**Multiple Unit**

Example: 5 physical education lessons per week

| | September October | November | |
|---|---|---|---|
| | 1 2 3 4 1 2 3 4 | 1 2 3 4 | 1 2 3 4 ... |
| **or Multiple Unit** Teach one game, one gymnastics, and one dance lesson, then repeat cycle. | | | |

**Multiple Unit: Example Week 1**

| Monday | Tuesday | Wednesday | Thursday | Friday |
|---|---|---|---|---|
| Games Unit 1 Lesson 1 | Dance Unit 1 Lesson 1 | Gymnastics Unit 1 Lesson 1 | Games Unit 1 Lesson 2 | Dance Unit 1 Lesson 2 |

**Solid Unit Worksheet**

Schedule unit 1 of your program by blocking out the number of weeks required to complete the unit. Continue pattern with each unit throughout the year.

| September | October | November | December | January | February | March | April | May | June |
|---|---|---|---|---|---|---|---|---|---|
| 1 2 3 4 | 1 2 3 4 | 1 2 3 4 | 1 2 3 4 | 1 2 3 4 | 1 2 3 4 | 1 2 3 4 | 1 2 3 4 | 1 2 3 4 | 1 2 3 4 |

**Variation of Solid Unit**

First, plan two or more solid units of game, dance, or gymnastic activities. Block game lessons for week 1, gymnastic lessons for week 2, and dance lessons for week 3. Continue pattern until the last lesson of each unit has been completed. Adjust any part of this system to meet local conditions.

| September | October | November | December | January | February | March | April | May | June |
|---|---|---|---|---|---|---|---|---|---|
| 1 2 3 4 | 1 2 3 4 | 1 2 3 4 | 1 2 3 4 | 1 2 3 4 | 1 2 3 4 | 1 2 3 4 | 1 2 3 4 | 1 2 3 4 | 1 2 3 4 |

## Modified Unit Worksheet

First, set aside the number of reserved days for other activities at the bottom of each week. Next, schedule a modified unit, as if it was a solid unit, into the available but shorter teaching weeks. Schedule in the other activities in the reserved days of the unit. Continue pattern to end of year.

|  | September | | | | October | | | |
|---|---|---|---|---|---|---|---|---|
|  | Week 1 | Week 2 | Week 3 | Week 4 | Week 1 | Week 2 | Week 3 | Week 4 |
|  | M T W Th F | M T W Th F | M T W Th F | M T W Th F | M T W Th F | M T W Th F | M T W Th F | M T W Th F |
| **Main Unit** | | | | | | | | |
| **Reserved Days** | | | | | | | | |

|  | November | | | | December | | | |
|---|---|---|---|---|---|---|---|---|
|  | Week 1 | Week 2 | Week 3 | Week 4 | Week 1 | Week 2 | Week 3 | Week 4 |
|  | M T W Th F | M T W Th F | M T W Th F | M T W Th F | M T W Th F | M T W Th F | M T W Th F | M T W Th F |
| **Main Unit** | | | | | | | | |
| **Reserved Days** | | | | | | | | |

|  | January | | | | February | | | |
|---|---|---|---|---|---|---|---|---|
|  | Week 1 | Week 2 | Week 3 | Week 4 | Week 1 | Week 2 | Week 3 | Week 4 |
|  | M T W Th F | M T W Th F | M T W Th F | M T W Th F | M T W Th F | M T W Th F | M T W Th F | M T W Th F |
| **Main Unit** | | | | | | | | |
| **Reserved Days** | | | | | | | | |

|  | March | | | | | | | | | | | | | | | | | | | | April | | | | | | | | | | | | | | | | | | | |
| --- | --- | --- | --- | --- | --- | --- | --- | --- | --- | --- | --- | --- | --- | --- | --- | --- | --- | --- | --- | --- | --- | --- | --- | --- | --- | --- | --- | --- | --- | --- | --- | --- | --- | --- | --- | --- | --- | --- | --- | --- |
|  | Week 1 | | | | | Week 2 | | | | | Week 3 | | | | | Week 4 | | | | | Week 1 | | | | | Week 2 | | | | | Week 3 | | | | | Week 4 | | | | |
|  | M | T | W | Th | F | M | T | W | Th | F | M | T | W | Th | F | M | T | W | Th | F | M | T | W | Th | F | M | T | W | Th | F | M | T | W | Th | F | M | T | W | Th | F |
| Main Unit |  |  |  |  |  |  |  |  |  |  |  |  |  |  |  |  |  |  |  |  |  |  |  |  |  |  |  |  |  |  |  |  |  |  |  |  |  |  |  |  |
| Reserved Days |  |  |  |  |  |  |  |  |  |  |  |  |  |  |  |  |  |  |  |  |  |  |  |  |  |  |  |  |  |  |  |  |  |  |  |  |  |  |  |  |

|  | May | | | | | | | | | | | | | | | | | | | | June | | | | | | | | | | | | | | | | | | | |
| --- | --- | --- | --- | --- | --- | --- | --- | --- | --- | --- | --- | --- | --- | --- | --- | --- | --- | --- | --- | --- | --- | --- | --- | --- | --- | --- | --- | --- | --- | --- | --- | --- | --- | --- | --- | --- | --- | --- | --- | --- |
|  | Week 1 | | | | | Week 2 | | | | | Week 3 | | | | | Week 4 | | | | | Week 1 | | | | | Week 2 | | | | | Week 3 | | | | | Week 4 | | | | |
|  | M | T | W | Th | F | M | T | W | Th | F | M | T | W | Th | F | M | T | W | Th | F | M | T | W | Th | F | M | T | W | Th | F | M | T | W | Th | F | M | T | W | Th | F |
| Main Unit |  |  |  |  |  |  |  |  |  |  |  |  |  |  |  |  |  |  |  |  |  |  |  |  |  |  |  |  |  |  |  |  |  |  |  |  |  |  |  |  |
| Reserved Days |  |  |  |  |  |  |  |  |  |  |  |  |  |  |  |  |  |  |  |  |  |  |  |  |  |  |  |  |  |  |  |  |  |  |  |  |  |  |  |  |

**Multiple Unit Worksheet**

Activity 1 _____ Unit _____ Lessons _____
Activity 2 _____ Unit _____ Lessons _____
Activity 3 _____ Unit _____ Lessons _____

First, plan two or more solid units of games, dance, or gymnastic activities. Teach the first lesson of games unit 1, followed by the first lesson of dance unit 1, then, if necessary, the first lesson of the gymnastic unit. Continue repeating cycle on each available day until the last lesson of each unit is completed.

| | September | | | | October | | | |
|---|---|---|---|---|---|---|---|---|
| | Week 1 | Week 2 | Week 3 | Week 4 | Week 1 | Week 2 | Week 3 | Week 4 |
| | M T W Th F | M T W Th F | M T W Th F | M T W Th F | M T W Th F | M T W Th F | M T W Th F | M T W Th F |
| Activity | | | | | | | | |
| Unit No. | | | | | | | | |
| Lesson No. | | | | | | | | |
| Guide Reference | | | | | | | | |

| | November | | | | December | | | |
|---|---|---|---|---|---|---|---|---|
| | Week 1 | Week 2 | Week 3 | Week 4 | Week 1 | Week 2 | Week 3 | Week 4 |
| | M T W Th F | M T W Th F | M T W Th F | M T W Th F | M T W Th F | M T W Th F | M T W Th F | M T W Th F |
| Activity | | | | | | | | |
| Unit No. | | | | | | | | |
| Lesson No. | | | | | | | | |
| Guide Reference | | | | | | | | |

| | January | | | | February | | | |
|---|---|---|---|---|---|---|---|---|
| | Week 1 | Week 2 | Week 3 | Week 4 | Week 1 | Week 2 | Week 3 | Week 4 |
| | M T W Th F | M T W Th F | M T W Th F | M T W Th F | M T W Th F | M T W Th F | M T W Th F | M T W Th F |
| Activity | | | | | | | | |
| Unit No. | | | | | | | | |
| Lesson No. | | | | | | | | |
| Guide Reference | | | | | | | | |

| | March | | | | April | | | |
|---|---|---|---|---|---|---|---|---|
| | Week 1 | Week 2 | Week 3 | Week 4 | Week 1 | Week 2 | Week 3 | Week 4 |
| | M T W Th F | M T W Th F | M T W Th F | M T W Th F | M T W Th F | M T W Th F | M T W Th F | M T W Th F |
| **Activity** | | | | | | | | |
| **Unit No.** | | | | | | | | |
| **Lesson No.** | | | | | | | | |
| **Guide Reference** | | | | | | | | |

| | May | | | | June | | | |
|---|---|---|---|---|---|---|---|---|
| | Week 1 | Week 2 | Week 3 | Week 4 | Week 1 | Week 2 | Week 3 | Week 4 |
| | M T W Th F | M T W Th F | M T W Th F | M T W Th F | M T W Th F | M T W Th F | M T W Th F | M T W Th F |
| **Activity** | | | | | | | | |
| **Unit No.** | | | | | | | | |
| **Lesson No.** | | | | | | | | |
| **Guide Reference** | | | | | | | | |

## Step 4: Adapt Lesson Plans of Each Unit to Your Own Teaching Situation

Virtually every elementary physical education class will vary in ability levels, available equipment, and the number and length of each period. Because of these and many other considerations, the recommended lessons within each unit should be considered *themes*. Each theme, in turn, is capable of expanding or contracting to meet one or more of these teaching or administrative variations. The following example will illustrate how Ms. Brown uses each lesson as a flexible guideline in planning each lesson throughout her first unit instruction.

**Ms. Brown's First Week**

On Monday of the first week, lesson 1 was fairly successful in terms of "activities" completed. The class completed 1 and 2 of part 1 and 1 through 4 in part 2, leaving time to play a tag game in part 3.

**Games Unit 1: Solid Unit (see p. 14)**
(see p. 14)

| Monday | Tuesday | Wednesday | Thursday | Friday |
|---|---|---|---|---|
| 30-minute physical education class | | 30-minute physical education class | | 30-minute physical education class |
| Lesson 1, page 43, *Part 1:* Completed 1 and 2 *Part 2:* Completed 1, 2, and 3 and Simple Dodge Ball | No physical education scheduled | Lesson 1a, *Part 1:* Completed 1, 2, and 3 *Part 2:* Completed Simple Dodge Ball and Fly Trap | No physical education scheduled | Lesson 2, page 45, *Part 1:* Completed 1 and 2 *Part 2:* Completed 1, 2, 3, and 4 and completed Place Kickball |

The second lesson on Wednesday would indicate a need to relax a bit, and so the teacher started with a good warm-up, then shifted to part 2 to allow the children to enjoy a couple of vigorous and enjoyable games. Friday's lesson is similar to the first lesson on Monday, with quite a bit covered in each part of the lesson.

This illustrated week should indicate to all teachers that not everything within each lesson needs to be covered. Follow the general progression from lesson to lesson and use your own judgment with respect to the selection and emphasis within each part of the lesson.

For each unit that you select from the appropriate section in this guide, begin with lesson 1. On the basis of the amount you have covered, tentatively plan your next lesson. Continue this process until you have a good idea regarding how much you can actually cover in a typical lesson. When you reach this point, it is possible to plan the remaining lessons within your first unit. Follow the same procedure for the next one or two units. Generally speaking, by the third or fourth unit, you will be able to outline each lesson, allowing a few spare periods to "catch up" or add some ideas that you or your class may feel appropriate.

## A Final Note

The scope and sequence of each unit in this manual follows a reasonable progression of skill development as well as an increase in student freedom and commensurate responsibility. As you progress through each respective unit, do not hesitate to make notes on each lesson to indicate problem areas or better ideas either from your own experiences or from other resources.

# Game Activities

# Game Activities
## Developmental Level I
## Unit 1: Manipulative / Movement Skills

## Expected Learning Outcomes

**Psychomotor Skills**

1. Traveling and stopping
2. Performing animal-like movements
3. Moving safely
4. Traveling with individual parts of the body leading
5. Changing speed
6. Changing direction
7. Balancing small equipment on parts of body
8. Running, jumping, and landing
9. Throwing an object with different parts of the body
10. Catching a ball or object with different parts of the body
11. Bouncing a ball with different parts of the body

**Cognitive and Affective Knowledge and Skills**

1. Meaning of "section places"
2. Meaning of "personal" and "general" space
3. Understanding rules of simple games
4. Moving with care and concern for other members of the class
5. Meaning of directional movements
6. Names of parts of the body
7. Ability to work with a partner
8. Ability to develop a simple creative game
9. Ability to share ideas with a partner

**Level I** **Unit 1:** Manipulative/Movement Skills
**Lesson 1.** Running and stopping
**Main Theme** Traveling and stopping
**Subthemes** Personal and general space; Animal and mechanical movements
**Equipment** No equipment necessary

**Additional Lessons** The following lesson outlines will illustrate how each teacher might spread one lesson over two or three days to expand upon various parts before progressing to lesson 2.

| Content | Teaching Strategies | References | Lesson 1a | 1b | 1c |
|---|---|---|---|---|---|
| **Entry Activity** | Leave out. Begin free play activities in lesson 2. | Free practice, p. 106 | | | |
| **Part 1: Introductory Activities** (*5 to 6 minutes*) Finding personal space —understanding the meaning of "section places" —listening and moving to verbal commands —moving safely | Organize children into four groups. Call them "section places" or give them your own name. Tell the children the four boxes represent the outer boundaries of their playing area. Marking off a designated playing area indoors or outdoors is very helpful in controlling the class and in giving verbal commands. Explain on command "go," children in "section 1" must walk quickly, without touching anyone or anything, and find their own space in the playing area. Wait a few seconds then call "section 2, 3, and 4." Call children back and repeat procedure. Finally, let all move at the same time. *Note:* This basic organizational procedure, particularly for Level I children, will take several lessons to establish. Lesson 1 simply sets the stage. Repeat this procedure several times during the next three or four lessons. | Teaching strategies, p. 124 Teaching game activities, p. 259 Planning a lesson, p. 106 | Repeat finding section places. | Repeat finding section places. | Repeat finding section places. |
| **Part 2: Skill Development** (*15 to 25 minutes*) Traveling and stopping —walking and stopping —animal and mechanical movements and stopping —running and stopping | When children are scattered and standing in their own personal spaces, pose the following questions: 1. "Can you walk around in your own space without touching anyone?" As the children start walking the teacher should also walk to a new location and call "stop." 2. "Now, see if you walk anywhere in the playing area without touching anyone." Wait a few moments then call "and stop." 3. "See if you can walk like a giant." Choose one or two to demonstrate to the class. Continue this challenge changing from a giant to a lame puppy, a robot, and so on. 4. Repeat 3, but change the walk to a run. *Note:* Do not always choose the "best" performer to demonstrate a particular skill or movement pattern. Choosing the less-talented performers provides an opportunity to help their self-images. These games will enhance the main skills of this lesson: 5. Games: *Simple Tag*—This game develops running, dodging, and tagging skills. One child is "it" and tries to tag others. *Mousetrap*—This game develops running and dodging skills. Children are chosen to be mice and the rest form a circle trap. When the trap is open, the mice move in and out. On the signal, "snap," the trap closes. Any mice caught in the trap join the circle and play continues until all mice are caught. | Skill development, p. 44 Games, p. 260 Simple Tag, p. 263 Mousetrap, p. 264 | Repeat 1 and 2. | Repeat 1, 2, and 3. | From scattered position, repeat 4. |
| **Part 3: Closure** (*1 to 3 minutes*) Section places Listening | Stress moving quickly to section place. Stress importance of listening to teacher. | Closure, p. 107 | Play one or two games. | Play one or two games. | Play one or two games. |

Equipment Boxes — Section Places

23

**Level I    Unit 1:** Manipulative/Movement Skills
**Lesson 2.** Directions
**Main Theme** Change of direction
**Subthemes** Running and stopping: Individual parts leading
**Equipment** A variety of small equipment (8½" balls, individual ropes, etc.) placed in four containers

**Additional Lessons** An understanding of the concept of "change of direction" is important. Where necessary, continue with a few more lessons as outlined below before moving to lesson 3.

| Content | Teaching Strategies | References | Lesson 2a | 2b | 2c |
|---|---|---|---|---|---|
| **Entry Activity** | Prior to lesson 2, the general routine of changing, moving into section places, and listening to the teacher's commands should be reasonably well established. Explain to the children that as soon as they are changed, they may select one piece of equipment and play with it in their own space (boxes of equipment already set out in four corners). When everyone has changed say, "put equipment away and go to your section places." | | Repeat free play activities. | Repeat free play activities. | Repeat free play activities. |
| **Part 1: Introductory Activities** *(5 to 6 minutes)*<br><br>Running and stopping<br>Traveling with individual parts of the body leading | While children are sitting in section places, tell them you would like to see them run, using all the space, no bumping, and to listen for your next challenge (or task). "Go." Wait a few moments then call "stop." Present the following sequence of challenges:<br>1. "Can you travel with your fingers leading? Your side leading? head?" and so on.<br>2. "Can you find another part of your body that can lead?"<br>3. "See if you can run and when I say change, make a new part of your body lead."<br>*Note:* After presenting each challenge, watch one or two children complete their task. A very close observation of one or two children will indicate whether the challenge is being understood and the general level of performance. | Equipment placement, p. 116<br>Locomotor skills, p. 43 | Repeat 1 and 2 | Repeat 1, 2, and 3. | Repeat 3 and make up your own challenge. |
| **Part 2: Skill Development** *(15 to 25 minutes)*<br><br>Change of direction<br>—walk forward, sideward, backward, and diagonally<br>—run forward, backward, sideward, and diagonally<br>—combine walk, run, and a change of direction | The major task here is to teach children to move in a variety of directions. Present the following challenges:<br>1. "See how many different ways you can run." As they run ask them to look forward, sideward, and backward to look for a space, then change direction to fill it.<br>2. "See if you can run anywhere you like, and when I say 'stop,' see if you can stop very quickly!"<br>3. Repeat 2, but ask children to "touch the floor" with both hands when you say "stop." Touching with both hands requires each child to control his or her stopping action.<br>4. "Can you run with your body high, then very low?"<br>The following games will help develop the main skills of this lesson. | Methods of teaching, p. 125<br>Stopping, p. 52 | Repeat 2 and 3. | Leave out. | Repeat 3 and 4. |

24

| Content | Teaching Strategies | References | Lesson 2a | 2b | 2c |
|---------|---------------------|------------|-----------|-----|-----|
| | 5. Games:<br>*Automobiles*—This game develops running and stopping skills. Children run in a designated direction pretending to be automobiles and may "pass" others. On signal, everyone must come to a full stop. Automobiles who fail to stop or who bump into other autos incur a consequence. | Games, p. 260<br>Automobiles, p. 263 | Play one or two games. | Play one or two games. | Play one or two games. |
| | *Foxes and Squirrels*—This game develops running and the movement concepts of personal and general space. Pairs of children join hands overhead to form trees. In each tree is a squirrel. A squirrel in a tree is "safe." Scattered about the trees are foxes who are "it." When squirrels are out of their trees they can be tagged by the foxes. When a fox tags a squirrel, they change positions. | Foxes and Squirrels, p. 262 | | | |

**Part 3: Closure**
*(1 to 2 minutes)*

| | | | | | |
|---------|---------------------|------------|-----------|-----|-----|
| Change of direction<br>Stopping | Discuss different directions and stopping with control. | | | | |

**Level I**   **Unit 1:** Manipulative/Movement Skills
**Lesson 3.** Balancing and Gripping Equipment
**Main Theme** Running and balancing equipment
**Subthemes** Running and stopping; Change of direction
**Equipment** One beanbag for each child

**Additional Lessons** Many of the game activities of this age level will require the child to both manipulate and throw a piece of small equipment. If necessary, teach one or two additional lessons to emphasize this skill.

| Content | Teaching Strategies | References | Lesson 3a | 3b | 3c |
|---|---|---|---|---|---|
| **Entry Activity** | Place beanbags in four boxes. Instruct children to take one beanbag to their own space and see how many parts of their bodies they can balance it on while waiting for everyone to change. | | Repeat free play activities. | Repeat previous. | Repeat previous. |
| **Part 1: Introductory Activities** *(5 to 6 minutes)* <br><br> Running and stopping <br> Change of direction | Once all children are in their own space, begin your lesson. Ask children to leave their beanbags on the floor and pose the following tasks: <br> 1. "See if you can run, using *all* the space and show me how many beanbags you can touch." <br> 2. "Can you run to a beanbag, walk around it, then run and find a new beanbag and do the same?" <br> As children are traveling, call key words such as "can you move sideways, across, backward," etc. From this scattered arrangement begin the second part of the lesson. | | Repeat 1 and 2. | Repeat 1 and 2 adding a change of speed and a change of level. | Design your own lesson adding one or two new challenges. |
| **Part 2: Skill Development** *(15 to 25 minutes)* <br><br> Balancing small equipment on parts of body <br> —on elbows, hands, shoulders, etc. <br> —perform skill from standing, sitting, or other position chosen by each child <br> —running and stopping and change of direction | The basic skills to emphasize are balancing, gripping, and holding a variety of small equipment on or between parts of the body. Pose the following questions or challenges: <br> 1. "Can you show me all the different ways you can balance the beanbag on parts of your body?" As children try different positions, stop the class and allow the children to watch. Allow time for all to practice new positions. <br> 2. "Can you balance the beanbag on your head? your elbow? knee?" etc. <br> 3. "Sit on the floor (or any other new position) and try to balance the beanbag on your knee," etc. <br> 4. "See if you can hold the beanbag between your elbows, knees," etc. <br> 5. "Balance the beanbag on your head and walk anywhere in the playing area." "Now you can run." <br> 6. Pose other questions combining balancing, gripping, and traveling. <br> The previous two parts of this lesson have been very active. If the children are tired, choose a less active game. | Beanbag activities, p. 506 <br><br><br><br><br><br><br><br><br><br> Games, p. 260 | Complete any part of 1 to 6. <br><br><br><br><br><br><br><br><br><br> Play one or two games. | Leave out. <br><br><br><br><br><br><br><br><br><br> Play one or two games. | |

| Content | Teaching Strategies | References | Lesson 3a | 3b | 3c |
|---|---|---|---|---|---|
| | 7. Games:<br>*Beanbag Pile*—This is a relatively quiet game for children. Students are seated in several rows and beanbags are passed one at a time to the last person in line. The last person stacks the beanbags one on top of the other. The first team to pile their beanbags, which stand without assistance, is the winning team. | Classroom Games, p. 224<br>Beanbag Pile, p. 226 | | | |
| | *Traffic Light*—This game develops the skills of running, walking, and stopping. Children are scattered about the gymnasium in their own space. Signals are taught: red means stop; yellow means walk; and green means run. Children move according to signals given. | Traffic Light, p. 260 | Traffic Light, p. 260 | | |

**Part 3: Closure**
*(1 to 2 minutes)*

Balancing        Discuss different ways and parts of body things can be balanced on.

**Level I  Unit 1:** Manipulative/Movement Skills
**Lesson 4.** Jumping
**Main Theme** Jumping
**Subthemes** Traveling and stopping, Change of direction
**Equipment** A variety of small equipment (beanbags, individual ropes, etc.) placed in four containers

**Additional Lessons** If additional lessons are planned, concentrate on jumping skills and simple individual or partner games.

| Content | Teaching Strategies | References | Lesson 4a | 4b | 4c |
|---|---|---|---|---|---|
| **Entry Activity** | Place a variety of small equipment (beanbags, individual ropes, and hoops) in each box. Ask each class member to take one piece of equipment and play with it in their own space. | | Repeat previous. | Repeat previous. | Repeat previous. |
| **Part 1: Introductory Activities** (*5 to 6 minutes*)<br><br>Running and stopping<br>Change of direction | When everyone is ready, pose the following challenges:<br>1. "Leave your equipment on the ground, and travel any way you like around all the equipment."<br>2. "Run toward a piece of equipment, change direction, and run toward another piece of equipment." Continue pattern.<br>3. Add other challenges involving combinations of run, stop, and change of direction. | | Repeat 1 and 2. | Repeat 3. | Design your own lesson adding one or two new challenges. |
| **Part 2: Skill Development** (*15 to 25 minutes*)<br><br>Jumping<br>—from one or two feet landing on two feet<br>—from one or two feet landing on one foot<br>—run, jump, and land<br>—run, jump, change direction, and land.<br>—run, change of speed | With each child standing and facing his own piece of small equipment, pose the following challenges:<br>1. "Show me how many ways you can jump over your equipment."<br>2. Add challenges involving taking off on one or two feet and landing on one or two feet.<br>3. "See if you can run anywhere and jump over any piece of equipment, land, and touch the floor with both hands." Touching the floor encourages a good knee bend and good body control.<br>4. Shadow Game: "Find a partner. When I say 'go' number one runs and tries to keep number two from touching him. If you are tagged, change positions and continue your game."<br>The following games will help develop the main skills of this lesson.<br>5. Games:<br>*Jump the Shot*—This game develops jumping and turning. The class is divided into groups of 5 or 6. A designated player, the "turner," moves to the center of the group. This turner swings a rope in a circle about one foot off the ground. Circle players try to jump the rope. If hit, the player is charged with a "shot." Game continues for a designated time period. The player with the least number of shots against him is the winner and becomes the "turner" for the next game.<br>*Do as I Do*—This game develops locomotor movements and creativity. One child starts the game by making a movement and all must follow doing the same. | Jumping skill, p. 46<br>Leaping skill, p. 47<br>Hopscotch, p. 270<br><br><br>Games, p. 260<br><br><br><br>Jump the Shot, p. 268<br><br><br><br><br><br><br>Do as I Do, p. 264 | Repeat 1 and 2.<br><br><br><br><br><br><br>Repeat partner activity with both players balancing a beanbag on their hands, elbows, etc. | Leave out.<br><br><br><br><br><br><br>Play one or two games. | |
| **Part 3: Closure** (*1 to 2 minutes*)<br><br>Jumping<br>Landing and bending knees | Stress landing with gradual bending of knees, plus the fingers touching floor. | | | | |

**Level I   Unit 1:** Manipulative/Movement Skills
**Lesson 5.** Rolling
**Main Theme** Rolling and stopping
**Subthemes** Change of speed; Traveling and stopping
**Equipment** One ball (8½″ or larger) for each child plus a variety of small equipment placed in four containers

**Additional Lessons** The progression that has been followed is from individual to *partner* activities. However, since five- and six-year-olds are basically egocentric, the shift to partner activities should be gradual and requires a lot of cooperation and a minimum of competition between each player.

| Content | Teaching Strategies | References | Lessons 5a | 5b | 5c |
|---|---|---|---|---|---|
| **Entry Activity** | Place enough balls (8½″ or larger) in the four containers. Ask children to take one ball and play with it in their own space. | | Repeat previous. | Repeat previous. | Repeat previous. |
| **Part 1: Introductory Activities** *(5 to 6 minutes)* <br><br> Traveling and stopping <br> Change of speed <br> Change of direction | This is a good test of your class control. When everyone is working in their own space say, "Equipment away and section places." Pose the following challenges: <br> 1. "When I say 'go,' start traveling any way you like—crab, lame puppy—and stop when I call the word. Away you go." <br> 2. "Now, just run, but when I call 'change,' run very quickly. 'Change,' run very slowly, 'change' run quickly," etc. | Crab walk, p. 465 <br> Lame puppy walk, p. 463 | Repeat 2. | Develop one or two new challenges. | Repeat new challenges. |
| **Part 2: Skill Development** *(15 to 25 minutes)* <br><br> Rolling a ball <br> —roll and stop <br> —roll with individual parts of body <br> —roll to wall and stop rebound | *Individual activities* <br> Explain the importance of getting a ball, carrying it to a space, holding it, and waiting for a challenge. Try the following sequence of tasks: <br> 1. "See if you can roll your ball around the ground and try to keep it close to you." <br> 2. "Can you roll it with any other part of your body?" Wait a few moments, then call out such parts as "your elbow, knee, head," and so on. <br> 3. "Can you roll the ball around your body? around part of your body?" <br> 4. "See if you can roll it toward the wall and stop it when it comes back." | | Repeat 1 to 3. | Repeat 4. | Leave out. |
| | *Partner activities:* <br> Pose the following challenges to partners each in their own space: <br> 1. "See if you can roll the ball to your partner; partner try to stop it." <br> 2. "Roll ball through legs of chair." <br> 3. "Roll ball between two beanbags." <br> 4. "Roll ball and try to knock milk cartons down." <br> 5. Repeat 4 with ball rolled backward through legs. <br> 6. "See if you can make up your own game, in your own space, and your game must require a roll." Give them a few minutes and watch for one or two interesting games, then have class stop and watch. | Creative games, p. 254 | Repeat 1 to 3. | Repeat 4 and 6. | Repeat 6. |
| **Part 3: Closure** *(1 to 2 minutes)* <br><br> Rolling an object | Discuss rolling a ball or an object with different parts of the body. | | | | |

29

**Level I    Unit 1:** Manipulative/Movement Skills
**Lesson 6.** Carrying
**Main Theme** Carrying an object
**Subthemes** Running, jumping, and stopping
**Equipment** One class set of beanbags, hoops, or any other small equipment and a few extra small pieces of equipment to be placed in containers

**Additional Lessons** Emphasize a variety of ways an object may be carried while traveling.

| Content | Teaching Strategies | References | Lesson 6a | 6b | 6c |
|---|---|---|---|---|---|
| **Entry Activity** | Place a variety of small equipment in each of the four containers. Tell the class to get one ball and one piece of equipment and play with it in their own space. | | Repeat previous. | Repeat previous. | Repeat previous. |
| **Part 1: Introductory Activities** *(5 to 6 minutes)*<br><br>Running, jumping, and stopping | Ask children to put equipment away, then get a hoop, find a space, place hoop on floor, and sit in the middle.<br>Begin with challenges involving running. changing direction, and jumping over hoops. After two or three individual challenges, play Nine Lives.<br>*Nine Lives:* On command, tell children to run anywhere. Remove two hoops, then call "stop." Everyone tries to stand inside a hoop. The two children remaining lose *one* life each but stay in the game. Continue pattern removing *two* hoops each time. Beanbags can also be used in this game. When "stop" is called they must place one foot (or head, elbow, etc.) on bag. | | Repeat Nine Lives. | Repeat 1. | Repeat Nine Lives with different equipment. |
| **Part 2: Skill Development** *(15 to 25 minutes)*<br><br>Carrying an object<br>Carrying an object and changing speed | *Individual activities:*<br>The important task here is to assist children in learning to carry a variety of small equipment with different parts of their bodies. The following sequence of tasks can be given using either beanbags, hoops, balls, or other small equipment.<br>1. "See if you can walk around the space carrying (or balancing) your beanbag on your elbow (wait a few moments between each part), head, back," and so on.<br>2. Repeat with run, skip, slide, or gallop.<br>3. "Balance beanbag on your knee, toss into air from knee, and catch." Designate other body parts to propel beanbag and catch. | Beanbag activities, p. 506<br>Hoop activities, p. 522<br>Wand activities, p. 524 | Repeat 1. | Leave out. | Leave out. |
| | *Partner activities:*<br>Arrange partners with one hoop between them in their own space.<br>1. Begin in stationary position. "How many ways can you and your partner balance your hoop?"<br>2. "How many ways can you and your partner balance your hoop while walking, running, or other locomotor movements?"<br>3. "Can you make up a carrying game with your partner and your hoop?" If too difficult, make the challenge very specific. | | Repeat 1 and 3. | Repeat 3. Add a new challenge. | Design new challenges for children to invent their own carrying game. |
| **Part 3: Closure** *(1 to 2 minutes)*<br><br>Balancing an object while moving | Discuss carrying an object with different parts of body. | | | | |

**Level I    Unit 1:** Manipulative/Movement Skills
**Lesson 7.** Throwing
**Main Theme**  Throwing
**Subthemes**  Running and dodging
**Equipment**  Hoops, beanbags, fifteen small strips of cloth (12″ long)

**Additional Lessons**  If the level of throwing skill is very low, several more lessons may be required before progressing to lesson 8. Concentrate on various ways of throwing.

| Content | Teaching Strategies | References | Lesson 7a | 7b | 7c |
|---|---|---|---|---|---|
| **Entry Activity** | Place hoops and beanbags in each of the four containers. Tell children to take one hoop and one beanbag, find a space, and play with their equipment. | | Repeat previous. | Repeat previous. | Repeat previous. |
| **Part 1: Introductory Activities**<br>(5 to 6 minutes)<br><br>Running and dodging | When everyone is ready, tell the class to place their beanbags in center of hoop. Play the game Tails: In partners, one child has a twelve-inch piece of cloth tucked in back of shorts. On the command ''go,'' partner chases the other trying to grasp the tail of his or her partner. Change around and continue game.<br>*Note:* Watch for unnecessary roughness when grabbing tails. Correct immediately. | | Play Tails. | Play Nine Lives (p. 30 of this guide). | Design your own lesson stressing throwing. |
| **Part 2: Skill Development**<br>(15 to 25 minutes)<br><br>Throwing an object<br>—throwing with individual parts of the body<br>—throwing with one or two hands<br>—throwing from a variety of positions<br>—throwing toward a target | The central focus of this lesson is to help children explore various ways of throwing an object. The following sequence of tasks will help develop this general skill. With children holding a beanbag and standing two ''giant steps'' away from their hoops, pose the following challenges:<br>1. ''How many ways can you throw the beanbag into your hoop?''<br>2. ''Can you throw it with two hands? one hand? with another part of your body?''<br>3. ''See if you can sit and throw it into the hoop.'' Later add from other parts— lying, on side, kneeling, etc. | Beanbag activities, p. 506<br>Hoop activities, p. 522 | Place a circle (chalk or tape) on wall and repeat 1 and 2 toward new target. | Repeat 1 and 2 with 8½″ ball and wall target. | |
| | Children at this age level have normally acquired a very basic catching skill, hence, throwing a beanbag or other small equipment to a partner may cause injuries as well as create an undesirable learning environment. Because of this, wait until lesson 7b or 7c or lesson 8 before introducing partner activities involving throwing and catching.<br>4. ''See if you can make up a throwing game in your own space.'' Later, add specific skills, such as two hands and a run.<br>5. ''Can you make up a new throwing game with a beanbag and a new piece of equipment?'' Allow children to choose their new equipment. | Hopscotch, p. 270<br>Beanbag horseshoes, p. 267 | Repeat 5 using circle target on wall. | Repeat 5 using circle target on wall. | |
| **Part 3: Closure**<br>(1 to 2 minutes)<br><br>Throwing an object | Discuss different ways of throwing an object. | | | | |

**Level I  Unit 1:** Manipulative/Movement Skills
**Lesson 8.** Catching
**Main Theme** Catching
**Subthemes** Throwing; Running, jumping, and stopping
**Equipment** Class set of beanbags, 8½" balls, and a variety of other small equipment

**Additional Lessons** Additional lessons should be planned to emphasize throwing and catching at different levels, throwing with each hand, and throwing at a specific target.

| Content | Teaching Strategies | References | Lesson 8a | 8b | 8c |
|---|---|---|---|---|---|
| **Entry Activity** | Place beanbags in each of the four containers. Tell children to take a ball or beanbag to their space and play with it. | | Repeat previous. | Repeat previous. | Repeat previous. |
| **Part 1: Introductory Activities** (5 to 6 minutes)<br><br>Traveling, jumping, stopping | Equipment away and "section places." Pose challenges involving running, skipping, jumping, landing, and touching floor with fingertips (control on landing). | Skipping skill, p. 51 | Play Tails (p. 31 of this guide). | Play Nine Lives (p. 30 of this guide). | |
| **Part 2: Skill Development** (15 to 25 minutes)<br><br>Two-hand catch—from below and above waist<br>Catching with different parts of body | *Individual activities:*<br>Arrange children in own space with one beanbag for each child.<br>1. "See how many ways you can throw your beanbag up and catch it."<br>2. "How many different ways can you catch it?" (above your head, below your chest, with your knees, etc.)<br>3. Exchange beanbag for ball and repeat 1 and 2. | Throwing, pp. 58, 404<br>Catching, pp. 61, 406 | Repeat 3. | Leave out. | Repeat 3. |
| Throw and catch to partner | *Partner activities:*<br>1. In partners about six to eight feet apart, ask "How many ways can you throw and catch the ball with your partner?"<br>2. "Can you make up a throwing and catching game with your partner?" Later, add the wall, a basket, or a hoop to this challenge. | | Repeat 2 using a beanbag and an individual rope. | Repeat 2 using a chair and a beanbag. | Repeat 2 using a hoop and a ball. |
| **Part 3: Closure** (1 to 2 minutes)<br><br>Catching an object | Discuss the position of fingers and thumbs when ball is caught from a high or low throw. Low throw: little fingers together; high throw; thumb and index fingers together. | | | | |

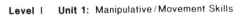

**Level I**  **Unit 1:** Manipulative/Movement Skills
**Lesson 9.** Bouncing
**Main Theme** Bouncing a ball
**Subthemes** Catching and throwing: Change of direction and level
**Equipment** Class set of utility balls (8½'')

**Additional Lessons** Several additional lessons should be developed to emphasize the skills in the second part of this lesson. Begin with a brief introductory activity, and devote the remainder of time to bouncing skills and partner activities.

| Content | Teaching Strategies | References | Lesson 9a | 9b | 9c |
|---|---|---|---|---|---|
| **Entry Activity** | Place balls in each of the four containers. Tell children to take a ball, find a space, and play. | | Repeat previous. | Repeat previous. | Repeat previous. |
| **Part 1: Introductory Activities**<br>*(5 to 6 minutes)*<br><br>Traveling and stopping<br>Change of levels | "Equipment away and find a space." Pose the following challenges:<br>1. "Can you show me how you can bounce like a ball? Can you bounce very low? very high?"<br>2. "See if you can run, stop when you like, bounce four times, then run to a new space and do it again."<br>  *Note:* Bouncing requires a lot of strength and endurance, so intersperse bouncing with other locomotor movements.<br>3. "Show me how to bounce very slowly, walk to a new space, and bounce very quickly." Repeat, but skip to a new space. | Bouncing, p. 63 | Play Nine Lives (p. 30 of this guide). | Play Tails (p. 31 of this guide). | Repeat 1 to 3. |
| **Part 2: Skill Development**<br>*(15 to 25 minutes)*<br><br>Bounce ball with one hand<br>Bounce and catch a ball | Begin the following sequence of challenges in a stationary position, then gradually add catching, traveling, and change of speed and direction.<br>1. "Show me how many different ways you can bounce and catch your ball."<br>2. "Can you bounce the ball with both hands?"<br>3. "How many different parts of your body can bounce the ball?"<br>4. "Can you bounce the ball very high? very low?" Continue pattern.<br>By now children have developed numerous skills that can be incorporated with the bouncing skill. Further, each child should have learned to share and cooperate with small group activities. In many instances, these children will prefer partner activities, particularly with the inventive game activities. Present the following challenges:<br>5. Individually: "Can you make up a bouncing game with a hoop?" (or beanbag, rope, etc.)<br>6. Individually: "See if you can make up a new bouncing game using your hoop and the wall."<br>7. Partners: "Can you make up a bouncing game with your partner?" (no equipment). Repeat, adding one or more pieces of small equipment to the challenge. | Bouncing, p. 63 | Repeat 1 and 2. Add "quick and slow" to this challenge.<br><br>Repeat 6. | Repeat 3 and 4. Add "near and far" to 4.<br><br>Repeat 6 adding equipment to the challenge. | Repeat 1 and 4. Add "traveling" and "directions" to 3 and 4.<br><br>Repeat 7 adding your own additional challenges. |
| **Part 3: Closure**<br>*(1 to 2 minutes)*<br><br>Bouncing a ball | Stress bouncing ball with one or two hands and in different directions. | | | | |

# Game Activities
## Developmental Level I
## Unit 2: Ball Skills
## (Foot- and Hand-Eye)

## Expected Learning Outcomes

**Psychomotor Skills**

1. Traveling and stopping
2. Rolling and stopping a ball with parts of the body
3. Moving safely
4. Kicking a stationary ball
5. Changing levels
6. Traveling in different directions
7. Kicking a stationary ball toward a target
8. Kicking a moving ball
9. Controlling a moving ball with feet
10. Striking a ball with hands or arms
11. Striking a ball with an implement
12. Controlling a moving ball with an implement

**Cognitive and Affective Knowledge and Skills**

1. Moving with care and concern for others
2. Ability to work with a partner
3. Ability to develop creative games independently and with a partner
4. Understanding of the meaning of kicking, striking movements
5. Understanding of space awareness

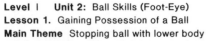

Level I    Unit 2: Ball Skills (Foot-Eye)
Lesson 1. Gaining Possession of a Ball
Main Theme  Stopping ball with lower body
Subthemes  Traveling and stopping; Using individual parts; Rolling a ball
Equipment  Class set of 8½" balls (volleyballs or larger utility balls are adequate)

**Additional Lessons** Gaining possession using the lower parts of the body requires children to judge where they must be before attempting to stop the ball. In addition, many games require the child to be in different positions (kneeling, crabwalk stance, or on his or her back). Stress these skills.

| Content | Teaching Strategies | References | Lesson 1a | 1b | 1c |
|---|---|---|---|---|---|
| **Entry Activity** | Place balls in four containers. Tell class to get a ball, find a space, and play with their balls. | | | | |
| **Part I: Introductory Activities** *(5 to 6 minutes)*<br><br>Traveling and stopping<br>Traveling and stopping on individual parts | Equipment away and section places. The following tasks begin with traveling, stopping with control, then stopping on individual parts. The latter is an extremely important aspect of lowering the body in preparation for controlling the ball with the lower body. Shadow Game:<br>1. "Travel any way you like, but when I call 'stop,' see how nicely you can stop and touch the floor with your fingertips."<br>2. "Next, travel, stop, touch the floor, then balance on any part of your body."<br>3. Tell children they are going to repeat this task, but tell them ahead of time you want them to end up balancing on knees, one foot and one knee, left side, other lower parts of body. | | Repeat 1 and 2. | Repeat 1 to 3. | Play Nine Lives (p. 30 of this guide). |
| **Part 2: Skill Development** *(15 to 25 minutes)*<br><br>Rolling and stopping ball with individual parts of body<br>Roll ball to wall and stop with legs, shins, and feet | The main task here is to encourage children to move into position, then lower body and use legs, shins, or feet to control the ball. Each child has a ball in his or her own space.<br>1. "See if you can roll the ball in your own space and stop it without using your hands."<br>2. "Can you roll and stop it with two legs, your knees, one foot, or any way you like?"<br>3. Roll the ball toward the wall and repeat tasks in 2. | Trapping skills, p. 317 | Repeat 1 and 2. | Leave out. | Repeat 3. |
| | The skill development part of this lesson has not required excessive vigorous activity. Develop one or more creative games, individually or in partners, and include traveling, change of speed and direction, as well as gaining possession.<br>4. "Can you make up a rolling game with your partner, but do not use your hands?"<br>5. "Can you make up a game with your partner that has a roll, a stop, and two beanbags?"<br>The following structured games are also helpful in developing good ball control.<br>6. Games:<br>*Tunnel Ball*—This game develops rolling and catching skills. Children form a circle and create many "tunnels" with their legs by standing with legs apart. One child in the center attempts to roll a ball out of the circle between the legs of any circle player. Circle players may use their hands to stop the ball.<br>*Roll Ball*—This game develops rolling skills. One player rolls the ball at cartons or pins. Partner resets cartons and returns ball. After several turns, partners change places. | Games, p. 260<br><br><br><br><br><br>Tunnel Ball, p. 266<br><br><br><br>Roll Ball, p. 265 | Repeat 4. | Play one or two games. | Repeat 5. |
| **Part 3: Closure** *(1 to 2 minutes)*<br><br>Controlling the ball | Discuss different ways of stopping the ball. | | | | |

**Level I    Unit 2:** Ball Skills (Foot-Eye)
**Lesson 2.** Kicking a Stationary Ball
**Main Theme** Kicking a stationary ball
**Subthemes** Stopping a ball with lower body; Traveling in different directions
**Equipment** Class set of 8½" balls plus a variety of small equipment

**Additional Lessons** Additional lessons may be indicated to help children gain a little more control and skill in using both feet. If possible, use a variety of different size balls to help children judge speed, force, position, body, and methods of gaining control.

| Content | Teaching Strategies | References | Lesson 2a | 2b | 2c |
|---|---|---|---|---|---|
| **Entry Activity** | Place balls and a variety of small equipment (beanbags, milk cartons, individual ropes, etc.) in containers. Tell children to take out a ball and one piece of equipment and play with them in their own space. | | Repeat previous. | Repeat previous. | Repeat previous. |
| **Part 1: Introductory Activities** (5 to 6 minutes) | Leave equipment on floor and put balls away. Pose the following challenges: | Dodging, p. 53 Sliding, p. 51 | Repeat 1 and 2. | Play Tails (p. 31 of this guide). | Play Tails. |
| Traveling and change of direction Jumping and dodging | 1. "Can you travel around the space and change direction every time you meet another player or a piece of equipment?" Encourage moving sideways by sliding. 2. "Now, run and jump over as many pieces of equipment as you can." 3. "Next, move sideways (reinforce either the slide or side-step) and jump over as many pieces of equipment as you can." | | | | |
| **Part 2: Skill Development** (15 to 25 minutes) | *Individual activities:* Children of this age level should be given opportunities to explore the many ways they can propel a ball with their lower body. Begin with general tasks, then progress to using the various parts of the right and left foot—stress both feet. Emphasis should be on simple control rather than accuracy, force, or distance. Try the following tasks: | Kicking, pp. 64, 314 | Repeat 1 and 2. | Leave out. | Repeat 1 and 2. |
| Kicking a stationary ball with leg, knee, parts of foot Kicking and stopping a ball Moving toward and kicking a stationary ball Kicking a ball toward a target | 1. "Place your ball three giant steps away from the wall. See if you can strike (or kick) the ball with your foot, hit the wall, and stop it as it rebounds back to you." 2. "Try it again and see if you can stop it with any part of your lower body." 3. "Make a target on the wall; then make up your own kicking game." | | Repeat 2. | Repeat 3. | Play one or two games. |
| | *Partner activities:* 1. "One kicks, the other gains possession, then kicks it back to the partner." Add moving back from ball before kicking it, placing two goals between players, and kicking through goals. 2. "Make up a kicking game with your partner." Add a limitation with each new game. | | | | |
| **Part 3: Closure** (1 to 2 minutes) | | | | | |
| Kicking a ball | Discuss different ways of kicking a ball. | | | | |

Level I    Unit 2: Ball Skills (Foot-Eye)
Lesson 3. Kicking a Moving Ball
**Main Theme** Kicking a moving ball
**Subthemes** Gaining possession; Rolling
**Equipment** Class set of 8½'' utility balls (or volleyballs) and a variety of small equipment

**Additional Lessons** Additional lessons should stress moving into position, kicking the ball when it is moving, and gaining possession.

| Content | Teaching Strategies | References | Lesson 3a | 3b | 3c |
|---|---|---|---|---|---|
| **Entry Activity** | Place balls and a variety of small equipment in containers. Ask children to get a ball—no equipment—and play with it in their own space or with their partner. | | Repeat previous. | Repeat previous. | Repeat previous. |
| **Part 1: Introductory Activities** (3 to 5 minutes)<br><br>Traveling and change of direction and levels<br>Rolling and jumping | In own space with a ball. Explain to children when you say ''roll,'' everyone must roll his or her ball anywhere, then quickly run and jump over as many rolling balls (stopped balls do not count) before you say ''stop.'' Do not wait for last ball to stop rolling before ''stop.'' Repeat several times. | | Repeat rolling and jumping. | Play Nine Lives (p. 30 of this guide). | Repeat rolling and jumping. |
| **Part 2: Skill Development** (15 to 25 minutes)<br><br>Kicking a stationary ball<br>Kicking a moving ball<br>Gaining possession of a moving ball<br>Kicking a moving ball toward a target | *Individual activities:*<br>Kicking a moving ball is far more difficult than striking it when in a stationary position. This skill requires moving into position so that the opposite kicking leg is near the side of the ball. Later, peripheral vision (looking at ball and target) will also be required in the game setting.<br>1. Start with a stationary kick against the wall. After a few kicks ask the class to ''see if you can kick the returning ball back to the wall.''<br>2. ''See if you can roll the ball, chase after it, and kick it.''<br>3. Repeat 2, adding ''then run after it and stop it.'' | Kicking, pp. 64, 314 | Repeat 1 and 2. | Leave out. | Repeat 3. |
| | *Partner activities:*<br>Continue with creative games with partners stressing kicking skills and cooperation rather than competition.<br>1. ''With your partner, can you keep your ball moving anywhere in the playing area?''<br>2. ''With your partner, make two goals (cones, beanbags, etc.) and see how many times you and your partner can kick the ball through the goals.''<br>3. ''Can you make up a kicking game where the ball is always moving?'' | Games, p. 260 | Repeat 1 and 2. | Repeat 2 and 3. | Make up your own challenge. |
| **Part 3: Closure** (1 to 2 minutes)<br><br>Kicking a moving ball | Discuss how important it is to be able to kick a ball with either foot. | | | | |

**Level I  Unit 2:** Ball Skills (Foot-Eye)
**Lesson 4.** Controlling a Moving Ball
**Main Theme** Controlling a moving ball
**Subthemes** Striking a ball with feet; Change of direction and pathway
**Equipment** Class set of 8½" utility balls (or volleyballs) and a variety of small equipment

**Additional Lessons** Each additional lesson should stress controlling a moving ball and be supplemented with previously acquired skills.

| Content | Teaching Strategies | References | Lesson 4a | 4b | 4c |
|---|---|---|---|---|---|
| **Entry Activity** | Place balls and a variety of small equipment in the containers. Ask class to get a ball and one piece of small equipment and play with it in their own space. | | Repeat previous. | Repeat previous. | Repeat previous. |
| **Part 1: Introductory Activities** *(3 to 5 minutes)*<br><br>Travel and change direction<br>Travel on different parts | Balls away, but leave equipment scattered around play area.<br>1. "Show me how many different ways you can travel (sideways, backward, and so on)."<br>2. "Travel on three parts of your body and when you meet another player, change direction and travel on three new parts." | | Repeat 1 and 2. Change 2 to traveling on 2, 3, 4 parts, etc. | Play Nine Lives (p. 30 of this guide). | Repeat 1 and 2 adding or changing the basic challenge. |
| **Part 2: Skill Development** *(15 to 25 minutes)*<br><br>Traveling and keeping ball close to body<br>Controlling ball while moving on different parts of body | Dribbling or controlling the ball while moving is a form of controlled striking. The following challenges will assist in developing this skill:<br>1. "Can you move around the playing area keeping the ball very close to you?" Mention "push" rather than kick the ball.<br>2. "Shift to a crab walk position and show me how you can move the ball with your feet."<br>3. "See if you can find another way of traveling and moving your ball."<br>4. Ask children to get two pieces of equipment and find a new space. "Place your equipment (may be individual ropes, cones, or beanbags) any way you like and see if you can move your ball around them."<br>5. "Place equipment a few yards from a wall. Move your ball around your equipment then kick it to the wall." Add "gain possession after kicking it."<br>6. Repeat 4 and 5 with a partner and allow them to develop their own game with equipment and space. | Dribbling, pp. 64, 318<br>Walk, p. 44 | Repeat 1 to 3.<br><br><br><br>Repeat 4 and 5. | Leave out.<br><br><br><br>Play one or two games. | Repeat 1 and 3.<br><br><br><br>Play one or two games. |
| **Part 3: Closure** *(1 to 2 minutes)*<br><br>Controlling a moving ball | Discuss and illustrate the importance of pushing rather than kicking the ball in order to keep the ball close to the feet for control. | | | | |

**Level I    Unit 2:** Ball Skills (Hand-Eye)
**Lesson 5.** Striking a Ball
**Main Theme** Striking with arm or hand
**Subthemes** Individual parts; Running and jumping
**Equipment** One large ball (beach or 12″ utility) for each child; One balloon for each child

**Additional Lessons** The material in this lesson cannot be thoroughly covered in one lesson. Spread over two or three lessons and do not overuse the balloon in the following lessons.

| Content | Teaching Strategies | References | Lesson 5a | 5b | 5c |
|---|---|---|---|---|---|
| **Entry Activity** | Place large (12″ utility or beach) balls in containers and have one balloon for each child. (Blow up in class.) Play in own space with a ball. | | Repeat previous. | Repeat previous. | Repeat previous. |
| **Part 1: Introductory Activities** *(3 to 5 minutes)*<br><br>Traveling with individual parts leading<br>Running and jumping | Equipment away and find a new space.<br>1. "Travel anywhere in the play area with your right foot leading, now your left toe, elbow." Call out a few more parts.<br>2. "Run and when you find a nice open space, jump as high as you can, land, and continue."<br>3. "See if you can travel on 'all fours' with your tummy the highest point." | | Repeat 1. | Repeat 2 and 3. | Play Nine Lives (p. 30 of this guide). |
| **Part 2: Skill Development** *(15 to 25 minutes)*<br><br>Striking with parts of upper body<br>Striking and traveling<br>Striking ball from different levels | *Individual activities:*<br>Showing children the difference between throwing and striking as well as striking with parts of the upper body can be accomplished with a balloon. Later move to a large play ball.<br>1. Each child with a balloon in his or her own space. "Can you keep the balloon in the air?"<br>2. "Try hitting it with your elbow, head, or shoulder, or find your own part."<br>3. "Can you move around the play area keeping your balloon in the air?" "With different body parts?"<br>4. "Can you keep the balloon in the air hitting it with your hand, head, and then your shoulder?" Use other sequences.<br><br>*Partner activities:*<br>1. "Make up a balloon game with your partner." After this challenge, put balloons away.<br>2. "Can you make up a new hitting game with your partner with a beach ball?"<br>3. Repeat 2 adding small equipment. | Striking, p. 63 | With large ball: "How many ways can you strike ball toward wall?" "Can you drop it, then hit it toward the wall?" "Can you throw ball up and hit it toward the wall?"<br><br>Repeat 2 involving striking and bouncing. | Repeat 1 and 2 of lesson 5a.<br><br><br><br><br><br><br><br>Free play with balloon. | Leave out.<br><br><br><br><br><br><br><br>Free play with balloon or design partner games. |
| **Part 3: Closure** *(1 to 2 minutes)*<br><br>Striking a ball with hands or arms | Discuss striking a ball with different parts of the body. | | | | |

**Level I   Unit 2:** Ball Skills (Hand-Eye)
**Lesson 6.** Striking a Ball with an Implement
**Main Theme** Striking a ball
**Subthemes** Change of direction; Change of level
**Equipment** One homemade "coat hanger" bat for each child; Nerf balls or crunched newspaper balls

**Additional Lessons** Additional lessons should stress striking skills combined with a change of direction, speed, and level. Game development should also emphasize partner activities.

| Content | Teaching Strategies | References | Lesson 6a | 6b | 6c |
|---|---|---|---|---|---|
| **Entry Activity** | Place balls (or pom-poms, newspaper balls) in containers. Tell children to get a ball and play with it in their own space. | | Repeat previous. | Repeat previous. | Repeat previous. |
| **Part 1: Introductory Activities** (3 to 5 minutes)<br><br>Running, jumping, and dodging | Equipment away and find a space.<br>1. Begin with children running, then change direction and speed.<br>2. Explain they are to repeat, but when you beat the drum (or call "jump") they must jump up as high as they can and hit an imaginary ball.<br>3. Repeat with opposite hand and with both hands. | Dodging, p. 53 | Repeat 1 and 2. | Use balloons, run, and strike balloon in the air. | Play Tails (p. 31 of this guide). |
| **Part 2: Skill Development** (15 to 25 minutes)<br><br>Striking a ball with a bat<br>Striking a ball from different levels<br>Striking a ball with right and left hand and with both hands | *Individual activities:*<br>Introducing children to striking skills with an implement can be enjoyable and safely accomplished by using nylon bats, pom-poms, and nerf balls. Have children make their own paddles in the classroom by bending a coat hanger into a diamond shape, bend hook flat, and wrap with masking tape. Pull two nylons over top of paddle and top of handle, then cut off remaining part of stocking. Balls can be made by crunching up newspaper and wrapping with masking tape. Arrange class in scattered formation, sitting down with paddle and nerf (pom-pom, wrapped paper, or balloon).<br>1. "See if you can throw your ball into the air and catch it on your paddle."<br>2. Kneel and repeat 1.<br>3. "Now, see if you can keep hitting your ball into the air—how many times?" If skill is low, have children begin by hitting ball along the ground, around obstacles, or toward wall.<br>4. "Can you hit the ball against the wall?"<br>5. "Can you hit the ball into the air by alternating sides of the paddle"? | Inexpensive equipment, Appendix B, p. 625<br>Striking, p. 65 | Repeat 1 to 3. | Repeat 1 to 3 with a balloon. | Leave out. |
| | *Partner activities:*<br>Striking skills for this age level can be effectively learned through simple and cooperative games between partners.<br>1. Use a hoop, basket, target on wall, etc., with each hitting ball into or at a target.<br>2. Stretch rope across two chairs and have partners hit it back and forth.<br>3. Develop a series of challenges that encourage partners to make up their own creative games. | Games, p. 260 | Repeat 1 and 2. | Repeat 2 with a balloon. | Repeat 3. |
| **Part 3: Closure** (1 to 2 minutes)<br><br>Striking with an implement | Stress hitting a ball very gently and with elbows bent. Demonstrate "stiff arm" hit, then a hit with elbow bent. | | | | |

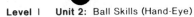

**Level** I **Unit 2:** Ball Skills (Hand-Eye)
**Lesson 7.** Controlling a Moving Ball with an Implement
**Main Theme** Dribbling with an implement
**Subthemes** Passing, change of speed and direction
**Equipment** One homemade coat hanger paddle or nylon stick; Nerf or plastic balls; A variety of small equipment

**Additional Lessons** Additional lessons should stress controlling the ball while moving. At this stage, partner activities are popular and constructive ways of learning this skill.

| Content | Teaching Strategies | References | Lesson 7a | 7b | 7c |
|---|---|---|---|---|---|
| **Entry Activity** | Place nylon paddles, sticks, and balls in containers. Tell children to get a paddle and ball and play with it in their own space. | | Repeat previous. | Repeat previous. | Repeat previous. |
| **Part 1: Introductory Activities** (*3 to 5 minutes*) | 1. Pose challenges involving running around small equipment (beanbags, cones, milk cartons, etc.) changing direction and speed. 2. Play Tails or Nine Lives. | Tails (p. 31 of this guide). | Repeat 1. | Play Nine Lives (p. 30 of this guide). | Repeat 1. |
| Traveling Change of direction | | | | | |
| **Part 2: Skill Development** (*15 to 25 minutes*) | *Individual activities:* Dribbling a ball with a paddle or stick is a lot of fun for this age group. Stress proper spacing and not swinging their paddle any higher than waist high. | | Repeat 1 and 2. | Repeat 1 and 3. | Leave out. |
| Dribbling ball with nylon bat or plastic stick Dribble around obstacles | 1. With a nylon paddle or plastic stick and a ball (nerf or other type of light ball), "Can you walk and 'push' the ball, keeping it very close to you? Try changing directions, running slowly, moving sideways," etc. 2. "Standing a few feet from the wall, see if you can hit the ball to the wall and stop it with your paddle." 3. "Can you hit the ball to the wall more than two times in a row?" 4. "How many times can you hit the ball against the wall before missing?" 5. "See if you can make up your own game." | | | | |
| | *Partner activities:* 1. "Can you make up a passing game with your partner?" 2. Add beanbags or milk cartons. One person dribbles a ball around obstacle, then passes ball back to partner. 3. Add target (legs of chair or two milk cartons), pass ball through stopping ball with paddle. | | Repeat 1. | Repeat 2. | Repeat 2 and 3. |
| **Part 3: Closure** (*1 to 2 minutes*) | | | | | |
| Moving a ball along ground with an implement | Stress keeping implement close to the ground when pushing the ball along the floor. | | | | |

# Game Activities
## Developmental Level II
## Unit 1: Manipulative/ Movement Skills

## Expected Learning Outcomes

**Psychomotor Skills**

1. Traveling and stopping
2. Using personal and general space
3. Traveling in different directions and pathways
4. Changing speed
5. Rolling a ball
6. Gripping an object with various parts of the body
7. Carrying an object while changing speed and direction
8. Throwing an object while changing speed and direction
9. Catching a ball from above and below the waist
10. Bouncing a ball with right or left hand

**Cognitive and Affective Knowledge and Skills**

1. Understanding personal and general space
2. Concern for safety of self and others
3. Understanding rules and regulations of games
4. Ability to work with two or more other players
5. Ability to design and explain inventive games involving two or more players
6. Moving with care and concern for other players
7. Appreciation of others' strengths and weaknesses

**Level** II    **Unit 1:** Manipulative/Movement Skills
**Lesson 1.** Traveling and Stopping
**Main Theme** Traveling and stopping
**Subthemes** Personal and general space; Jumping and landing
**Equipment** Variety of small equipment such as beanbags, traffic cones, hoops, and individual ropes

**Additional Lessons** On the basis of routine procedures, using space, safety, as well as the level of skill demonstrated in running, landing, and jumping, one or two more lessons may be necessary before moving to lesson 2.

| Content | Teaching Strategies | References | Lesson 1a | 1b | 1c |
|---|---|---|---|---|---|
| **Entry Activity** | Leave until beginning of second lesson. | | Free play with equipment. | Repeat previous. | Repeat previous. |
| **Part 1: Introductory Activities** (5 to 6 minutes)<br><br>Using personal and general space<br>Moving safely<br>Traveling and stopping | By the second grade, most children should be able to move in an orderly manner to, from, and within a designated playing area. Organize class into four groups and give them special names and set a place for each group to line up when you call "section places" or "teams." If you have a large playing area (indoors or outside), mark off a small area with four containers or cones. Use this space for your class instruction. Expand boundaries as needed. From section places, try the following:<br>1. "On the command go, everyone run and find their own space." Watch general movement and notice if children group together leaving large open spaces. Return to section places and repeat.<br>2. With children in own personal space, "See if you can run using all the space and when I call stop, lower body, and touch the floor with fingers of both hands. Go . . . stop . . . go." Touching floor ensures a safe and controlled stopping action. Add "stop . . . go . . . dodge . . . stop."<br>3. "Next, run again and whenever you see a safe space, stop, touch the floor, then continue and do it four times." | Section places, p. 113<br>Tag games, p. 273 | Repeat 3 and play a tag game. | Repeat 2 and 3. | Play a tag game. |
| **Part 2: Skill Development** (15 to 25 minutes)<br><br>Jumping and landing from one or two feet to one or both feet | Ask children to get one piece of small equipment and find a space. (Beanbags, hoops, milk cartons, traffic cones, etc.)<br>1. With equipment on floor, "How many ways can you jump over your equipment?" Watch for different takeoff and landing movements. Choose one or two to demonstrate, then allow children to continue. As they continue, walk around calling out key words or phrases such as "Can you jump sideways, with a turn in the air, land on one foot?" etc.<br>2. "Next, run anywhere you like and jump as high as you can over any piece of equipment. Remember as you land, bend your knees and touch the floor with fingertips."<br>3. Pose challenges involving a run, jump and turn, other tricks, landing, and continue. | Teaching strategies p. 124 | Leave out. | Repeat 1 and 2. | Leave out. |
| | The previous part of the lesson has been quite vigorous. Select one or two games and watch for listening skills, interpersonal cooperation, and other social behavior.<br>*Note:* Explain to children that from now on equipment will be available in four containers before the lesson begins. (Use team captains to get out equipment.) As soon as a child is changed, he or she may select a piece of equipment and play with it while waiting for the rest of the class to change. | Games, p. 273 | Play one or two games. | Play one or two games. | Play one or two games. |

| Content | Teaching Strategies | References | Lesson 1a | 1b | 1c |
|---|---|---|---|---|---|
| | 4. Games: | | | | |
| | *Simple Dodge Ball*—This game develops throwing and catching skills. Two teams are formed and each team takes a place on either side of the center line. Players try to hit each other with nerf balls. If hit, player runs to a marker and back and rejoins the group. | Simple Dodge Ball, p. 268 | | | |
| | *Red Stop, Green Go*—This game develops running, tagging, and dodging skills. Several players are designated as "catchers" or "releasers." The remaining players scatter. "Catchers" try to tag as many players as possible. When tagged, players are frozen. "Releasers" tag frozen players who are then free to move again. | Red Stop, Green Go p. 278 | | | |

**Part 3: Closure**
*(1 to 4 minutes)*

| | | | | | |
|---|---|---|---|---|---|
| Running and stopping | Discuss moving safely in terms of self and others. | | | | |

**Level** II   **Unit 1:** Manipulative/Movement Skills
**Lesson 2.** Direction and Pathway
**Main Theme** Direction and pathway
**Subtheme** Change of speed
**Equipment** Class set of individual ropes

**Additional Lessons** Your observations of the children's performances in the previous lesson may indicate one or two more lessons are needed for skill development or to clearly establish an efficient yet informal teaching atmosphere.

| Content | Teaching Strategies | References | Lesson 2a | 2b | 2c |
|---|---|---|---|---|---|
| **Entry Activity** | Place individual ropes in four containers. After changing, each child comes into gymnasium, selects a rope, and plays with it in his own space. | | Repeat previous. | Repeat previous. | Repeat previous with new equipment. |
| **Part 1: Introductory Activities** *(5 to 6 minutes)*<br><br>Traveling and stopping<br>Change of direction | Prior to the beginning of this lesson, the general routine of changing, moving efficiently into teams (or "section places"), and listening to your verbal instructions (no whistle is necessary) should be reasonably well established. When everyone is changed, "Equipment away and section places."<br>　1. "On command, let me see you run in as many different directions as you can . . . go." Wait a few minutes then call "stop" or "freeze." Repeat.<br>　2. Explain you will call out different ways of traveling as they move and change direction. "Go . . . backward, on all fours, sideways, one foot and two hands," etc. | | Repeat 1 and 2. | Design your own lesson. | Design your own lesson. |
| **Part 2: Skill Development** *(15 to 25 minutes)*<br><br>Traveling in different pathways<br>Traveling and changing speed | Ask children to get an individual rope from the nearest box and return to their space. Main emphasis here is to encourage children to move in a variety of pathways and with a change of speed.<br>　1. "Make a straight line with your rope and show me how many ways you can travel up and down your rope." Later add "move on one foot, backward, sideways," etc.<br>　2. Repeat 1 with rope making a triangle, circle, or square pattern.<br>　3. Ask children to make a letter with their ropes and repeat 1.<br>　4. Ask children to make up any design they like with their ropes, then move anywhere they like. When they find a rope they should "hop" through its pattern.<br>　5. Repeat 4, but each time they find a new rope, change their way of traveling across the rope. Continue pattern.<br>This lesson is similar to lesson 1 in that the previous part of the lesson has been extremely vigorous. Depending upon fatigue factors, select one or two games from the following list. | Locomotor skills, p. 43 | Repeat 3 and 4. | | |

| Content | Teaching Strategies | References | Lesson 2a | 2b | 2c |
|---|---|---|---|---|---|
| | 6. Games: | Games, p. 273 | Play one or two | | |
| | *Numbers*—This game develops running, dodging, stopping, and hitting skills. Class is in scattered formation. On signal, players move about doing designated locomotor skill. A number is called out and all players must form a group of that particular number. Those who do not must "make a funny face." Game continues with different locomotor movements and a variety of numbers being called. | Numbers, p. 277 | games. | | |
| | *Loose Caboose*—This game develops running, dodging, and tagging skills. Groups of three create a train by each member holding onto the waist of the player in front of them. The front player is the "engine," the second the "baggage car," and the last person in line is the "caboose." There are several "loose cabooses" who try to attach themselves to the back of a train. When this happens, the engine becomes a new "loose caboose." | Loose Caboose, p. 275 | | | |
| **Part 3: Closure**<br>*(1 to 2 minutes)* | Discuss the difference between directional movements and pathways of movement. | Space awareness, p. 39 | | | |

**Level** II  **Unit 1:** Manipulative/Movement Skills
**Lesson 3.** Rolling
**Main Theme** Rolling a ball
**Subthemes** Jumping and dodging; Change of direction
**Equipment** Class set of hoops and balls

**Additional Lessons** If children are not used to developing their own inventive games or if the teacher is trying this for the first time, develop one or two more lessons stressing rolling and one or more skills of traveling and change of direction.

| Content | Teaching Strategies | References | Lesson 3a | 3b | 3c |
|---|---|---|---|---|---|
| **Entry Activity** | Place hoops and 8½" utility balls in four containers. Take a hoop and play with it in your own space. | | Repeat previous. | Repeat previous. | Repeat previous. |
| **Part 1: Introductory Activities** (5 to 6 minutes)<br><br>Running and jumping<br>Change of direction | When everyone is ready, ask them to stop and place their hoops on the floor. Pose the following challenges:<br>1. "Show me how many ways you can cross over your hoop." Watch for a few moments. Add, "Cross with one foot and land on two feet bending knees as you land." Then add "sideways, hands only," etc.<br>2. "See if you can run anywhere and jump over as many hoops as you can." Stress good knee bending on landing. Add "land in middle of hoop and jump, making a shape in the air," etc.<br>3. "Can you run and when you meet another player or a hoop shift sideways and continue?"<br>4. Repeat 3 and change direction or speed each time you shift. | Tag games, p. 273 | Play tag game, Tails (p. 31 of this guide). | Play Tails (p. 31 of this guide). | Design your own lesson. |
| **Part 2: Skill Development** (15 to 25 minutes)<br><br>Rolling a ball | *Individual activities:*<br>Ask children to get a ball and take it to a hoop.<br>1. "Can you roll the ball around your hoop, keeping it very close to you?"<br>2. "See if you can roll it with your elbow, tummy, knee," etc. Continue pattern.<br><br>*Partner activities:*<br>1. In partners with one ball, and hoops put away, pose challenges involving a roll to each other with different parts of the body; roll under different parts of the body; roll when facing in different directions.<br>If the class has not previously been introduced to making up their own creative games, they should be ready by now. Keep your first challenges very simple.<br>2. In partners, with one hoop, "Can you make up a game, in your own space, that has a roll and uses your equipment?" Give the class a few minutes, watch for one or two interesting games, then have the class stop and watch these games.<br>3. Pose another challenge, but add one more piece of equipment to the challenge. Select one or two for demonstration. | Inventive games, pp. 215, 254, 272 | Repeat 1 and 2.<br><br><br><br><br>Repeat 1 and 2 with beanbag or traffic cones. | Leave out.<br><br><br><br><br>Repeat 1 and 2 with wall target or chairs. | |
| **Part 3: Closure** (1 to 2 minutes)<br><br>Rolling a ball | Discuss the importance of "pushing" action in rolling a ball. | | | | |

**Level** II  **Unit 1:** Manipulative/Movement Skills
**Lesson 4.** Carrying
**Main Theme** Carrying
**Subtheme** Traveling in different ways
**Equipment** Class set of hoops and 8½″ utility balls

**Additional Lessons** Each additional lesson should stress carrying a different kind of small equipment (beanbag, wand, individual rope, etc.) and traveling with individual parts leading.

| Content | Teaching Strategies | References | Lesson 4a | 4b | 4c |
|---|---|---|---|---|---|
| **Entry Activity** | Place small equipment, including one hoop for each child, in containers. Free play with hoops only. | | Repeat previous. | Repeat previous. | Repeat previous. |
| **Part 1: Introductory Activities** *(4 to 5 minutes)* <br><br> Running, jumping, skipping, and sliding <br> Traveling on different parts | With children in scattered formation and standing next to a hoop, <br> 1. Play Nine Lives; <br> 2. Repeat game with skipping only; <br> 3. Repeat game with sliding only. | Skipping, p. 51 <br> Sliding, p. 51 | Repeat 1 to 3. | Play a tag game. | Play a tag game. |
| **Part 2: Skill Development** *(15 to 25 minutes)* <br><br> Gripping an object with various parts of body <br> Manipulating an object <br> Carrying an object while changing speed and direction | *Individual activities:* <br> In many game activities, players are required to grip, manipulate, and carry a bat or small equipment with dexterity and safety. The following challenges stress this carrying skill. <br> 1. "Show me how many different parts of your body you can balance the hoop on." <br> 2. "How many different parts of your body can you grip it with?" <br> 3. "Hold the hoop behind your back and run in different directions without losing it or hitting anyone." Repeat with other parts of the body. <br> 4. "Place the hoop on your head (or any other part) and travel, changing direction." Use a drum or whistle to signify a change in direction and/or level. | | Repeat 1 to 3. | Leave out. | Repeat 4. |
| | *Partner activities:* <br> 1. In partners, follow the leader with the leader constantly changing ways of balancing a hoop as he or she travels. <br> 2. "With your partner and two hoops, can you make up a game in which both players carry their hoops?" <br> 3. Introduce a ball to the above game. <br> 4. Create other challenges involving carrying an object plus traveling and changing direction. | Inventive games, pp. 215, 254, 272 | Repeat 2. | Play one or two structured games. | Repeat 3. |
| **Part 3: Closure** *(1 to 2 minutes)* <br><br> Carrying an object | Emphasize the importance of carrying an object with care and concern for others. | | | | |

**Level** II   **Unit 1:** Manipulative/Movement Skills
**Lesson 5.** Throwing
**Main Theme** Throwing
**Subthemes** Rolling a ball; Traveling; Change of direction
**Equipment** Class set of utility balls; Variety of small equipment

**Additional Lessons** As emphasized in lesson 5, this should be an exploratory lesson to observe and determine the level of skill and to plan additional lessons as the skill needs dictate. The following lessons provide additional time for observation and for practicing throwing skills.

| Content | Teaching Strategies | References | Lesson 5a | 5b | 5c |
|---|---|---|---|---|---|
| **Entry Activity** | Place a variety of balls and small equipment in each container. Free play with equipment. | | Repeat previous. | Repeat previous. | Repeat previous. |
| **Part 1: Introductory Activities** (*4 to 5 minutes*)<br><br>Traveling with a change of direction and speed | 1. Ask children to put equipment away and return with a ball. Stress that balls must remain stationary. Children run around or jump over any ball.<br>2. Add a change of speed to challenge. | | Repeat 1 and 2 adding a change in level to challenge. | Play tag game. | Design your own lesson. |
| **Part 2: Skill Development** (*15 to 25 minutes*)<br><br>Rolling a ball<br><br>Throwing an object with one or two hands<br><br>Throwing from a variety of positions<br><br>Throwing while on the move | The central emphasis of this lesson is to determine the level of throwing skill of the class. Adjust challenges according to the needs and interests of your class.<br>1. Tell children to get a ball and stand about six to eight feet away from the wall. Review rolling ball to wall with each hand and from a variety of positions.<br>2. "Let me see how well you can throw the ball against the wall with your right hand, left hand, two hands."<br>3. Draw a target (or place milk cartons or beanbags near the wall) on the wall and try to hit it.<br>4. "Kneel (or sit, stand sideways, etc.) and try and hit your target."<br>5. With partners about eight feet apart and with one ball, throw and catch the ball.<br><br>This lesson has been restricted to throwing skills with little concern for stopping or catching the ball. Continue lesson with partners inventing their own games adding small equipment as desired. The structured games listed below also stress throwing and give the teacher an opportunity to observe the general level of throwing skill.<br>6. Games:<br>*Keep Away*—This game develops passing, catching, and guarding skills. Class is divided into two teams. One team has the ball and passes it to teammates. Opposing players attempt to intercept the ball or break up the pass.<br>*Bombardment*—This game develops throwing, catching, and guarding skills. Class is divided into two teams. Each team has an equal number of milk cartons set up near their respective endlines. Teams must remain on their own half of the playing area. Each team tries to knock down all of the opponent's milk cartons by rolling and throwing balls (nerf, foam). | Throwing skills, p. 58<br><br><br><br><br><br><br><br><br><br><br><br><br><br><br><br><br><br>Games, p. 273<br>Keep Away, p. 281<br><br><br><br><br>Bombardment, p. 279 | Repeat 5 adding throw with right and left hands from kneeling and sitting positions and with both partners moving.<br><br><br><br><br><br>Play one or two structured games. | Repeat 5 with additional challenges.<br><br><br><br><br><br><br><br><br><br>Play one or two structured games. | |
| **Part 3: Closure** (*1 to 2 minutes*) | Discuss the need to throw a ball with either hand. | | | | |

**Level II   Unit 1:** Manipulative/Movement Skills
**Lesson 6.** Catching
**Main Theme** Catching an object
**Subtheme** Throwing
**Equipment** Class set of utility balls, plus variety of small equipment

**Additional Lessons** Once the basic throwing and catching skills have been introduced, concentrate on one catching skill and several throwing and/or traveling skills. Although children enjoy inventing their own games, they also enjoy lead-up or modified team games. Include both types of games.

| Content | Teaching Strategies | References | Lesson 6a | 6b | 6c |
|---|---|---|---|---|---|
| **Entry Activity** | Place a variety of balls and small equipment in each container. Free play with equipment. | | Repeat previous. | Repeat previous. | Repeat previous. |
| **Part 1: Introductory Activities** (3 to 5 minutes)<br><br>Running, jumping, and landing<br>Change of direction and pathway | Put equipment away, then pick up a beanbag and find a space.<br>1. "Run and jump over as many beanbags as you can."<br>2. Repeat 1; however, after beanbag, change direction.<br>3. "Using the beanbags, can you run, skip, slide, or hop and trace out a circle (or square, triangle, zigzag) as you move from one beanbag to another?" | | Repeat 1 and 2. | Play a tag game. | Design your own lesson. |
| **Part 2: Skill Development** (15 to 25 minutes)<br><br>Two-hand underhand catch<br>Two-hand overhand catch | *Individual activities:*<br>In this part of the lesson stress catching, but also review throwing, adding from below waist and above shoulders. Also review throwing.<br>1. "Show me how many different ways you can throw your beanbag up and catch it with both hands."<br>2. Repeat above, but catch bag when it is "above" shoulders or "below" waist. This limitation encourages children to anticipate and move into a good set position prior to catching the beanbag.<br>3. Exchange beanbag for a ball, move to wall. Roll to wall, stop, rebound; one-hand underhand throw to wall, catch, rebound; one-hand overhand throw and catch, rebound; throw at a target on wall and catch, rebound. | Throwing, p. 58<br>Catching, pp. 61, 406<br>Softball skills, p. 404 | Repeat 3. | Leave out. | |
| | *Partner activities:*<br>1. Practice throwing and catching (eight to ten feet apart).<br>2. Change level (sit, kneel) and throw and catch.<br>3. Practice throwing and catching: one partner stationary and one moving; both partners moving.<br>4. "Can you make up a throwing and catching game with your partner, one ball, and one other piece of equipment? One more thing—both players must always be on the move." | Structured games, pp. 273, 412 | Play one or two games. | Play one or two games. | |
| **Part 3: Closure** (1 to 2 minutes)<br><br>Catching skills | Discuss and illustrate different ways of catching a ball. | | | | |

**Level** II **Unit 1:** Manipulative/Movement Skills
**Lesson 7.** Bouncing
**Main Theme** Bouncing
**Subthemes** Throwing and catching
**Equipment** Variety of balls and small equipment

**Additional Lessons** Additional lessons should enhance bouncing skills as well as provide opportunities for children to develop inventive games in groups. Begin with a brief introductory activity, then devote the remaining time to bouncing skills combined with previously learned skills.

| Content | Teaching Strategies | References | Lesson 7a | 7b | 7c |
|---|---|---|---|---|---|
| **Entry Activity** | Place a variety of balls and a selection of small equipment in containers. Free play activities. | | Repeat previous. | Repeat previous. | Repeat previous. |
| **Part 1: Introductory Activities** *(3 to 5 minutes)* <br><br> Hopping and jumping <br> Change of speed <br> Change of direction | Equipment away and take a hoop to your own space. <br> 1. "Hop around hoop and in and out of hoop." <br> 2. "Jump around hoop and jump in and out of hoop." <br> 3. "Run anywhere jumping over first hoop, change direction, and hop to next hoop." <br> 4. "Run and jump over first hoop, change speed, and move to a new hoop." | | Repeat 3 and 4. | Repeat 3 and 4 and add a change of level to challenge. | Play a tag game. |
| **Part 2: Skill Development** *(15 to 25 minutes)* <br><br> Bouncing and catching <br> Traveling and bouncing | The following sequence of challenges begin in a stationary position, then gradually add catching, traveling, and change of speed and direction. <br> 1. "Show me how many parts of your body you can bounce the ball with." <br> 2. "Bounce the ball very low . . . very high . . . to the right . . . under your leg," etc. <br> 3. "Can you bounce the ball and do a trick before it bounces again?" <br> 4. Pose challenges to include bounce and catch, and bounce against wall and catch. | Bouncing a ball, p. 63 <br> Basketball skills, p. 383 | Repeat 3 and 4. | Repeat 4 and lengthen distance from wall. | Leave out. |
| | This age level, particularly third graders, enjoys playing on teams and displays good competitive spirit. Continue to stress both inventive games, involving two or more children, as well as structured games such as those listed below. <br> 5. Games: <br> *Guard Ball*—This game develops throwing, catching, and guarding skills. Players in section A try to pass balls to their teammates in section C. Players in the center section (B) attempt to block passes with their hands. Points are awarded for successful passes. | Structured games, p. 273 <br> Basketball lead-up games, p. 390 <br> Guard Ball, p. 280 | Repeat 3 and change type of equipment. | Repeat 3 with new equipment. | Play one or more structured games. |

X    X    X        Team A
_____

⊗    ⊗    ⊗        Team B
_____

○    ○    ○        Team C

| Content | Teaching Strategies | References | Lesson 7a | 7b | 7c |
|---|---|---|---|---|---|
| | *Four Square*—This game develops bouncing and striking skills. One player stands in each square. The game begins by one player bouncing the ball and then hitting it with one or both hands so that it bounces into one of the other squares. Player receiving the ball hits it after one bounce to any of the other squares. Game proceeds until a player fails to return the ball properly or commits a foul. When this happens, the offending player goes to the end of the line and all players move up one square toward square D. | Four Square, p. 278 | | | |

**Part 3: Closure**
*(1 to 2 minutes)*

| Bouncing skill | Discuss importance of "pushing" rather than "slapping" the ball toward the floor. |
|---|---|

# Game Activities
## Developmental Level II
## Unit 2: Ball Skills

## Expected Learning Outcomes

### Psychomotor Skills

1. Trapping ball with legs, shins, or feet
2. Traveling with change of speed and direction
3. Throwing and catching a ball
4. Kicking a stationary or moving ball
5. Gaining possession of a moving ball
6. Dribbling a ball using right and left foot
7. Striking a ball with hand or arm
8. Striking a ball with a racquet
9. Hitting a ball with a bat
10. Controlling a moving ball with an implement

### Cognitive and Affective Knowledge and Skills

1. Understanding space awareness with respect to other players, equipment, and general space
2. Understanding and appreciation of rules and regulations
3. Ability to play as a leader or follower in a game setting
4. Ability to plan and share creative ideas relating to partner or group inventive game activities
5. Appreciation of others' creative talents and limitations
6. Concern for safety of others and self

**Level** II **Unit 2:** Ball Skills
**Lesson 1.** Gaining Possession of a Ball
**Main Theme** Gaining possession of a ball
**Subthemes** Traveling and stopping; Rolling
**Equipment** Class set of utility balls; Variety of small equipment

**Additional Lessons** Gaining possession of a ball with the legs, shin, or feet is an important skill for many low organization games and an integral part of soccer. Allow children to practice controlling the ball and basic trapping skills. Stress both conscious practice and general exploration.

| Content | Teaching Strategies | References | Lesson 1a | 1b | 1c |
|---|---|---|---|---|---|
| **Entry Activity** | Place balls and a variety of small equipment in containers. Free play. | | Repeat previous. | Repeat previous. | Repeat previous. |
| **Part 1: Introductory Activities**<br>*(5 to 6 minutes)*<br><br>Traveling and stopping<br>Change of direction | Equipment away and section places.<br>　1. "Run, change direction, stop when you see an open space, touch ground with fingertips, and continue."<br>　2. Repeat above, changing to "a skip, slide, hop, or gallop after each stop."<br>　3. "Run, jump, make a shape in the air, land, and continue pattern." | Shadow game (p. 35 of this guide). | Repeat 2 and 3. | Play Tails (p. 31 of this guide). | Play a tag game. |
| **Part 2: Skill Development**<br>*(15 to 25 minutes)*<br><br>Rolling and stopping with lower body<br>Throwing and stopping with lower body | *Individual activities:*<br>Central focus is to encourage children to move into a ready position, then to use leg, shin, or feet to stop or trap the ball. Each child has a ball and stands about eight feet away from the wall.<br>　1. "See if you can roll the ball toward the wall and stop it when it rebounds back without using your hands." Choose children using upper leg, shins, or one foot to demonstrate.<br>　2. Roll and stop with shins.<br>　3. Roll and stop with right, then left foot.<br>　4. Repeat 1, 2, and 3 with a throw.<br>　5. "Find a space. Throw the ball up, let it bounce, then try to trap it with your shins or feet. Repeat without a bounce." | Trapping skills, p. 317<br>Relays, pp. 225, 228 | Repeat 2 and 3. | Repeat 4 and 5. | Leave out. |
| | *Partner activities:*<br>　1. Present challenges involving the following:<br>　　a. roll ball to each other stopping it with any part of lower body;<br>　　b. roll and stop with shins, right leg, left leg, from side of foot, etc.;<br>　　c. bounce ball to each other, stopping it with parts of lower body;<br>　　d. throw to each other stopping with legs, shins, or feet;<br>　　e. roll or throw to wall stopping rebound with legs, shins, or feet;<br>　　f. roll or throw to target, stopping rebound with legs, shins, or feet;<br>　　g. one stationary, rolls, partner moves to control and trap ball.<br>　2. "See if you can make up a game with your partner that includes a ball, one piece of equipment, stopping the ball with your feet, and in your own space." | Structured games, p. 273<br>Soccer lead-up games, p. 324 | Repeat 1. | Repeat 2. | Play one or two structured games. |

| Content | Teaching Strategies | References | Lesson 1a | 1b | 1c |
|---|---|---|---|---|---|
| | *Group activities:* | | | Repeat 1. | |
| | 1. In fours: "Make up a game in your group of four, with two goals (use any small equipment), no goalie, and include some form of a trap." | | | | |
| | 2. Games: | | | | |
| | *Boundary Ball*—This game develops kicking and trapping skills. Class is divided into two teams who must remain on their own half of the playing area. Players move about freely on their own half. Each team tries to kick balls across the opponent's goal line. Players try to prevent balls from crossing their own goal line. One point is awarded each time a ball crosses the opponent's goal line. | Boundary Ball, p. 283 | | | |
| | *Battle Ball*—Kicking and trapping skills are developed. Class is divided into two teams who then take positions on opposing lines and hold hands with team members. Each team tries to kick the ball (foam) over the opponent's line. | Battle Ball, p. 283 | | | |

**Part 3: Closure**
*(1 to 2 minutes)*

| | | | | | |
|---|---|---|---|---|---|
| Trapping a ball | Discuss the different parts of the body that can be used to gain possession of a ball. | | | | |

**Level** II  **Unit 2:** Ball Skills
**Lesson 2.** Kicking a Stationary Ball
**Main Theme** Kicking a stationary ball
**Subthemes** Gaining possession; Traveling
**Equipment** Class set of utility balls; Variety of small equipment

**Additional Lessons** Additional lessons should concentrate on kicking a stationary ball. Use the direct method to teach children the form and the limitation method to encourage creativity in game development.

| Content | Teaching Strategies | References | Lesson 2a | 2b | 2c |
|---|---|---|---|---|---|
| **Entry Activity** | Place balls, milk cartons, skittles, and traffic cones in containers. Free play with balls and equipment. | | Repeat previous. | Repeat previous. | Repeat previous. |
| **Part 1: Introductory Activities** (*5 to 6 minutes*) | Leave equipment on floor and balls away. | Tag games, p. 273 | Play a tag game. | Play Nine Lives (p. 30 of this guide). | Design your own lesson. |
| | 1. "Begin traveling any way you like and when you meet a piece of equipment, jump over it and change direction." | | | | |
| Traveling | 2. Repeat 1, hopping only, skipping only, sliding only, etc. | | | | |
| Change of direction | 3. Play a tag game. | | | | |
| **Part 2: Skill Development** (*15 to 25 minutes*) | *Individual activities:* Children of this age level should be able to kick the ball reasonably well with their strongest kicking foot and with proportionately less proficiency with the other foot. This is an important time to allow for experimentation but also to consciously stress kicking with either foot. Emphasize proper form rather than distance or accuracy. | Kicking skills, p. 64 Soccer kicking skills, p. 314 | Repeat 1 and 2. | Leave out. | |
| Kicking a stationary ball with right or left foot | | | | | |
| Kicking toward a target | | | | | |
| Stopping a ball | 1. Each child places his ball about eight feet from the wall. "See if you can kick the ball toward the wall and stop the rebound with any part of your body." Look for children who kick with instep and toe down. Have one or two demonstrate. | | | | |
| | 2. With ball stationary, have children stand with nonkicking foot next to the ball. Kick with instep—first with right foot, then with left foot. | | | | |
| | 3. Repeat above with player beginning three or four steps away from ball. | | | | |
| | 4. Repeat 3, but approach from the left, then right, side before kicking ball. | | | | |
| | *Partner activities:* The skill level normally possessed by children of this age range would indicate simple partner activities with short kicking distances. Group games involving kicking are normally very slow and inactive for the less-skilled performer. If this is the case, concentrate on simple partner activities including lots of small equipment, then progress to games involving three, four, or five children. | Soccer lead-up games, p. 324 | Repeat 1 and 2. | Repeat 2. | |
| | 1. In partners about ten to twelve feet apart— | | | | |
| | a. one kicks, the other traps; | | | | |
| | b. kick between goals; | | | | |
| | c. kick to knock over milk carton; | | | | |
| | d. kick to moving partner. | | | | |
| | 2. "Make up a kicking game with a partner." Add limitations. | | | | |

| Content | Teaching Strategies | References | Lesson 2a | 2b | 2c |
|---|---|---|---|---|---|
| | *Group activities:* | | | | |
| | 1. Games: | | | | |
| | *4 Goal Soccer*—This game develops kicking, dribbling, passing, and trapping skills. Class is divided into two teams and four goals are placed about the playing area. One team tries to kick the ball through the goals on the north and west side of the field while the other team scores by kicking through the goals on the south and east sides. This game is played without goalies. Major soccer rules apply. | 4 Goal Soccer, p. 281 | | | |
| | *Place Kickball*—This game develops running, kicking, and catching skills. This game takes place on a softball diamond with one team positioned in the field and the other team taking up its place behind home plate as the kicking team. Each player on the kicking team is given one stationary kick and must then try to cross home plate before the fielded ball beats him or her there. The kicker is out if the ball is caught on a fly or if the ball beats the kicker home. | Place Kickball, p. 283 | | | |

**Part 3: Closure**
*(1 to 2 minutes)*

| Content | Teaching Strategies | | | | |
|---|---|---|---|---|---|
| Kicking a stationary ball | Discuss importance of keeping toe down when kicking a ball. | | | | |

**Level** II **Unit 2:** Ball Skills
**Lesson 3.** Kicking a Moving Ball
**Main Theme** Kicking a moving ball
**Subthemes** Gaining possession; Traveling
**Equipment** Class set of utility balls and hoops; Variety of small equipment

**Additional Lessons** Continue lesson structure, as illustrated in lesson 3, stressing kicking a moving ball.

| Content | Teaching Strategies | References | Lesson 3a | 3b | 3c |
|---|---|---|---|---|---|
| **Entry Activity** | Place hoops, balls, and other small equipment in the containers. Free play with equipment. | | Repeat previous. | Repeat previous. | Repeat previous. |
| **Part 1: Introductory Activities** *(5 to 6 minutes)* | Equipment away, then ask class to get a hoop and find a space. Place hoop on ground. | Tag games, p. 273 | Repeat 1 to 3. | Repeat 1 and 3 and change equipment. | Design your own lesson. |
| | 1. Run and jump over hoops. | | | | |
| Traveling | 2. Repeat 1, but change speed and direction after each jump. | | | | |
| Change of speed | 3. Repeat 2 with change of speed, direction, and level after each jump. | | | | |
| Change of level | 4. Play tag games. | | | | |
| **Part 2: Skill Development** *(15 to 25 minutes)* | *Individual activities:* Equipment away, get a ball, and find a space about fifteen feet from the wall. | Kicking Skills, pp. 64, 314 Trapping skills, p. 317 | Repeat 3. | Leave out. | |
| Kicking a moving ball | *Note:* This skill requires the player to move into position so that the nonkicking foot is near the side of the ball. | | | | |
| Gaining possession of a moving ball | 1. Start by rolling the ball toward the wall, run after it, and kick it toward the wall. Use any part of the body to stop it and repeat pattern. | | | | |
| | 2. Repeat above with opposite foot. | | | | |
| | 3. Roll ball into open space, run after it, kick it, chase it, and trap it with feet. Repeat with opposite foot. | | | | |
| | *Partner activities:* | Inventive games, pp. 215, 254, 272 | Repeat 3 and 4. | Repeat 5 in groups of four. | |
| | 1. One rolls to partner who kicks it back. | | | | |
| | 2. Both kicking it back and forth without trapping the ball. | | | | |
| | 3. Kicking back and forth through a goal (two milk cartons) or toward a target. | | | | |
| | 4. "Make up a game that requires the ball to be kicked while it is moving, a milk carton, and in your own space." | | | | |
| | 5. "In groups of three, make up a game with three milk cartons and require a kick, a trap, and everyone always moving." | | | | |
| | *Note:* Three rather than two goals will normally lead to a cooperative game rather than a two-on-one competitive game. | | | | |
| | 6. Game: Boundary Ball (see lesson 1 of this unit, p. 000) | Boundary Ball, p. 283 | | | |
| **Part 3: Closure** *(1 to 2 minutes)* | | | | | |
| Kicking a moving ball | Discuss importance of getting into proper position before kicking a moving ball. | | | | |

**Level** II  **Unit 2:** Ball Skills
**Lesson 4.** Dribbling and Controlling a Ball
**Main Theme** Dribbling and controlling a ball
**Subthemes** Gaining possession; Kicking; Change of direction and pathway
**Equipment** Class set of utility balls; Variety of small equipment

**Additional Lessons** In almost every classroom situation, all the activities listed in this lesson cannot be thoroughly covered in a typical lesson. Hence, with additional lessons, begin with a brief introductory activity, then stress the second and third parts of the lesson.

| Content | Teaching Strategies | References | Lesson 4a | 4b | 4c |
|---|---|---|---|---|---|
| **Entry Activity** | Place balls, milk cartons, traffic cones, and beanbags in containers. Free play with equipment. | | Repeat previous. | Repeat previous. | Repeat previous. |
| **Part 1: Introductory Activities** *(5 to 6 minutes)*<br><br>Traveling<br>Change of direction and pathway | Equipment away and children standing in own spaces.<br>1. Running with change of direction.<br>2. Begin with a run and each time you change direction, change your method of traveling (skip, slide, etc.).<br>3. In partners, "Follow the leader with leader moving from one pathway to another (from circle to zigzag, etc.)." | | Repeat 2 and 3. | Play a tag game. | Design your own lesson. |
| **Part 2: Skill Development** *(15 to 25 minutes)*<br><br>Dribbling with right and left foot<br>Dribble and stop the ball<br>Dribble, kick, and trap | *Individual activities:*<br>Dribbling is basically controlled striking, and thus requires the player to "push" rather than kick or strike the ball.<br>1. With players standing in their own space with a ball, "See if you can move the ball around your own space without losing control—begin with your strongest foot, try your other foot, now try using both."<br>2. "Try dribbling anywhere and stop the ball when you get too close to another player." Continue pattern.<br>3. "Can you dribble with your feet and change direction?"<br>4. "Can you move the ball sideways?"<br>5. "Get three pieces of small equipment and place them in a straight line. See if you can move the ball in and out of your equipment."<br><br>*Partner activities:*<br>1. In partners, "Follow the leader around obstacles."<br>2. "Make up a game with your partner that has a dribble and a pass and two pieces of equipment."<br><br>*Group activities:*<br>1. In threes, with one ball and one hoop, make up a game that requires a dribble and two hoops. Repeat above game with two hoops.<br>2. Repeat 3 and add one more player. | Soccer dribbling skills, p. 318 | Repeat 2 to 4.<br><br><br><br><br><br><br><br>Repeat 1 and 2.<br><br><br><br><br>Repeat 1 and 2. | Repeat 5. | |
| **Part 3: Closure** *(1 to 2 minutes)*<br><br>Dribbling a ball | Discuss importance of "pushing" rather than striking a ball. | | | | |

**Level II   Unit 2:** Ball Skills
**Lesson 5.** Hitting a Ball with Arm or Hand
**Main Theme** Hitting
**Subtheme** Individual parts
**Equipment** Variety of play and utility balls

**Additional Lessons** Additional lessons should stress hitting the ball with hand or arm.

| Content | Teaching Strategies | References | Lesson 5a | 5b | 5c |
|---|---|---|---|---|---|
| **Entry Activity** | Place a variety of large (8½'' or beach ball) lightweight balls in containers. Free play with balls. | | Repeat previous. | Repeat previous. | Repeat previous. |
| **Part 1: Introductory Activities** (*4 to 5 minutes*) <br><br> Traveling <br> Traveling on different parts | Equipment away. <br> 1. ''Run, changing direction and speed.'' <br> 2. ''Travel anywhere with left toe, right elbow, other parts leading.'' <br> 3. ''Travel on hands and one foot, four parts, other parts of body.'' <br> 4. Play a tag game. | Tag games, p. 273 | Repeat 1 to 3. | Play Nine Lives (p. 30 of this guide) | Play Tails (p. 31 of this guide) |
| **Part 2: Skill Development** (*15 to 25 minutes*) <br><br> Striking with parts of upper body <br> Striking ball from different levels | *Individual activities:* <br> Children in this grade level should know the difference between throwing, striking, and pushing a ball. However, since the level of skill is still rather weak, use large balls and begin hitting a stationary ball on the ground, then from different levels, and finally while traveling. If skill level is extremely low, review level I, unit 2, lesson 5, balloon activities (p. 00). <br> 1. Each child has a ball and stands about eight to ten feet from the wall. ''Show me how you can hit the ball with one or two hands toward the wall. Stop the rebound with your hands or feet.'' <br> 2. ''Can you hit (or strike) the ball with any other part of your upper body?'' Watch for head, shoulder, and back, and have children demonstrate. <br> 3. ''See if you can drop the ball, then hit it toward the wall. Try both hands.'' <br> 4. ''Try throwing a ball up, let it bounce, then strike it toward the wall.'' | Hitting a ball, p. 63 <br> Volleyball hitting skills, p. 367 <br> Relays, pp. 225, 228 | Repeat 1 and 2, varying distance from wall. | Leave out. | Leave out. |
| | *Partner activities:* <br> 1. In partners: Hitting to each other along ground from a bounce, in the air, at different levels, and with different parts of upper body. <br> 2. Tether Ball—This game develops striking skills. Players are on opposite sides of the restraining line. Players strike the ball with their hand. The first player who winds the ball around the pole is the winner. | Volleyball lead-up games p. 370 <br> Tether Ball, p. 272 | Play Two or Four Square. | Design challenge involving three players and striking. | Play one or two games. |
| | *Group activity:* <br> 1. Four Square | Four Square, p. 278 | | | |

Restraining line

| | | | | | |
|---|---|---|---|---|---|
| **Part 3: Closure** (*1 to 2 minutes*) <br><br> Striking with hands or arms | Illustrate why it is important not to relax the fingers, wrist, or arm just before or while performing a striking action. | | | | |

**Level** II  **Unit 2:** Ball Skills
**Lesson 6:** Striking a Ball with a Racquet
**Main Theme** Striking a ball with a racquet
**Subtheme** Gaining possession
**Equipment** A variety of racquets, paddles, pom-poms, or nerf balls

**Additional Lessons** Additional lessons should stress hitting the ball with an implement (bat or racquet) and not with hand or arm.

| Content | Teaching Strategies | References | Lesson 6a | 6b | 6c |
|---|---|---|---|---|---|
| **Entry Activity** | Place racquets, nerf balls, pom-poms, paper balls, and old tennis balls in container. Free play with balls only. | | Repeat previous. | Repeat previous. | Repeat previous. |
| **Part 1: Introductory Activities** (*4 to 5 minutes*) | 1. Travel using a run, slide, or skip and change speed and direction.<br>2. Tag game. | Tag games, p. 273 | Repeat 1 and 2. | Play a tag game. | Design your own lesson. |
| Traveling<br>Change of speed and direction | | | | | |
| **Part 2: Skill Development** (*15 to 25 minutes*)<br><br>Hitting a ball with a racquet | *Individual activities:*<br>If children have not been introduced to hitting through the use of nylon paddles and nerf balls, review lesson 6 of level I games, unit 2 (p. 00). This lesson will stress hitting a ball with a modified plastic racquet, a paddle ball bat, or other one-hand striking implements.<br>1. Arrange class in own space with racquet and ball. Stress proper grip, wrist action, and safety skills when using racquets. Demonstrate proper grip.<br>2. Using racquet and pom-pom, nerf ball, or paper ball, "Try throwing ball into air and catching it on your racquet. Kneel and repeat."<br>3. Hit ball toward wall, along ground, and from an overhand hit.<br>4. "How many times can you hit the ball into the air?"<br>5. "Can you run and keep hitting your ball into the air?"<br>6. "Can you hit the ball into the air by alternating sides of the racquet?"<br><br>*Partner activities:*<br>1. In partners: Hit ball back and forth along ground, from a bounce, while kneeling, and when both are facing back to back.<br>2. "Make up a game with your partner that has a striking action and a net or target."<br><br>*Group activity:*<br>1. "In groups of four, make up a game that involves a net (rope across two chairs) and a pass to your partner before it goes over the net." | Level I, unit 2, lesson 6, p. 40<br>Batting skills, p. 65<br><br><br><br><br><br><br><br><br><br><br><br>Individual and dual hitting games, pp. 410, 412 | Repeat 3 and 4 varying distance from wall.<br><br><br><br><br><br><br><br><br><br><br><br>Repeat 1 and 2.<br><br><br><br><br><br>Repeat 1. | Repeat 4 and 6. | |
| **Part 3: Closure** (*1 to 2 minutes*)<br><br>Striking with an implement | Discuss safety of other players while using an implement. | | | | |

**Level** II   **Unit 2:** Ball Skills
**Lesson 7.**  Striking a Ball with a Bat
**Main Theme**  Hitting
**Subthemes**  Throwing; Gaining possession
**Equipment**  15, 6½" balls, 15 bats, and a variety of small equipment

**Additional Lessons**  The following lessons are designed to introduce other types of hitting skills.

| Content | Teaching Strategies | References | Lesson 7a | 7b | 7c |
|---|---|---|---|---|---|
| **Entry Activity** | Place balls and bats and a variety of small equipment in containers. Free play with equipment. | | Repeat previous. | Repeat previous. | Repeat previous. |
| **Part 1: Introductory Activities** *(4 to 5 minutes)* <br><br>Traveling <br>Change of speed and direction | 1. Travel, stressing sideways, diagonal, and backward movements. <br> 2. Traveling on different parts. <br> 3. Play one or two tag games. | | Play Tails or a tag game (p. 31 of this guide). | Repeat 1 and 2. | Design your own lesson. |
| **Part 2: Skill Development** *(15 to 25 minutes)* <br><br>Hitting a ball with a bat <br>Throwing and catching | *Individual activities:* <br>Striking a ball with a bat is one of the basic skills of softball and should be learned by the end of the third grade. This skill is also used in other games such as Rounders, Modified Cricket, and in numerous inventive games developed by children. Stress proper grip, good swinging action, and a safe release of the bat. <br> 1. Explain, demonstrate, and practice skill. <br><br>*Partner activities:* <br> 2. In partners: With one bat, 6½" play ball or nerf ball, and approximately fifteen feet apart, practice underhand throw and hitting with your partner. <br>   a. Place ball on traffic cone (or batting T) and hit off cone. <br>   b. Vary distance between partners. <br>   c. Experiment with different types of balls. <br>   d. Repeat a, b, and c with one partner fungo hitting to the other. <br><br>*Group activities:* <br>Inventive games involving three or more players can be developed to enhance hitting and fielding skills. <br> 1. "In groups of six, make up a hitting game with two bases (traffic cones) and three hoops." <br> 2. Game: <br> *Swing at Four* (group of five or six)—This game develops pitching, hitting, throwing, and catching skills. Players take positions in the infield. The batter hits a pitched ball into the infield. Infield players retrieve the ball and throw it to first base. Each batter hits the ball four times and then positions are rotated. | Softball batting skills, p. 408 <br><br><br><br><br><br><br><br><br><br><br><br> Individual hitting games, p. 410 <br> Softball lead-up games, p. 412 <br> Swing at Four, p. 414 | Demonstrate and practice a one-hand hitting skill using a bat. <br><br><br><br><br><br><br><br><br><br><br><br> Play Rounders or make up a challenge involving this skill. | Demonstrate hockey-type hitting. <br><br><br><br><br><br><br><br><br><br><br><br> Play a modified floor or grass hockey game. | |
| **Part 3: Closure** *(1 to 2 minutes)* <br><br>Striking with a bat | Stress importance of good grip, swing, and follow-through. | | | | |

**Level** II **Unit 2:** Ball Skills
**Lesson 8.** Controlling a Moving Ball with an Implement
**Main Theme** Controlling a moving ball with an implement
**Subthemes** Passing; Change of direction; Change of speed
**Equipment** Class set of wands or hockey sticks, nerf or small play balls

**Additional Lessons** Additional lessons should stress dribbling and controlling a ball combined with one additional skill such as passing, checking, or shooting.

| Content | Teaching Strategies | References | Lesson 8a | 8b | 8c |
|---|---|---|---|---|---|
| **Entry Activity** | Place wands, plastic hockey sticks, nerf or small balls, and a variety of small equipment in containers. Free play with equipment. | | Repeat previous. | Repeat previous. | Repeat previous. |
| **Part 1: Introductory Activities** *(4 to 5 minutes)*<br><br>Traveling<br>Change speed and direction | 1. Pose challenges involving travel and changes of direction and speed.<br>2. Play a tag game. | Shadow game (p. 35 of this guide) or a tag game, p. 273 | Play a tag game. | Play a tag game. | Design your own lesson. |
| **Part 2: Skill Development** *(15 to 25 minutes)*<br><br>Dribbling with a stick<br>Dribbling, passing, and shooting | *Individual activities:*<br>1. Explain and demonstrate dribbling a ball or puck with a wand. Both require controlled passing movements. Practice.<br>2. Demonstrate proper grip, dribbling, and shooting skills.<br>3. Practice moving ball (ring or puck) around obstacles.<br>4. Shoot ball against wall and control rebound with stick.<br><br>*Partner activities:*<br>1. In partners, set up practice activities or develop skills involving dribbles around each other, follow the leader, side by side dribbles, and dribble and pass to each other.<br>2. Practice activities that involve passing to each other.<br>3. Practice dribble and pass to each other.<br>4. Set up two cones with balls on each set and practice shooting and stopping the puck. | Dribbling with a stick, p. 341<br>Relays, pp. 225, 228 | Repeat 1 to 3. | Repeat 4. | |
| | Children of this age level, like their older brothers and sisters in the intermediate grades, thoroughly enjoy playing field and floor hockey. Too often, however, it becomes a mass game with the better players generally dominating the playing. For this reason, emphasize participation games, progressing to games involving three, four, five, or six players and use a variety of small equipment. Divide into four or more groups to provide maximum participation.<br>1. "In partners, with a ball and two traffic cones, make up a game involving dribble and shoot." | Field hockey games, p. 346 | Repeat 1 with a modified game. | | |

| Content | Teaching Strategies | References | Lesson 8a | 8b | 8c |
|---|---|---|---|---|---|

*Group activities:*

1. "In fours, make up your own hockey game using four beanbags or four hoops."

2. Game:

    *Line Field Hockey*—This game develops shooting, passing, and receiving skills. The ball is placed in the center of the field. On signal, the first player from each team runs out, tries to gain possession, and attempts to score a goal by shooting the ball over the opponent's goal line. Players rotate positions after every goal.

Line Field
Hockey, p. 348

Repeat 1 with a modified game.

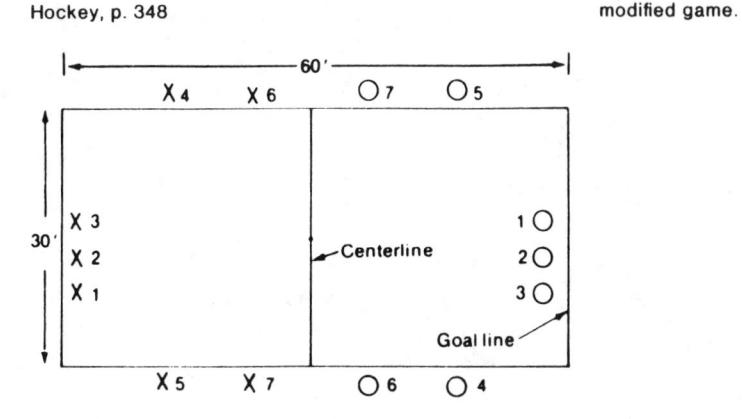

**Part 3: Closure**
*(1 to 2 minutes)*

Dribbling with a stick | Stress importance of keeping stick below waist level.

# Game Activities
## Developmental Level III
## Unit 1: Soccer

## Expected Learning Outcomes

**Psychomotor Skills**

1. Ability to kick a stationary and moving ball with the instep and side of foot
2. Ability to trap a ball with the upper body, leg, and foot
3. Ability to dribble a ball with reasonable control
4. Ability to pass a ball with reasonable accuracy
5. Ability to perform heading skills from a stationary and a moving position
6. Ability to perform a throw-in skill with reasonable speed and accuracy
7. Ability to demonstrate positional play and basic team strategy
8. Ability to move with the ball and demonstrate space awareness with respect to players and field of play

**Cognitive and Affective Knowledge and Skills**

1. Understanding of one's level of ability prior to and after a unit of soccer
2. Understanding basic positional play—defensively and offensively
3. Appreciation of individual differences of other children
4. Understanding of the basic rules and regulations of soccer
5. Respect and appreciation of officials and referees
6. Understanding and appreciation of the qualities of sportsmanship, team loyalty, and fair play
7. Ability to invent individual, partner, or group soccer practice activities or creative games involving one or more skills of the game

## Soccer Skill Evaluation

The general level of skill of each respective class can be determined through two evaluation techniques. The first is to have the children play one or more soccer-type lead-up games and to observe and record individual and general levels of skill and playing ability. This general overview provides a basis for the selection and emphasis of skills, practice activities, and lead-up games.

The following lead-up games can be used to provide a general overview of the class's general level of skill and playing ability.

| Game | Page in text |
|------|-------------|
| Sideline Soccer | 332 |
| Forwards and Backs | 333 |
| Seven-Person Soccer | 334 |

An Evaluation checklist (subjective), such as the one shown below, can be used to record performance on specific skills as well as to note general weaknesses or problems common to most children. (Kirchner, 8th ed., p. 337)

### Evaluation Checklist

*Rating*

1 needs practice                1st Evaluation _____

2 shows progress                2nd Evaluation _____

3 has acquired skill or concept   3rd Evaluation _____

| Name | Pass | Trap | Dribble | Shoot | Tackle | Uses Space | Moves Through Space | Change of Direction | Change of Pathway | Change of Speed |
|------|------|------|---------|-------|--------|-----------|--------------------|--------------------|------------------|-----------------|
| | | | | | | | | | | |
| | | | | | | | | | | |

A standardized or teacher-made test is the second technique used to assess a class's level of skill and playing ability. In the majority of classroom situations, a teacher-made test outline is normally used for this purpose. It is strongly recommended that teachers use a test similar to the one shown in the accompanying reference and modify this test to meet the level of skill, need, and interest of each respective class.

| Soccer Skill Test | Page in text |
|---|---|
| Kick and Trap | 338 |
| Dribbling | 338 |
| Shooting | 338 |
| Subjective Evaluation | 338 |

## Soccer Skill Test

| Name | Kick and Trap (total pts.) | Dribbling | Shooting | Subjective Evaluation | Total Score | Grade |
|---|---|---|---|---|---|---|
| 1<br>2<br>3<br>4<br>5 | | Rank total scores for the class, then convert to letter grades or ratings (superior, good, etc.). | | | | |

**Level** III **Unit 1:** Soccer
**Lesson 2.** Kick and Trap
**Main Theme** Kicking and trapping
**Subthemes** Traveling; Change of direction
**Equipment** Class set of soccer or other suitable balls

**Additional Lessons** The amount that can actually be covered in this lesson will depend upon time allotment, skill level, and general behavior of the class. If the teacher feels more time is necessary to cover skills or to establish more efficient procedures and class tone, develop one or more lessons.

| Content | Teaching Strategies | References | Lesson 2a | 2b | 2c |
|---|---|---|---|---|---|
| **Entry Activity** | Place a variety of balls (soccer, old volley balls, or utility balls) in containers. Free play with balls. | | Repeat previous. | Repeat previous. | Repeat previous. |
| **Part 1: Introductory Activities** *(5 to 6 minutes)*<br><br>Traveling—run, jump, slide, skip<br>Change of direction—forward, sideway, backward | When all students are changed and in the playing area, tell them to leave balls on the ground. Try the following challenges:<br>1. "When I call go, run anywhere in the playing area, do not touch balls, and listen for my next command . . . go." Wait a few moments, watching for spacing and directional movements, then call "stop" or "freeze."<br>2. "Begin running and change direction on signal . . . go . . . sideways . . . backward . . . stop . . . forward . . ." etc.<br>3. "Next, begin running and change direction and your way of traveling each time you meet a ball or another player." | Teaching strategies, p. 124 | Repeat 1 to 3. | Repeat 1 to 3. | Play a shadow game (p. 35 of this guide). |
| **Part 2: Skill Development** *(20 to 35 minutes)*<br><br>Instep kick—stationary ball, moving ball<br>Trapping—foot trap, shin trap | Arrange class into a large semicircle.<br>Practice skills with right and left foot.<br>1. Demonstrate instep kick and foot and shin trap. Use teacher or student to demonstrate, but be simple, clear, and brief.<br>2. Partner practice activities—passing and trapping, wall passing and trapping.<br>Teaching points: It is extremely important at this stage that children learn to move about the instructional area by your verbal commands and with care and concern for other children in the class. If movements are wreckless and too noisy or if students bunch up in one or more areas, call them back and repeat procedures. Also, the teacher should move to different parts of the instructional area throughout the lesson, giving advice, praise, and encouragement where needed. | Instep kick, p. 314<br>Foot trap, p. 317<br>Practice activities, p. 322 | Repeat 2, extending distance between players. | Leave out. | Repeat 2, extending distance between players. |
| | This part of the lesson should be used to complement the skills learned in previous parts of this lesson. | Techniques of teaching, p. 128<br>Lead-up games, p. 330<br>Soccer Dodge Ball, p. 330<br>Boundary Ball, p. 283 | Play one or two lead-up games. | Play one or two lead-up games. | Play one or two lead-up games. |
| | 3. Lead-up games:<br>*Soccer Dodge Ball*—A large circle is formed by half the players with the other half scattered inside. Attempts are made to eliminate members within the circle by hitting them with the ball (foam) below the waist. Student joins outside of circle when hit.<br>*Boundary Ball*—Two teams divided by centerline. Players try to kick ball across opponent's goal while trapping balls in own territory to prevent opponents from scoring. | | Before choosing one or more lead-up games, divide instructional area into halves or quadrants to encourage maximum participation.<br><br>Team (1) ↑ Team (3) ↑<br>Team (2) ↓ Team (4) ↓ | | Traffic cones to divide area. |

| Content | Teaching Strategies | References | Lesson 2a | 2b | 2c |
|---|---|---|---|---|---|

*Pin Soccer*—Two teams at endlines (shooting line) with pins along centerline. Players kick ball and attempt to knock over pins. Points are awarded for every pin knocked down.

Pin Soccer, p. 331

Team A                                                    Team B

X                              ⎘                              ○

X        X ← Team                ⎘                              ○
              captain

X                              ⎘        Team                   ○
                                        captain →

X                              ⎘                    ○           ○

X                              ⎘                              ○

X                              ⎘                              ○

              20'                            ← Pins        20'

↑
Shooting
line

---

**Part 3: Closure**
*(1 to 2 minutes)*

Kicking                    Discuss importance of keeping toe down when kicking a soccer ball.

---

**Level** III    **Unit 1:** Soccer
**Lesson 3.** Pass and Trap
**Main Theme** Passing and trapping
**Subthemes** Traveling; Change of speed
**Equipment** Variety of balls and small equipment

**Additional Lessons** A teacher may wish to continue with one or two more lessons to develop passing and trapping skills as well as to become more competent with the inventive games approach before progressing to lesson 4.

| Content | Teaching Strategies | References | Lesson 3a | 3b | 3c |
|---|---|---|---|---|---|
| **Entry Activity** | Place a variety of balls and small equipment in four containers. Free play with equipment. | | Repeat previous. | Repeat previous. | Repeat previous. |
| **Part 1: Introductory Activities** (5 to 6 minutes)<br><br>Traveling—run, jump, slide, skip<br>Change of speed<br>Change of direction | Balls away and scatter small equipment around instructional area.<br>1. "Travel and jump over small equipment."<br>2. "Travel, jump over equipment, change direction and speed, jump over another piece of small equipment, change direction and speed, and continue pattern."<br>3. Repeat 2 in partners and play Follow the Leader. | | Repeat 1 to 3. | Play a shadow game (p. 35 of this guide). | Design your own lesson. |
| **Part 2: Skill Development** (20 to 35 minutes)<br><br>Passing—inside and outside of foot, stationary or moving ball<br>Trapping—foot, shin, and side of foot | Arrange class in partners with one ball to each pair.<br>1. Review kicking and foot trap using right and left foot.<br>2. Form semicircle and demonstrate passing and trapping with outside of foot.<br>3. Practice partner activities (emphasizing side of foot)—passing and trapping.<br>Begin with simple tasks and gradually increase difficulty.<br>Sample Challenge:<br>4. "Can you make up a game with your partner, using one ball, two pieces of small equipment, a pass, and stay in your own space?" Allow time for partners to develop and practice their game. Choose one or two games for demonstration. Continue for a few more minutes, then give the following challenge.<br>5. "Now try and make up a game that has two balls, a pass, in your own space, and one piece of equipment." Develop other challenges emphasizing passing and trapping.<br>6. During this part of the lesson, three types of group activities may be used. First, if for various reasons more structure and tighter control is indicated, choose one or two lead-up games. Second, choose a lead-up game such as Circle Soccer. Let children play for a few minutes, then stop and say, "Play the same game, but team A (then B) must add one new rule to your game." Gradually allow children to change the game or add your own new rules, such as "and everyone must be always moving." Third, continue with inventive games involving three children. For example: "Make up a game in groups of three with one ball, four hoops, and requiring a pass and a trap." | Inventive games, pp. 215, 254, 294<br>Instep kick, p. 314<br>Side of foot kick, pp. 314, 315<br><br><br><br><br><br><br><br><br><br>Lead-up games, p. 332<br>Circle Soccer, p. 330 | Repeat 3, 4, and 5.<br><br><br><br><br><br><br><br><br><br><br><br><br><br><br><br>Choose one type of activity to repeat. | Leave out.<br><br><br><br><br><br><br><br><br><br><br><br><br><br><br><br>Develop inventive game in groups of three or four. | |
| **Part 3: Closure** (1 to 2 minutes)<br><br>Passing | Discuss the role of inventive games (to help develop skill and/or to allow children to use their creative abilities). | | | | |

**Level** III **Unit 1:** Soccer
**Lesson 4.** Dribble and Pass
**Main Theme** Dribbling and passing
**Subtheme** Traveling
**Equipment** Variety of balls and small equipment

**Additional Lessons** If one or more additional lessons are desired, concentrate on the basic skills of dribbling and passing.

| Content | Teaching Strategies | References | Lesson 4a | 4b | 4c |
|---|---|---|---|---|---|
| **Entry Activity** | Place a variety of balls and small equipment in four containers. Free play with equipment. | | Repeat previous. | Repeat previous. | Repeat previous. |
| **Part 1: Introductory Activities** *(5 to 6 minutes)* <br><br> Traveling—in different ways, (run, jump, etc.) | Equipment away with children standing in their own space. <br> 1. "Run, change direction and speed." <br> 2. "Run, jump, land, change direction, and continue." <br> 3. Play a tag game. | Tag games, pp. 273, 286 | Repeat 1 and 2. | Play a shadow game (p. 35 of this guide). | Design your own lesson. |
| **Part 2: Skill Development** *(20 to 35 minutes)* <br><br> Dribble—inside and outside of foot <br> Passing—stationary ball, moving ball | Arrange class in partners with one ball to each pair. Always practice with right and left foot. <br> 1. Review pass and trap. <br> 2. Arrange in semicircle. Demonstrate dribbling with inside and outside of foot and moving in different directions. <br> 3. Practice activities <br>   a. Individual Activities: dribble and stop on whistle, voice, or hand signal; dribble around obstacles; dribble in different directions. <br>   b. Partner Activities: follow the leader, dribble and pass. <br> Develop challenges that stress dribbling, using right and left foot, and passing to partner. Example: <br> 4. "Make up a game with your partner that involves a dribble with outside of foot, a change of direction, and one piece of equipment." <br> 5. "Can you make up a game that requires both players to dribble with the outside of their feet, a pass, and three pieces of equipment?" <br> 6. Lead-up game: <br>   *Forwards and Backs*—This game develops passing, dribbling, and trapping. Only "forwards" can score goals and "backs" serve as defensive players guarding their own endline. "Forwards" must play in front of their own center zone line and "backs" may not cross the center zone line that is on their half of the playing field. Forwards try to kick the ball over the opponent's goal line while backs try to gain possession and advance the ball to its offense (forwards). Forwards and backs change positions every few minutes. | Dribbling, p. 318 <br> Practice activities, p. 322 <br> Follow the Leader, p. 327 <br> Dribble and pass, p. 327 <br><br><br><br><br><br> Forwards and Backs, p. 333 | Repeat 3. <br><br><br><br><br><br><br><br> Repeat 5 and develop a new challenge for partners. | Leave out. <br><br><br><br><br><br><br><br> Repeat 5 and play one lead-up game. | |

71

| Content | Teaching Strategies | References | Lesson 4a | 4b | 4c |
|---|---|---|---|---|---|
| **Part 3: Closure**<br>*(1 to 2 minutes)* | | | | | |
| Dribbling | Emphasize the importance of "pushing" rather than kicking the ball when dribbling; look around while dribbling to know where opponents and teammates are; keep ball close to feet when opponents are near; dribble with short controlled steps. | | | | |

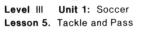

**Level** III **Unit 1:** Soccer
**Lesson 5.** Tackle and Pass
**Main Theme** Tackling and passing
**Subthemes** Traveling; Change of direction; Change of level
**Equipment** Soccer or utility balls and a variety of small equipment

**Additional Lessons** As suggested in the previous lesson, continue concentrating on tackling and passing with each supplementary lesson.

| Content | Teaching Strategies | References | Lesson 5a | 5b | 5c |
|---|---|---|---|---|---|
| **Entry Activity** | Place a variety of balls and small equipment in the four containers. Free play with equipment. | | Repeat previous. | Repeat previous. | Repeat previous. |
| **Part 1: Introductory Activities** (4 to 5 minutes) | One ball for each child—all other equipment away. Children standing in their own space with ball on ground. | Shadow game (p. 35 of this guide). | Repeat 1 and 2. | Play a shadow game (p. 35 of this guide). | Design your own lesson. |
| Traveling—in different ways Change of direction Change of level | 1. "Run, jump over ball, land, change direction and level, and continue." 2. "Run, jump, make a shape in air, land, change direction and speed, and continue." 3. Play a shadow game. | | | | |
| **Part 2: Skill Development** (20 to 35 minutes) | Arrange class in partners with two pieces of equipment and one ball for each pair. Review passing skills. | Tackling, p. 321 Partner Keep Away, p. 328 | Repeat 4 and 5 adding a new challenge. | Leave out. | |
| Passing—moving ball Tackling | 1. Passing between partners—both on the move. 2. Passing between goals—from right, left side, and center. 3. Arrange in semicircle. Demonstrate tackling skill. 4. Practice activities—Partner Keep Away. Keep ball away from partner by dribbling, dodging, stopping, and pivoting. 5. Inventive games: Pose the following types of challenges, stressing tackling and passing. "With your partner, a ball, and one other piece of equipment, can you play a game that involves tackling and passing?" "See if you can make up a passing and tackling game using two balls and no other equipment." | | | | |
| **Final Activity** (15 to 20 minutes) | 6. Lead-up games: | | Play one or two lead-up games. | Inventive games involving four players. | |
| Lead-up games Inventive games involving four players | *Shuttle, Dribble, and Tackle*—This game develops the movement concepts of using space, moving into space, change of direction and speed. Dribbling and tackling skills are developed. Player #1 dribbles the ball toward the other line while player #2 moves out to "tackle" player #1. Player #1 tries to reach the opposite line without being tackled. Allow about 20 seconds of play and then start the next two players. | Shuttle, Dribble, and Tackle, p. 330 | | | |
| | *One versus Two Players*—Two players (offense) attempt to keep the ball away from a third player (defense). This game is similar to keep away. Dribbling, passing, and tackling skills are used. | One versus Two, p. 330 | | | |
| | 7. For inventive games, begin with a question such as, "Can you make up a game in your group of four that has a tackle, a pass, and two hoops?" Continue changing limitations (rules, skills, equipment). | | | | |
| **Part 3: Closure** (1 to 2 minutes) | | | | | |
| Tackling | Explain and illustrate the correct method of tackling an opponent. Be quick and decisive; tackle when opponent is off balance; be ready to pass the ball quickly when possession is gained. | | | | |

**Level III    Unit 1:** Soccer
**Lesson 6.** Throw-in and Trap
**Main Theme** Throwing and trapping
**Subthemes** Traveling; Passing; Tackling
**Equipment** Soccer or utility balls and a variety of small equipment

**Additional Lessons** Additional lessons may be required to cover all the skills, practice activities, and games suggested. Stress throw-in, chest, and leg trap in one or all additional lessons.

| Content | Teaching Strategies | References | Lesson 6a | 6b | 6c |
|---|---|---|---|---|---|
| **Entry Activity** | Place a variety of balls and small equipment in the four containers. Free play with equipment. | | Repeat previous. | Repeat previous. | Repeat previous. |
| **Part 1: Introductory Activities** *(4 to 5 minutes)* <br><br> Traveling—different ways <br> Change of speed | 1. Leave balls scattered on ground. "Run, change direction, and stop in front of any ball." Continue pattern. <br> 2. "Repeat 1, but stop in front of ball with feet parallel . . . one in front of the other . . . parallel and continue pattern." <br> 3. Play partner tag, but do not touch any ball in the playing area. | Tag games, pp. 273, 286 | Repeat 1 to 3. | Repeat 3. | Play a shadow game (p. 35 of this guide). |
| **Part 2: Skill Development** *(20 to 35 minutes)* <br><br> Throw-in—feet parallel, feet apart <br> Trapping | 1. Arrange in semicircle and demonstrate throw-in skill with feet parallel or with one foot in front of the other. <br> 2. Practice Activities: Passing and trapping; throw-in to partner and trap; Wall passing and trapping; Throw-in to wall and partner traps rebound. <br> 3. Demonstrate chest and leg trap. <br> 4. Inventive games. Pose challenges that require either a throw-in, a trap, or both skills. Also, specify the type of throw-in or trapping skill. The following challenges will illustrate the type of questions to pose: "Make up a game with your partner in your own playing area and with one ball, using a throw-in pass and trapping the ball with your chest or upper leg." "With your partner use the wall and make up a drill or game to improve your throw-in and trapping skills." | Throw-in skill, p. 320 <br> Trapping skills, p. 317 <br> Wall passing, p. 326 | Repeat 4. | Leave out. | Leave out. |
| | 5. Arrange class into groups of five, then divide each group into two versus three players. Start with one player from group of three throwing ball up between two opposing players. Each side tries to keep possession. After a few minutes, ask groups to add one new rule to their games. A few minutes later, ask each group to add another new rule. Continue pattern. <br> 6. Keep two versus three situation, provide two goals, and play two versus three soccer. <br> 7. Allow each group of five to make up their own game with the only requirement being a throw-in. | Lead-up games, p. 322 | Repeat 6. | Repeat 7. | Play one or two lead-up games. |
| **Part 3: Closure** *(1 to 2 minutes)* <br><br> Throw-in | Discuss the advantages of a forward stride position rather than feet parallel position when executing a throw-in. | | | | |

**Level** III    **Unit 1:** Soccer
**Lesson 7.** Heading, Throw-in, and Dribble
**Main Theme** Throw-in, trap, and dribble
**Subthemes** Traveling; Change of direction
**Equipment** Soccer or utility balls and a variety of small equipment

**Additional Lessons** If additional lessons are required, follow the pattern illustrated below.

| Content | Teaching Strategies | References | Lesson 7a | 7b | 7c |
|---|---|---|---|---|---|
| **Entry Activity** | Place a variety of balls and small equipment in the four containers. Free play with equipment. | | Repeat previous. | Repeat previous. | Repeat previous. |
| **Part 1: Introductory Activities** (4 to 5 minutes)  Traveling—in different ways  Change of direction | Equipment away and find a space. 1. Have children run, skip, or slide in any direction. When you call out a number, such as three, everyone must try to get into groups of three. Continue pattern keeping numbers low (three, two, five, four). Later, for fun, increase number to ten or fifteen and watch what happens! 2. Individual dribbling. Ask class to take one ball each and find a space. Dribble in different directions; later, teacher calls out directions—"shift right, backward," etc. | | Repeat 1 and 2. | Play a tag game. | Design your own lesson. |
| **Part 2: Skill Development** (20 to 35 minutes)  Throw-in—feet parallel, feet apart  Trap—foot, shin, leg, chest  Dribble—right and left foot, inside and outside of foot  Heading | *Partner activities:* 1. Review throw-in, trap, and dribble. 2. Develop series of challenges involving throw-in, trap, and dribbling. For example: "In partners, with two hoops, a traffic cone, and one ball, see if you can invent a game that includes a trap and a throw-in." 3. Repeat previous challenge and substitute a dribble for trap and throw-in. 4. Practice partner activities "throw and head." 5. Partner "throws in" to partner who heads ball forward and down to first partner's feet. | Heading skills, p. 319  Throw and head, p. 326  Practice activities, p. 322 | Repeat 2 and 3. | Repeat 4. | |
| | *Group activities:* 1. Arrange class into groups of eight. Divide into four versus four. Use cones or milk cartons as goal posts (about six feet apart). Play four versus four and require two (or three) passes before a team can attempt to score a goal. Ball crossing side or endlines is put into play with a throw-in. No goalie for either team. 2. After a few minutes ask groups to add or modify one rule. Continue pattern every three or four minutes. 3. Allow groups of eight to make up their own games, involving one or more balls and their own selection of equipment. | | Repeat 3. | Repeat 3. | |

| Content | Teaching Strategies | References | Lesson 7a | 7b | 7c |
|---------|--------------------|-----------|-----------|----|----|

4. Lead-up game:

*Seven-Person Soccer*—Utilization of all soccer skills. Playing field can be divided in half to allow two games to be played for maximum participation. Official rules of soccer are followed.

Seven-Person
Soccer, p. 334

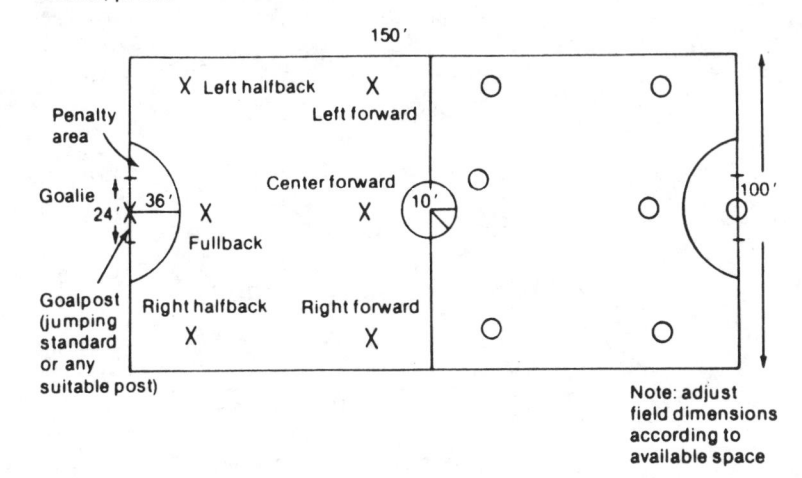

**Part 3: Closure**
*(1 to 2 minutes)*

Throw-in and trap     Discuss the importance of good teamwork.

**Level** III **Unit 1:** Soccer
**Lesson 8.** Pass, Trap, and Dribble
**Main Theme** Pass, trap, and dribble
**Subthemes** Traveling; Change of direction
**Equipment** Soccer or utility balls and a variety of small equipment

**Additional Lessons** If additional lessons are planned, it is suggested the final activity of each lesson stress 1 to 3 in the final activity of this lesson rather than playing eleven-person soccer.

| Content | Teaching Strategies | References | Lesson 8a | 8b | 8c |
|---|---|---|---|---|---|
| **Entry Activity** | Place a variety of balls and small equipment in four containers. Free play with equipment. | | Repeat previous. | Repeat previous. | Repeat previous. |
| **Part 1: Introductory Activities** (4 to 5 minutes) | Leave small equipment scattered over instructional area, balls away, and children standing in their own space. | Tag games, pp. 273, 286 | Repeat 2. | Play a tag game. | Repeat 2. |
| | 1. Individual running, skipping, sliding around and over obstacles. | | | | |
| Traveling | 2. Play shadow game around obstacles, teachers call out "move forward, move | | | | |
| —in different ways | sideways, move backward," as game progresses. | | | | |
| Pathways | 3. Play tag games. | | | | |
| —square, circle, zigzag | | | | | |
| **Part 2: Skill Development** (20 to 35 minutes) | Leave equipment scattered, ask children to get a ball and find a space. | | Leave out. | Leave out. | Leave out. |
| | 1. Individual dribbling around obstacles: dribble to an obstacle, circle it, and continue; dribble and make up pattern to and around objects. | | | | |
| Passing | 2. Equipment away and arrange class into partners with one ball between each | | | | |
| —right or left foot | pair; dribble and pass around instructional area; follow pathways such as | | | | |
| —inside or outside of foot | circle, square, etc., as partners dribble and pass around area. | | | | |
| Dribbling | 3. "Make up a game with your partner, in your own space, use two hoops, and | | | | |
| —with right or left foot | require a pass, dribble, and trap." | | | | |
| —with inside or outside of foot | 4. Develop other challenges involving a pass, dribble, and trapping skills. | | | | |
| Trapping | | | | | |
| —with chest, leg, shin, or foot | Arrange class into groups of twelve or fourteen and play one or more of the following activities: | Sideline Soccer, p. 332 | Play one or two lead-up games. | Repeat 2. | Repeat 3. |
| | 1. Lead-up games: Sideline Soccer, Forwards and Backs, Seven-Person Soccer. | Forwards and Backs, p. 333 | | | |
| | 2. Five versus Five, Six versus Six, Mini-Soccer. | Seven-Person Soccer, p. 334 | | | |
| | 3. Inventive games involving five or more players. | | | | |
| | *Note:* Subjective evaluation of each player's playing ability, improvement, and interpersonal development should be completed in this lesson. The evaluation checklist at the beginning of this unit should be used. | | | | |
| **Part 3: Closure** (1 to 2 minutes) | General discussion of soccer unit. | | | | |

**Level** III **Unit 1:** Soccer
**Lesson 9.** Evaluation
This lesson and additional lessons if needed should be used to administer the skill tests at the beginning of this unit.

Administer the skill tests used at the beginning of this unit (p. 67 of this guide).

# Game Activities
## Developmental Level III
## Unit 2: Touch Football

### Expected Learning Outcomes

**Psychomotor Skills**

1. Ability to punt a football
2. Ability to throw a spiral and lateral pass
3. Ability to catch a forward pass while running
4. Ability to center a ball with reasonable accuracy
5. Ability to block according to the rules of the game
6. Ability to play a variety of offensive and defensive positions

**Cognitive and Affective Knowledge and Skills**

1. Understanding of one's level of ability prior to and after a unit of football
2. Understanding of defensive and offensive positional play
3. Understanding of basic rules and regulations of touch football
4. Appreciation of individual differences of other children
5. Respect and appreciation of officials and referees
6. Ability to design simple offensive plays
7. Ability to modify or invent practice activities or inventive games involving touch football skills
8. Understanding and appreciation of good sportsmanship, team loyalty, and fair play

## Touch Football Skill Evaluation

The general level of skill of each respective class can be determined through two evaluation techniques. The first is to have the children play one or more touch football-type lead-up games and to observe and record individual and general levels of skill and playing ability. This general overview provides a basis for the selection and emphasis of skills, practice activities, and lead-up games.

The following lead-up games can be used to provide a general overview of the class's general level of skill and playing ability.

| Games | Page in text |
|---|---|
| One-Down Football | 361 |
| Punt and Catch | 360 |

An observation sheet, such as the one shown below, can be used to record performance on specific skills, as well as to note general weaknesses or problems common to most children.

### Class Observation Sheet—Touch Football

| | Level of Ability | | |
|---|---|---|---|
| **Skills** | **High** | **Low** | **Comments** |
| Forward pass | | | |
| Lateral pass | | | |
| Catching while on the move | | | |
| Punting | | | |
| Positional play—defense | | | |
| Positional play—offense | | | |

A standardized or teacher-made test is the second technique used to assess a class's level of skill and playing ability. In the majority of classroom situations, a teacher-made test outline is normally used for this purpose. It is strongly recommended that teachers use a test similar to the one shown in the accompanying reference and modify this test to meet the level of skill, need, and interest of each respective class.

| Touch Football Skill Test | Page in text |
|---|---|
| Accuracy Pass | 363 |
| Punting | 363 |
| Ball Carrying | 363 |
| Subjective Evaluation | 363 |

**Touch Football Skill Test**

| Name | Accuracy Pass (total pts.) | Punting (total pts.) | Ball Carrying (total pts.) | Subjective Evaluation (50 pts.) | Total Score | Grade |
|------|------|------|------|------|------|------|
| 1 | | | | | | |
| 2 | | Rank total scores for the class, then convert to letter grades or ratings (superior, good, etc.) | | | | |
| 3 | | | | | | |
| 4 | | | | | | |
| 5 | | | | | | |

**Level** III  **Unit 2:** Touch Football
**Lesson 2.** Pass and Catch
**Main Theme** Pass and catch

**Additional Lessons** The amount that can actually be covered in this lesson will depend upon time allotment, skill level, and general behavior of the class. If the teacher feels more time is necessary to cover skills or to establish more efficient procedures and class tone, develop one or more lessons.

| Content | Teaching Strategies | References | Lesson 2a | 2b | 2c |
|---|---|---|---|---|---|
| **Entry Activity** | Practice throwing, catching, or kicking. | | | | |
| **Part 1: Introductory Activities**<br>(4 to 5 minutes) | 1. Walk, jog, and run around outer edges of the playing field.<br>2. Calisthenics. | Calisthenics,<br>p. 180 | Repeat 1 and 2. | Rope jumping,<br>p. 509 | |
| **Part 2: Skill Development**<br>(20 to 35 minutes)<br><br>Forward pass catching | 1. Explain and demonstrate forward pass and catching skills.<br>2. Practice partner activities.<br>  a. Pass and catch with both stationary, and with the other moving.<br>  b. Pass and catch with one partner moving.<br>  c. Partner centers, runs forward to catch other's pass.<br>  d. Inventive drills or games. Present challenges to encourage partners to make up their own creative drills or games using a ball and one or more pieces of small equipment. | Forward pass,<br>p. 354<br>Practice<br>activities,<br>p. 358 | Review forward pass. Repeat 2b. | Leave out. | |
| | *Group activities:*<br>1. Lead-up game:<br>*One-Down Football*—This game develops throwing, catching, and tagging skills as well as movement concepts. The offensive team is given one down to score a touchdown by running or passing the ball. If tagged before reaching the goal line, the ball is downed and the other team takes over.<br>2. Inventive games. Present challenges involving two or four players (one vs. one, two vs. one, or two vs. two), a ball, and small equipment. Stress forward passing and catching. | Lead-up<br>games, p. 358<br>One-Down<br>Football,<br>p. 361 | Play One-Down Football. | Boundary Ball,<br>p. 283 (modify) | |

| Content | Teaching Strategies | | |
|---|---|---|---|
| **Part 3: Closure**<br>(1 to 3 minutes)<br><br>Forward pass | Discuss position of fingers on the ball, particularly for the proportionately smaller hands of elementary school children. Other key points: Keep ball above shoulder when arm moves back; throw ball from behind ear with strong shoulder and wrist snapping action; follow through with fingers pointing toward receiver. | | |

*Note:* Entry Activities should be provided for at the beginning of each lesson. See soccer unit for types of small equipment that should be
available prior to the beginning of each lesson.

**Level III** **Unit 2:** Touch Football
**Lesson 3.** Pass and Catch
**Main Theme** Pass and catch

**Additional Lessons** A teacher may wish to continue with one or more lessons to enhance passing and catching skills. Expand each lesson as illustrated below.

| Content | Teaching Strategies | References | Lesson 3a | 3b | 3c |
|---|---|---|---|---|---|
| **Entry Activity** | Place a variety of small equipment and footballs in four containers. Free play with equipment and balls. | | | | |
| **Part 1: Introductory Activities** *(4 to 5 minutes)*<br><br>Running<br>Conditioning Exercises | 1. Walk, jog, run—extend jogging and running time and maintain or reduce walking time.<br>2. Calisthenics: Continue above series of exercises and increase repetitions by one for each exercise. | Jogging, p. 191<br>Calisthenics, p. 180 | Repeat 1 and 2. | Design your own lessons. | Design your own lessons. |
| **Part 2: Skill Development** *(20 to 35 minutes)*<br><br>Passing<br>Catching | *Partner activities:*<br>1. Review forward pass and catching skill.<br>  a. Pass and catch—one stationary, the other on the move.<br>2. Explain and demonstrate lateral pass.<br>3. Practice Activities for lateral passing.<br>  a. Partners running and lateral passing back and forth. Vary the distance between players and the speed as drill progresses.<br>  b. Inventive drills or games. Ask partners to use three traffic cones (or any other available small equipment), and make up a drill that stresses a lateral pass. Design other similar challenges. | Lateral pass, p. 354<br>Practice activities, p. 358 | Review forward and lateral pass, 1a, and 3b. | | |
| | *Group activities:*<br>1. Lead-up games:<br>One-Down Football<br>*Borden Ball*—This game utilizes throwing and catching skills. Moving in general space with speed and the ability to change direction are developed. It is similar to "keep away," with goals being scored for points.<br>2. Inventive Games: Present challenges involving two to six players, one or more balls, and a variety of small equipment.<br>3. Modify lead-up games. | Lead-up games, p. 358<br>Inventive games, pp. 215, 254, 294<br>One-Down Football, p. 361<br>Borden ball p. 289 | Lead-up games, p. 358. | | |
| **Part 3: Closure** *(1 to 2 minutes)*<br><br>Lateral pass | Explain when a lateral pass may be used in touch football. | | | | |

**Level** III **Unit** Touch Football
**Lesson 4.** Punt and Catch
**Main Theme** Punt and catch

**Additional Lessons** If one or more additional lessons are desired, concentrate on the basic skills of punting and catching.

| Content | Teaching Strategies | References | Lesson 4a | 4b | 4c |
|---|---|---|---|---|---|
| **Entry Activity** | Place a variety of small equipment and footballs in four containers. Free play with equipment and balls. | | | | |
| **Part 1: Introductory Activities**<br>*(4 to 5 minutes)*<br><br>Running<br>Conditioning exercises | 1. Walk, jog, run—continue pattern established in lesson 2.<br>2. Calisthenics—increase repetitions by one. | Calisthenics, p. 180 | Design your own lessons. | Design your own lessons. | Design your own lessons. |
| **Part 2: Skill Development**<br>*(20 to 35 Minutes)*<br><br>Punting<br>Catching | *Partner activities:*<br>1. Review forward pass and catch—one stationary, one on the move.<br>2. Explain and demonstrate punting.<br>3. Practice activities. Partners punting and catching. Vary distances and kick slightly to right, then left side of partner.<br><br>*Group activities:*<br>1. Lead-up games:<br>*Punt and Catch*—Develops skills of punting and catching. Develops movement concepts of moving into space, changing direction and speed. Ball is punted back and forth from team to team over neutral zone. Punted ball must be caught by opposing team. If ball is not caught, kicking team is awarded a point.<br>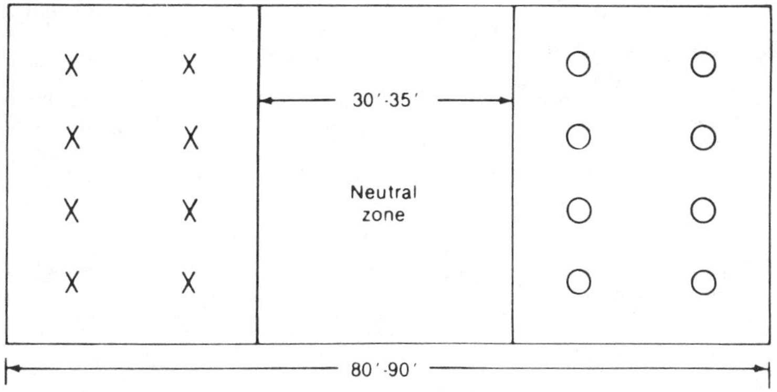<br><br>*Punt Back*—Develops punting, catching, speed, change of direction, and moving into space. The object of the game is to put the ball over the opponent's goal line.<br>Play above games with three or four on each team. Stress shorter kicks, but more accuracy. | Punting, p. 357<br>Practice activities, p. 358<br><br>Lead-up games, p. 358<br>Punt and Catch, p. 360<br><br>Punt Back, p. 360 | | | |
| **Part 3: Closure**<br>*(1 to 2 minutes)*<br><br>Punting | Discuss the key points of punting. Contact the ball as the leg begins its upward movement. Stress follow-through action. Keep eyes on ball until it is kicked. Drop rather than throw the ball to kicking foot. | | | | |

**Level III   Unit 2:** Touch Football
**Lesson 5.** Hike and Stance
**Main Theme** Hike and stance

| Content | Teaching Strategies | References | Lesson 5a | 5b | 5c |
|---|---|---|---|---|---|
| **Entry Activity** | Place footballs in one container. Free practice with footballs. | | | | |
| **Part 1: Introductory Activities** (*4 to 5 minutes*) | 1. Introduce continuous running.<br>2. Continue calisthenics or football obstacle course. | Calisthenics, p. 180 | Design your own lessons. | Design your own lessons. | Design your own lessons. |
| **Part 2: Skill Development** (*20 to 25 minutes*) | *Partner activities:*<br>1. Review lateral pass.<br>2. Explain, demonstrate, and practice centering ball and two types of stances.<br><br>*Group activities:*<br>1. Practice pass and defend—require receiver and defender to assume correct stance for each respective position; rotate players after each play.<br>2. Inventive games: Present challenges involving two to ten players, stressing centering, passing, and catching.<br>3. Lead-up games:<br>*Keep Away and Score*—Passing, catching, and moving into space are developed. Team with ball attempts to score touchdown by running, passing, and catching. Opposing team tries to intercept ball. When tagged with ball, opposing team takes over possession.<br>*Grab It*—Running, changing direction, speed, and tagging skills are utilized. Players wear football tags/flags. Players protect own flags from being stolen while stealing others. | Centering ball, p. 355<br><br>Inventive games, pp. 215, 254, 294<br>Lead-up games, p. 358<br>Keep Away and Score, p. 361<br>Grab It, p. 361 | | | |
| **Part 3: Closure** (*1 to 3 minutes*) | Discuss when to use 3- and 4-point stance. | | | | |

**Level** III **Unit 2:** Touch Football
**Lesson 6.** Blocking
**Main Theme** Blocking

| Content | Teaching Strategies | References | Lesson 6a | 6b | 6c |
|---|---|---|---|---|---|
| **Entry Activity** | Place footballs in one container. Free practice with footballs. | | | | |
| **Part 1: Introductory Activities**<br>*(4 to 5 minutes)* | 1. Continuous running.<br>2. Calisthenics or football obstacle course. | | Design your own lessons. | Design your own lessons. | Design your own lessons. |
| **Part 2: Skill Development**<br>*(20 to 35 minutes)*<br>—*passing and catching*<br>—*blocking* | *Partner activities:*<br>1. Review passing and catching.<br>   a. Pass and Defend: Center snaps to passer. Receiver moves forward and tries to catch pass. Defender tries to prevent receiver from catching ball.<br><br>2. Explain and demonstrate blocking.<br>3. Practice activities:<br>   a. Blocking Practice: On signal, offensive player attempts to get past defensive player by dodging, feinting, etc.<br><br>*Group activities:*<br>1. Lead-up games: One-Down Football, Borden Ball.<br>2. Inventive games: Present challenges involving three to twelve players, stressing passing, catching, and blocking. | Blocking, p. 357<br><br><br><br><br><br><br>Lead-up games, p. 358<br>One-down Football, p. 361<br>Bordon Ball, p. 289 | | | |
| **Part 3: Closure**<br>*(1 to 3 minutes)*<br><br>Blocking | Discuss key points of blocking: slight forward body lean; keep elbows out and forearms close to the chest; keep both feet on the ground and only touch the shoulders and body of the opponent. | | | | |

| Content | Teaching Strategies | References | Lesson 7a | 7b | 7c |
|---|---|---|---|---|---|
| **Entry Activity** | Place a variety of small equipment and footballs in four containers. Free play with equipment and balls. | | | | |
| **Part 1: Introductory Activities** <br> *(4 to 5 minutes)* <br><br> Running <br> Conditioning | 1. Continuous running. <br> 2. Football obstacle course. | | Repeat 1 and 2. | Design your own lessons. | Design your own lessons. |
| **Part 2: Skill Development** <br> *(20 to 35 minutes)* <br><br> Positional play <br> All skills | 1. Review: Develop a series of inventive game challenges involving two or three players, one ball, a variety of small equipment, and stressing passing, catching, and blocking skills. <br> 2. Explain offensive playing positions and a few simple play patterns. <br> 3. Play Seven-Person Touch Football. | Offensive positions, p. 362 <br><br> Seven-Person Touch Football p. 361 | Leave out. | | |

Field layout:

Offensive and defensive lineup positions:

Offense

Right halfback ◯    ◯ Fullback    Quarterback ◯    ◯ Left halfback

Right end ◯    ⊗ Center    ◯ Left end

Defense

Line of scrimmage

| Content | Teaching Strategies |
|---|---|
| **Part 3: Closure** <br> *(1 to 2 minutes)* <br><br> Offensive positions | Review offensive positions. |

**Level** III    **Unit 2:** Touch Football
**Lesson 8.** Positional Play
**Main Theme** Defensive positions

**Additional Lessons** If additional lessons are planned, stress one or more skills and play one or more lead-up games or seven-person football.

| Content | Teaching Strategies | References | Lesson 8a | 8b | 8c |
|---|---|---|---|---|---|
| **Entry Activity** | Place a variety of small equipment and footballs in four containers. Free play with equipment and balls. | | | | |
| **Part 1: Introductory Activities** *(4 to 5 minutes)* | 1. Continuous running.<br>2. Football obstacle course. | | Repeat 1 and 2. | Design your own lesson. | Design your own lesson. |
| Running<br>Conditioning | | | | | |
| **Part 2: Skill Development** *(20 to 35 minutes)*<br><br>Positional play<br>All skills | 1. Develop a series of inventive game challenges involving two or three players, one ball, a variety of small equipment, and stressing passing, catching, and blocking skills.<br>2. Explain defensive playing positions and a few simple play patterns.<br>3. Play Seven-Person Touch Football. | Defensive positions, p. 362<br><br>Seven-Person Touch Football, p. 361 | Leave out.<br><br>Repeat 1. | | |
| **Part 3: Closure** *(1 to 2 minutes)*<br><br>Offensive and Defensive positions | Review offensive and defensive positions. | | | | |
| **Level** III<br>**Unit 2:** Touch Football<br>**Lesson 9.** Evaluation | This lesson and additional lessons if needed should be used to administer the skill tests used at the beginning of this unit. | | | | |

Administer the skill tests used at the beginning of this unit (p. 79 of this guide).

# Game Activities
## Developmental Level III
## Unit 3: Field Hockey

## Expected Learning Outcomes

### Psychomotor Skills

1. Ability to drive a ball or puck with reasonable speed and accuracy
2. Ability to dribble, pass, or shoot
3. Ability to dribble and dodge away from an oncoming opponent
4. Ability to approach and fairly tackle an opponent
5. Ability to perform a face-off and roll-in skill
6. Ability to play a variety of offensive and defensive positions

### Cognitive and Affective Knowledge and Skills

1. Understanding of one's level of ability prior to and after a unit of field hockey
2. Understanding of defensive and offensive positional play
3. Understanding of the basic rules of field hockey
4. Appreciation of individual differences of other children
5. Respect and appreciation of officials and referees
6. Ability to design play patterns
7. Ability to modify or invent practice activities or inventive games involving field hockey skills
8. Understanding and appreciation of good sportsmanship, team loyalty, and fair play

## Field Hockey Skill Evaluation

The general level of skill of each respective class can be determined through two evaluation techniques. The first is to have the children play one or more field hockey-type lead-up games and to observe and record individual and general levels of skill and playing ability. This general overview provides a basis for the selection and emphasis of skills, practice activities, and lead-up games.

The following lead-up games can be used to provide a general overview of the class's general level of skill and playing ability.

| Games | Page in text |
|---|---|
| Zone Field Hockey | 347 |
| Line Field Hockey | 348 |
| Hockey Golf | 348 |

An observation sheet, such as the one shown below, can be used to record performance on specific skills, as well as to note general weaknesses or problems common to most children.

### Class Observation Sheet—Field Hockey

| Skills | Level of Ability | | Comments |
| | High | Low | |
|---|---|---|---|
| Driving a stationary ball | | | |
| Dribbling a ball | | | |
| Passing a stationary ball | | | |
| Passing while dribbling a ball | | | |
| Positional play—defense | | | |
| Positional play—offense | | | |

A standardized or teacher-made test is the second technique used to assess a class's level of skill and playing ability. In the majority of classroom situations, a teacher-made test outline is normally used for this purpose. It is strongly recommended that teachers use a test similar to the one shown in the accompanying reference and modify this test to meet the level of skill, need, and interest of each respective class.

| Field Hockey Skill Test | Page in text |
|---|---|
| Shoot and Stop | 338 |
| Dribbling | 338 |
| Shooting | 338 |
| Subjective Evaluation | 338 |

The above tests are taken from the chapter on soccer activities, which can be modified for field hockey.

**Additional Lessons** The amount that can actually be covered in this lesson will depend upon time allotment, skill level, and general behavior of the class. If the teacher feels more time is necessary to cover skills, or to establish more efficient procedures and class tone, develop one or more lessons.

| Content | Teaching Strategies | References | Lesson 2a | 2b | 2c |
|---|---|---|---|---|---|
| **Entry Activity** | Have equipment and balls available. Free dribbling with ball and stick. | | | | |
| **Part 1: Introductory Activities** *(4 to 5 minutes)* <br><br> Traveling-run <br> Change of direction | 1. Walk, jog, and run around outside boundaries of playing field. <br> 2. Return to marked-off smaller instructional area. <br>     a. Run and change direction by command. <br>     b. Play a shadow game. | Shadow game (p. 35 of this guide) | Repeat 1 and 2b. | Play a tag game, p. 286 | Design your own lessons. |
| **Part 2: Skill Development** *(20 to 35 minutes)* <br><br> Basic grip <br> Driving <br> Fielding | 1. Explain and demonstrate basic grip, driving, and fielding a ball. <br> 2. Practice activities <br>     a. Individual activities: Stand fifteen to twenty feet from wall, and field the rebounding ball; drive ball on field, run after it, and stop it. Continue pattern. <br>     b. Partner activities: Passing and fielding, driving directly onward, then to left and right of partner; drive at target on wall or between goals. <br><br> 3. Lead-up games: <br> *Hockey Golf*—This game develops the skills of shooting and receiving. Hockey golf is similar in style of play to that of croquet. Player A drives the ball through the first set of cones. If successful, one point is awarded. Player B retrieves the ball and takes his turn. Play continues through all sets of cones. | Grip, p. 341 <br> Drive, p. 343 <br> Practice activities, p. 345 <br> Partner activities, p. 345 <br> Inventive games, pp. 215, 254, 294 <br> Lead-up games, p. 345 <br> Hockey Golf, p. 348 | | | |

| Content | Teaching Strategies | References | Lesson 2a | 2b | 2c |
|---|---|---|---|---|---|

*Zone Field Hockey*—Develops all hockey skills and moving in space. This game is played like regular field hockey with the exception that players must remain in their own zone.

4. Inventive games—Example: "In groups of four, make up a game that has a drive and fielding skill, two goals, and no goalie." Develop other challenges requiring a drive and/or fielding the ball, and changing equipment or rules.

Zone Field Hockey, p. 347

Skills   All hockey skills

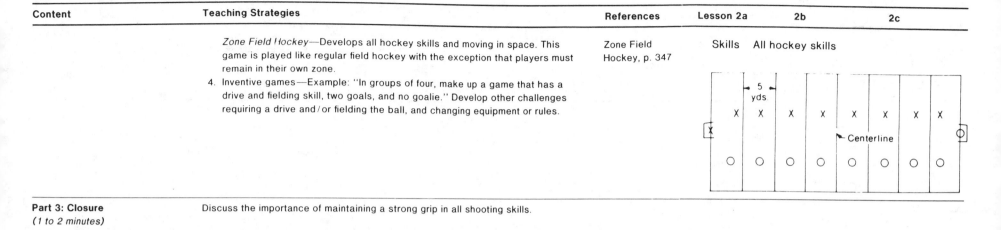

**Part 3: Closure**
*(1 to 2 minutes)*

Discuss the importance of maintaining a strong grip in all shooting skills.

*Note:* Entry activities should be provided at the beginning of each lesson. See soccer unit for types of small equipment that should be available prior to the beginning of each lesson.

**Level** III    **Unit 3:** Field Hockey
**Lesson 3.** Driving and Fielding
**Main Theme** Driving and fielding

**Additional Lessons** A teacher may wish to continue with one or more lessons to develop driving and fielding skills. Expand each lesson according to the needs of the class. Use sample lessons as a guide.

| Content | Teaching Strategies | References | Lesson 3a | 3b | 3c |
|---|---|---|---|---|---|
| **Entry Activity** | Practice dribbling and passing. | | | | |
| **Part 1: Introductory Activities**<br>*(4 to 5 minutes)*<br><br>Running<br>Change of speed | 1. Walk, jog, run.<br>2. In marked-off area, run with change of direction and speed. Add small equipment, such as traffic cones or hoops, to maneuver around or over. | Jogging,<br>p. 191 | Design your own lessons. | Design your own lessons. | Design your own lessons. |
| **Part 2: Skill Development**<br>*(20 to 35 minutes)*<br><br>Scoop shot<br>Hand stop | 1. Review driving and fielding through partner activities.<br>2. Explain and demonstrate scoop shot and aerial hand stop.<br>3. Practice activities<br>　a. Individual activities: Scoop shot on field, run after it, stop it; scoop shot into corner of goal.<br>　b. Partner activities: Pass and field; scoop shot to left, right, and directly to partner.<br>4. Inventive games: Develop a series of challenges involving six players (three vs. three), one ball, two goals, and any additional equipment or rules. Stress driving and fielding.<br>5. Lead-up games:<br>*Sideline Hockey*—This game is similar to sideline soccer with adaptations for hockey. Players in center may move anywhere within field of play. Sideline players may receive and pass to field players. Only players in field of play may score. (Only allow passing—no dribbling of the ball.)<br>6. Partner/small group activities:<br>Follow the Leader, dribble, and pass<br>Push Pass: Player #1 passes to #2. #2 returns pass to #1. #1 passes to #3 who returns pass to #1. | Scoop shot,<br>p. 343<br><br><br><br><br><br>Inventive games,<br>pp. 215, 254, 294<br>Lead-up games, p. 345<br>Sideline Hockey, p. 332 | | | |

Cones as goalposts (4' to 8' apart)

**Part 3: Closure**
*(1 to 2 minutes)*

Driving
Scoop shot

Discuss the difference between a drive and a scoop shot.

92

**Additional Lessons** If one or more additional lessons are desired, concentrate on the basic skills of dribbling and passing.

| Content | Teaching Strategies | References | Lesson 4a | 4b | 4c |
|---|---|---|---|---|---|
| **Entry Activity** | Practice dribbling and passing. | | | | |
| **Part 1: Introductory Activities** *(4 to 5 minutes)* | 1. Walk, jog, run. 2. Calisthenics. 3. Obstacle course running. | Jogging, p. 191 Calisthenics, p. 180 Obstacle course, p. 190 | Repeat 1 and 3. | Repeat 1 and 2. | Design your own programs. |
| Running Conditioning | | | | | |
| **Part 2: Skill Development** *(20 to 35 minutes)* | 1. Review partner practice activities for driving and fielding. 2. Explain and demonstrate dribbling skill. 3. Practice activities | Dribbling, p. 341 Practice activities, p. 345 | Leave out. Player 2 ⊗ ⟶ ⊗ Player 1 | Leave out. | |
| Dribbling Driving Fielding | a. Individual activities: Free dribbling, dribble around obstacles. b. Partner activities: Follow the leader, dribble, and pass. c. Small group activities: Push Pass | | ⊗ Player 3 | | |
| | 4. Inventive games: Develop a series of challenges involving eight players (four vs. four) stressing dribbling and passing. 5. Lead-up game: *Line Field Hockey*—This game develops shooting, passing, and receiving skills as well as movement concepts. Players are 1 versus 1 in field of play. Sideline players are able to receive and pass to their teammate in the field of play. Object is to shoot ball over opponent's goal line. | Lead-up games, p. 345  Line Field Hockey, p. 348 | Play Zone Hockey, p. 347 | Inventive games for 5 and 6 players. | |
| **Part 3: Closure** *(1 to 2 minutes)* | | | | | |
| Dribbling | Discuss similarities and differences in dribbling a soccer or hockey ball. | | | | |

**Level** III  **Unit 3:** Field Hockey
**Lesson 5.** Dribbling and Shooting
**Main Theme** Dribbling and shooting

| Content | Teaching Strategies | References | Lesson 5a | 5b | 5c |
|---|---|---|---|---|---|
| **Entry Activity** | Practice dribbling and stopping ball. | | | | |
| **Part 1: Introductory Activities** (*4 to 5 minutes*) <br><br> Running <br> Conditioning | 1. Continuous running. <br> 2. Calisthenics. <br> 3. Obstacle course running. | Jogging, p. 191 <br> Calisthenics, p. 180 <br> Obstacle course, p. 190 | Repeat 2 and 3. | Repeat 1 and 2. | Design your own lessons. |
| **Part 2: Skill Development** (*20 to 35 minutes*) <br><br> Dribbling <br> Shooting | 1. Review practice activities for dribbling. <br> 2. Demonstrate combined dribbling and shooting skills. <br> 3. Practice activities <br>    a. Partners on either side of goal (two traffic cones). Dribble from different angles and drive or scoop shot to goal. <br>    b. Inventive games: Develop challenges involving two players, goals, and dribbling, passing, and shooting. <br> 4. Inventive games: Develop a series of challenges involving four to ten players and including dribbling, passing, and shooting. <br> 5. Lead-up games: Line Field Hockey (p. 348), Zone Field Hockey (p. 347). | Practice activities, p. 345 <br><br><br><br><br><br> Lead-up games, p. 345 | Leave out. <br><br><br><br><br><br> Lead-up games. | Leave out. <br><br><br><br><br><br> Lead-up games. | |
| **Part 3: Closure** (*1 to 2 minutes*) <br><br> Dribbling <br> Shooting | Stress the importance of keeping the ball close to the stick while dribbling, and the correct position prior to striking the ball. | | | | |

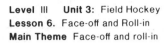

**Level** III    **Unit 3:** Field Hockey
**Lesson 6.** Face-off and Roll-in
**Main Theme** Face-off and roll-in

**Additional Lessons** As suggested in previous lessons, concentrate on face-off, roll-in, and dribbling skills.

| Content | Teaching Strategies | References | Lesson 6a | 6b | 6c |
|---|---|---|---|---|---|
| **Entry Activity** | Practice passing and stopping ball. | | | | |
| **Part 1: Introductory Activities** (*4 to 5 minutes*) <br><br> Running <br> Conditioning | 1. Continuous running. <br> 2. Calisthenics. <br> 3. Obstacle course running. | Jogging, p. 191 <br> Calisthenics, p. 180 <br> Obstacle course, p. 190 | Repeat 1 and 2. | Repeat 2 and 3. | Design your own lessons. |
| **Part 2: Skill Development** (*20 to 35 minutes*) <br><br> Face-off <br> Dribbling | 1. Review 3a and b from lesson 5. <br> 2. Explain and demonstrate face-off. <br> 3. Practice Activities: <br>   a. Zigzag Passing: Player A passes to B who passes to C. C passes back to A. Begin again. <br>   b. Face-off always to a full court. <br> 4. Inventive games: Develop a series of challenges involving four to twelve players, face-off goals, and other small equipment. <br> 5. Lead-up games: <br>   *Line Field Hockey* <br>   *Zone Field Hockey* <br>   *Pin Hockey*—This game is similar to Pin Soccer with adaptations for hockey. The object of this game is to drive the ball toward center pins in order to knock them over. Each team is awarded one point for every pin knocked down. | Practice activities, p. 345 <br><br><br><br><br><br> Lead-up games, p. 345 <br> Line Field Hockey, p. 348 <br> Zone Field Hockey p. 347 <br> Pin Hockey, p. 331 | Leave out. <br><br><br><br><br><br><br> Seven-Person Hockey, p. 334 | Leave out. <br><br><br><br><br><br><br> Seven-Person Hockey | |
| **Part 3: Closure** (*1 to 2 minutes*) <br><br> Face-off | Discuss and illustrate the rules and face-off skills. | | | | |

**Additional Lessons** If additional lessons are required, stress tackling and passing.

| Content | Teaching Strategies | References | Lesson 7a | 7b | 7c |
|---|---|---|---|---|---|
| **Entry Activity** | Practice dribbling, passing, and stopping. | | | | |
| **Part 1: Introductory Activities** (*4 to 5 minutes*) | 1. Continuous running. 2. Calisthenics. 3. Obstacle course running. | Jogging, p. 191 Calisthenics, p. 180 Obstacle course, p. 190 | | | Design your own lessons. |
| Running Conditioning | | | | | |
| **Part 2: Skill Development** (*20 to 35 minutes*) | 1. Review dribbling and passing.   a. Follow the Leader.   b. Dribble and Pass. 2. Explain and demonstrate tackling. 3. Practice Activities   a. Partner Keep Away.   b. Inventive games. | Practice activities, p. 345 | Repeat 3b. | Repeat 1 or 3b. | |
| Tackling Passing | Develop a series of partner challenges involving tackling and small equipment. 4. Inventive games: Begin with zone field hockey with seven on each team. After a few minutes, ask each team to add one new rule. Play with new rules, stop, add two new rules. Continue pattern as long as interest is shown or change to a new lead-up game. 5. Modified Field Hockey. | Lead-up games, p. 345 Modified Field Hockey, p. 348 | Seven-Person Hockey, p. 334 | Seven-Person Hockey. | |

| | | | | | |
|---|---|---|---|---|---|
| **Part 3: Closure** (*1 to 2 minutes*) | | | | | |
| Tackling | Discuss and illustrate the need to tackle fairly to prevent injuries. | | | | |

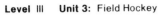

**Level** III **Unit 3:** Field Hockey
**Lesson 8.** Dodging
**Main Theme** Dodging

**Additional Lessons** If additional lessons are required, stress dodging, dribbling, and passing.

| Content | Teaching Strategies | References | Lesson 8a | 8b | 8c |
|---|---|---|---|---|---|
| **Entry Activity** | Practice dribbling, dodging, and tackling | | | | |
| **Part 1: Introductory Activities** (*4 to 5 minutes*) <br><br> Running <br> Conditioning | 1. Continuous running. <br> 2. Calisthenics. <br> 3. Obstacle course running. | Jogging, p. 191 <br> Calisthenics, p. 180 <br> Obstacle course, p. 190 | Repeat 1 and 2. | Repeat 2 and 3. | Design your own lesson. |
| **Part 2: Skill Development** (*20 to 35 minutes*) <br><br> Dodging <br> Dribbling and passing | 1. Review tackling and passing. <br>   a. Partner Keep Away. <br>   b. Dribble and Pass. <br> 2. Explain and demonstrate dodging. <br> 3. Partners activities: dodging drill. <br><br><br> 4. Modified Field Hockey. | Practice activities, p. 345 <br><br><br><br><br><br><br> Lead-up games, p. 345 <br> Modified Field Hockey, p. 348 | Leave out. <br><br><br><br><br><br><br> Modified Hockey. | Leave out. <br><br><br><br><br><br><br> Modified Hockey. | |

Path of dribbler X ⟶ ⊕    ◯ Defender
— Runs around to the left
‑ ‑ Passes ball to the right (the tackler's left side)

| | | | | | |
|---|---|---|---|---|---|
| **Part 3: Closure** (*1 to 2 minutes*) <br><br> Dodging | Explain the importance of good feinting skills. | | | | |
| **Level** III <br> **Unit 3:** Field Hockey <br> Lesson 9. Evaluation | This lesson and additional lessons if needed should be used to administer the skill tests used at the beginning of this unit. | | | | |
| Administer the skill tests used at the beginning of this unit (p. 89 of this guide). | | | | | |

# Game Activities
## Developmental Level III
## Unit 4: Volleyball

## Expected Learning Outcomes

### Psychomotor Skills

1. Ability to serve a volleyball using underhand and overhand skills
2. Ability to pass a volleyball using the bumping or two-hand overhand skill
3. Ability to set up or spike with a minimum of proficiency (lowered net)
4. Ability to block with minimum proficiency (lowered net)

### Cognitive and Affective Knowledge and Skills

1. Understanding of one's level of ability prior to and after a unit of volleyball
2. Understanding the basic rules and regulations of volleyball
3. Understanding of the defensive and offensive positional play and team strategies
4. Respect and appreciation for referees
5. Appreciation of individual differences of other players
6. Ability to design, modify, or create practice activities and inventive games involving volleyball skills
7. Understanding and appreciation of good sportsmanship, team loyalty, and fair play

## Volleyball Skill Evaluation

The general level of skill of each respective class can be determined through two evaluation techniques. The first is to have the children play one or more volleyball-type lead-up games and to observe and record individual and general levels of skill and playing ability. This general overview provides a basis for the selection and emphasis of skills, practice activities, and lead-up games.

The following lead-up games can be used to provide a general overview of the class's general level of skill and playing ability.

| Game | Page in text |
|------|------|
| Nebraska Ball | 375 |
| Newcomb | 376 |
| Modified Volleyball | 376 |

An observation sheet, such as the one shown below, can be used to record performance on specific skills, as well as to note general weaknesses or problems common to most children.

### Class Observation Sheet — Volleyball

| Skills | Level of Ability | | Comments |
|--------|------|------|------|
|  | High | Low |  |
| Overhand pass |  |  |  |
| Bumping |  |  |  |
| Underhand serve |  |  |  |
| Overhand serve |  |  |  |
| Positional play—defense |  |  |  |
| Positional play—offense |  |  |  |

A standardized or teacher-made test is the second technique used to assess a class's level of skill and playing ability. In the majority of classroom situations, a teacher-made test outline is normally used for this purpose. It is strongly recommended that teachers use a test similar to the one shown in the accompanying reference and modify this test to meet the level of skill, need, and interest of each respective class.

| Volleyball Skill Test | Page in text |
|------|------|
| Wall Volley | 379 |
| Serving Over the Net | 379 |
| Forearm Pass | 379 |
| Subjective Evaluation | 380 |

## Volleyball Skill test

| Name | Wall Volley (total pts.) | Service over Net (20 pts.) | Forearm Pass (20 pts.) | Subjective Evaluation (50 pts.) | Total Score | Grade |
|---|---|---|---|---|---|---|
| 1 | | | | | | |
| 2 | | Rank all total scores for the class, then convert to letter grades or ratings (superior, good, etc.) | | | | |
| 3 | | | | | | |
| 4 | | | | | | |

**Level** III  **Unit 4:** Volleyball
**Lesson 2.** Overhand Passing
**Main Theme** Overhand passing

**Additional Lessons** The amount that can actually be covered in this lesson will depend upon time allotment, skill level, and general behavior of the class. If the teacher feels more time is necessary to cover skills or to establish more efficient procedures and class tone, develop one or more lessons.

| Content | Teaching Strategies | References | Lesson 2a | 2b | 2c |
|---|---|---|---|---|---|
| **Entry Activity** | Practice striking and catching the ball. | | | | |
| **Part 1: Introductory Activities** (4 to 5 minutes)<br><br>Run and jump<br>Conditioning | 1. Running with change of direction by voice command, "right . . . back . . . sideways," etc.<br>2. Run, jump, land, continue pattern.<br>3. Calisthenics. | Calisthenics, p. 180 | Repeat 1 and 3. | Play a tag game, p. 260 | Design your own lesson. |
| **Part 2: Skill Development** (20 to 35 minutes)<br><br>Overhand pass | 1. Demonstrate overhand pass.<br>2. Practice activities<br>  a. Individual activities: Individual volleying, draw a line or target on wall and repeat.<br>  b. Partner activities: Partner tosses to other who catches in proper position; partner tosses to other who sets ball back; continue setting to each other.<br>3. Divide playing area into two or more courts.<br>4. Lead-up games:<br>*Volleyball Keep Away*—Class is divided into four or six teams of equal number. Each team is designated to compete against another in a limited playing area. Team with ball tries to keep ball away from other team by volleying. Team without ball attempts to intercept ball. The team volleying the greatest number of times before an interception is the winning team.<br>*Newcomb*—This game develops the serve and volley. Ball is served over the net. Receiving team returns the ball with any number of hits allowed. Play continues until ball drops. Only serving team scores. | Pass, p. 367<br>Practice activities, p. 370<br><br><br><br>Lead-up games, p. 370<br>Volleyball Keep Away, p. 377<br><br><br>Newcomb, p. 376 | Review overhand pass.<br><br><br><br><br>Lead-up games. | Leave out.<br><br><br><br><br>Lead-up games. | |
| **Part 3: Closure** (1 to 3 minutes) | Emphasize importance of moving into position to hit the ball, firm contact, and follow-through action. | | | | |

*Note:* Entry activities should be provided at the beginning of each lesson. See soccer unit for types of small equipment that should be available prior to the beginning of each lesson.

**Level** III    **Unit 4:** Volleyball
**Lesson 3.**  Underhand Serving
**Main Theme**  Underhand serving

**Additional Lessons** If one or more additional lessons are required, stress circuit training, overhand pass, and underhand serving.

| Content | Teaching Strategies | References | Lesson 3a | 3b | 3c |
|---|---|---|---|---|---|
| **Entry Activity** | Practice striking and catching the ball. | | | | |
| **Part 1: Introductory Activities** (*5 to 6 minutes*) <br><br> Circuit training | 1. Running with change of speed and direction. <br> 2. Circuit training. | Tag games, p. 286 <br> Circuit training, p. 189 | Repeat circuit. | Repeat circuit. | Repeat circuit. |
| **Part 2: Skill Development** (*20 to 35 minutes*) <br><br> Underhand serve <br> Overhand pass | 1. Review partner passing. <br> 2. Demonstrate underhand serve. <br> 3. Practice activities: <br>   a. Individual activities: Serve to wall and catch rebound; serve to wall and set rebound back to wall, catch and repeat. <br>   b. Partner activities: Serve back and forth; player serves and other catches and sets ball back. <br> 4. Inventive games with four players. Example: "In your group of four, try to make up a game using one ball, the wall, and requiring a serve and an overhand pass." Develop similar challenges varying equipment and rules. <br> 5. Lead-up games: <br> *Bound Ball*—This game utilizes the serve and volley. Similar to volleyball; however, there is no net and the ball must bounce between each hit. <br> *Modified Volleyball*—This game develops the serve, volley, and introduces an "S" rotation system. Traditional rules and scoring apply with the exception that the ball may be hit an unlimited number of times by either team as is necessary to return the ball over the net. | Practice activities, p. 370 <br> Serving, p. 368 <br><br><br><br><br><br> Lead-up games, p. 370 <br><br><br><br><br> Bound Ball, p. 375 <br> Modified Volleyball, p. 376 | Repeat 3b. <br><br><br><br><br><br> Lead-up games. | Leave out. <br><br><br><br><br><br> Lead-up games. | Repeat 3b. <br><br><br><br><br><br> Lead-up games. |

Diagram labels: Back line  Middle line  Front line; Team A; Team B; End line; Serving position; Net; circles (Team A) and X marks (Team B) arranged in three rows.

| **Part 3: Closure** (*1 to 2 minutes*) <br><br> Underhand serve | Discuss the importance of contacting the ball with the heel of the hand or the side of the fist—firm contact. | | | | |

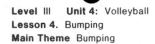

**Level** III **Unit 4:** Volleyball
**Lesson 4.** Bumping
**Main Theme** Bumping

**Additional Lessons** If additional lessons are required, stress bumping and serving.

| Content | Teaching Strategies | References | Lesson 4a | 4b | 4c |
|---|---|---|---|---|---|
| **Entry Activity** | Practice serving the ball with one hand. | | | | |
| **Part 1: Introductory Activities** (*5 to 6 minutes*) | 1. Running and sliding with a change of direction and speed. <br> 2. Circuit training. | Circuit training, p. 189 | Repeat circuit. | Repeat circuit. | Design your own lessons. |
| Circuit training | | | | | |
| **Part 2: Skill Development** (*20 to 35 minutes*) | 1. Review serving and passing, using inventive games with partners. Example: "See if you can make up a game with your partner that uses a serve, a pass, one hoop, and one ball." | Bumping, p. 367 | Repeat 3. | Repeat 1 and 3. | |
| Bumping <br> Serving | 2. Demonstrate bumping. <br> 3. Partner activities: Partner tosses ball to other who bumps ball back; continue bumping to each other. <br> 4. Lead-up games: <br> *Keep It Up*—The object is to keep the ball in the air by bumping. Ball may be bumped by any member of the group. <br> *Sideline Volleyball*—The game utilizes all volleyball skills. This game is played like regular volleyball with the addition of active sideline players. <br> 5. Develop inventive games involving six players. | Lead-up games, p. 370 <br> Keep It Up, p. 376 <br> Sideline Volleyball, p. 378 | Lead-up games. | Lead-up games. | |
| **Part 3: Closure** (*1 to 2 minutes*) | | | | | |
| Bumping | Key points concerning the bump: Contact the ball between the knees and waist; emphasize the "lifting" action of the body by straightening the legs. | | | | |

| Content | Teaching Strategies | References | Lesson 5a | 5b | 5c |
|---------|--------------------|-----------|----------|----|----|
| **Entry Activity** | Practice striking ball with two hands and practice overhand serve. | | | | |
| **Part 1: Introductory Activities** (5 to 6 minutes)  Circuit training | 1. Traveling with emphasis on jumping and change of speed. 2. Circuit training. | Circuit training, p. 189 | Repeat circuit. | Repeat circuit. | Design your own lessons. |
| **Part 2: Skill Development** (20 to 35 minutes)  Overhead serve Bumping | 1. Review passing overhand and forearm skills; partner activities. 2. Demonstrate overhand serving. 3. Practice activities: Individual activities; partner activities; group activities— baseline serving. 4. Inventive games with eight players (stress passing). 5. Lead-up games: *Donkey*—This game utilizes bumping and setting skills as well as moving into space. Players in a line and alternating turns attempt to keep the ball rebounding off the wall. Player who misses a volley gets the letter "D" and so on until a player spells D-O-N-K-E-Y. (Other words could be used such as V-O-L-L-E-Y.) *Mass Volleyball*—Similar to regular volleyball with the following exception: Anyone may hit the ball as many times as he or she wishes, but only three different players may touch the ball before returning it over the net. | Serving, p. 368  Lead-up games, p. 370 Donkey, p. 376 Mass Volleyball, p. 376 | Repeat 1 and 3.  Lead-up games. | Leave out.  Lead-up games. | |
| **Part 3: Closure** (1 to 3 minutes) | Discuss key points of overhand serve: Step with opposite foot to striking hand; shift weight to front foot as striking hand hits ball; snap wrist on contact. | | | | |

**Level** III  **Unit 4:** Volleyball
**Lesson 6.** Set-up
**Main Theme** Set-up

**Additional Lessons** If additional lessons are required, stress serving and passing.

| Content | Teaching Strategies | References | Lesson 6a | 6b | 6c |
|---|---|---|---|---|---|
| **Entry Activity** | | | | | |
| **Part 1: Introductory Activities** *(5 to 6 minutes)* | 1. Traveling, with emphasis on change of direction and level. <br> 2. Circuit training. | Circuit training, p. 189 | | | Design your own lessons. |
| Circuit training | | | | | |
| **Part 2: Skill Development** *(20 to 35 minutes)* <br><br> Set-up <br> Passing | 1. Review serving and passing—use circuit volleyball. <br> 2. Demonstrate set-up skill. <br> 3. Practice activities <br>    a. Hit the Square: Leader tosses ball to first player who tries to return a high arc set into the square. <br>    b. Set up the Ball: Player 1 tosses high arc to player 2 who sets ball to player 3. Player 3 attempts to pass ball over the net to receiver. | Serving, p. 368 <br> Set-up, p. 370 <br> Practice activities, p. 370 | Repeat 3. | Leave out. | |

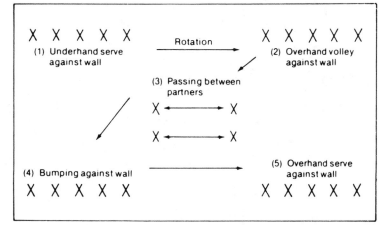

| Content | Teaching Strategies | References | Lesson 6a | 6b | 6c |
|---|---|---|---|---|---|
| | 4. Lead-up games: (use five players on each team)<br>*Modified Volleyball*<br>*Four-Way Volleyball*—Regular volleyball rules apply to this game involving four teams. | Lead-up games, p. 370<br>Modified Volleyball, p. 376<br>Four-Way Volleyball, p. 377 | Lead-up games. | Lead-up games. | |
| | Allow teams to add new rules according to their own interests. Give each team a turn and limit changes to a maximum of four rule changes. | | | | |

**Part 3: Closure**
*(1 to 2 minutes)*

Set-up      Discuss and illustrate the importance of a high volley in the set-up skill.

**Level** III **Unit 4**: Volleyball
**Lesson 7.** Set-up
**Main Theme** Set-up

**Additional Lessons** If additional lessons are required, continue to stress set-up and serving.

| Content | Teaching Strategies | References | Lesson 7a | 7b | 7c |
|---|---|---|---|---|---|
| **Entry Activity** | | | | | |
| **Part 1: Introductory Activities** *(5 to 6 minutes)* | 1. Traveling, jumping, change of speed and direction. 2. Circuit training. | Circuit training, p. 189 | | Design your own lessons. | Design your own lessons. |
| Circuit training | | | | | |
| **Part 2: Skill Development** *(20 to 35 minutes)* | 1. Review serving and passing using circuit volleyball. 2. Review set-up. 3. Practice activities. | Set-up, p. 370 | Repeat 3. | Leave out. | |
| Set-up Serving | | | | | |
| | 4. Lead-up games: (use six players on each team) Allow teams to create new rules as described in lesson 6. *Four-Way Volleyball* *Modifed Volleyball* *Volleyball* | Lead-up games, p. 370 Four-Way Volleyball, p. 377 Modified Volleyball, p. 376 Volleyball, p. 378 | Lead-up games. | Lead-up games. | |

| Left back | | Left forward |
|---|---|---|
| 3 | → | 4 |
| ↑ | | ↓ |
| Center back | | Center forward |
| 2 | | 5 |
| ↑ | | ↓ |
| Right back | | Right forward |
| 1 | ← | 6 |
| Start | | |

Six players

## Positions and Rotation Pattern (after opponents lose their serve)

| | | |
|---|---|---|
| **Part 3: Closure** *(1 to 2 minutes)* | Discuss the value of allowing players to add their own new rules to lead-up games. | |
| Modified Games | | |

| | | |
|---|---|---|
| **Level** III **Unit 4**: Volleyball **Lesson 8.** Evaluation | This lesson and additional lessons if needed should be used to administer the skill tests at the beginning of this unit. | |

Administer the skill tests used at the beginning of this unit (p. 99 of this guide).

# Game Activities
## Developmental Level III
## Unit 5: Basketball

## Expected Learning Outcomes

### Psychomotor Skills

1. Ability to pass a basketball using a two-hand, baseball, or bounce pass
2. Ability to catch a ball from varying heights and while stationary or on the move
3. Ability to dribble the ball with either hand, at various speeds, and in different levels and directions
4. Ability to shoot a ball using a two-hand underhand, overhand, or hand set, jump, and lay-up shot
5. Ability to pivot according to the rules of the game
6. Ability to check an opponent according to the rules of the game
7. Ability to play a variety of offensive and defensive positions

### Cognitive and Affective Knowledge and Skills

1. Understanding of one's level of ability prior to and after a unit of basketball
2. Understanding of the basic rules and regulations of basketball
3. Understanding of defensive and offensive positional play and team strategies
4. Respect and appreciation for referees
5. Appreciation of individual differences of other players
6. Understanding and appreciation of good sportsmanship, team loyalty, and fair play
7. Ability to design, modify, or create practice activities and inventive games involving basketball skills

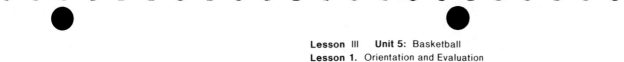

## Basketball Skill Evaluation

The general level of skill of each respective class can be determined through two evaluation techniques. The first is to have the children play one or more basketball-type lead-up games and to observe and record individual and general levels of skill and playing ability. This general overview produces a basis for the selection and emphasis of skills, practice activities, and lead-up games.

The following lead-up games can be used to provide a general overview of the class's general level of skill and playing ability.

| Games | Page in text |
|---|---|
| Keep Away | 397 |
| Sideline Basketball | 397 |
| Twenty-One | 398 |

An observation sheet, such as the one shown below, can be used to record performance on specific skills, as well as to note general weaknesses or problems common to most children.

### Class Observation Sheet—Basketball

| Skills | Level of Ability | | Comments |
|---|---|---|---|
| | High | Low | |
| Passing | | | |
| Catching | | | |
| Dribbling | | | |
| Shooting | | | |
| Pivoting | | | |
| Positional play—defense | | | |
| Positional play—offense | | | |

A standardized or teacher-made test is the second technique used to assess a class's level of skill and playing ability. In the majority of classroom situations, a teacher-made test outline is normally used for this purpose. It is strongly recommended that teachers use a test similar to the one shown in the accompanying reference and modify this test to meet the level of skill, need, and interest of each respective class.

| *Basketball Skill Test* | *Page in text* |
|---|---|
| Passing | 400 |
| Shooting | 400 |
| Dribbling | 400 |
| Subjective Evaluation | 400 |

## Basketball Skill Test

| Name | Passing (total pts.) | Dribbling (total pts.) | Shooting (50 pts.) | Subjective Evaluation (50 pts.) | Total Score | Grade |
|---|---|---|---|---|---|---|
| 1 | | | | | | |
| 2 | | Rank total scores for the class, then convert to letter grades or ratings (superior, good, etc.) | | | | |
| 3 | | | | | | |

**Level** III  **Unit 5:** Basketball
**Lesson 2.** Pass and Catch
**Main Theme** Passing and catching

**Additional Lessons** The amount that can actually be covered in this lesson will depend upon time allotment, skill level, and general behavior of the class. If the teacher feels more time is necessary to cover skills or to establish more efficient procedures and class tone, develop one or more lessons.

| Content | Teaching Strategies | References | Lesson 2a | 2b | 2c |
|---|---|---|---|---|---|
| **Entry Activity** | Place a container of basketballs in the gymnasium. Practice dribbling the ball. | | | | |
| **Part 1: Introductory Activities** *(4 to 5 minutes)* <br><br> Running <br> Conditioning | 1. Run in different directions. <br> 2. Run, stop, change direction to voice commands. <br> 3. Calisthenics. | Calisthenics, p. 180 | Repeat 1 and 3. | Repeat 1 and 3. | Design your own lessons. |
| **Part 2: Skill Development** *(20 to 30 minutes)* <br><br> Chest pass <br> Baseball pass <br> Catching | 1. Demonstrate chest and baseball pass and underhand and overhand catching. <br> 2. Practice activities: Wall passing (individuals); partner passing. | Chest pass, p. 383 <br> Practice activities, p. 390 | Introduce baseball pass, p. 385 | Review passing. | |
| | 3. Lead-up games: <br> *Guard Ball*—This game develops passing, catching, and guarding skills. Two teams pass ball(s) back and forth with third team trying to intercept as many passes as possible. Similar to "keep away," but each team has a designated area in which to play. <br> *Keep Away*—Players simply pass ball among themselves trying to keep the ball away from the other team. <br> *5 Passes*—This game develops passing and catching skills. When a team completes five passes in a row a point is scored. Opposing team tries to intercept or interrupt series of passes. | Lead-up games, p. 390 <br> Guard Ball, p. 396 <br> Keep Away, p. 397 <br> 5 Passes, p. 397 | Lead-up games. | Lead-up games. <br><br> X  X  X <br>_____ <br><br> ⊗  ⊗  ⊗ <br>_____ <br><br> C  ○  ○ | Team A <br><br><br> Team C <br><br><br> Team B |
| **Part 3: Closure** *(1 to 2 minutes)* <br><br> Passing | Explain and illustrate wrist action and follow-through when executing a pass. <br> Discuss when to use an underhand and overhand catch. | | | | |

*Note:* Entry activities should be provided at the beginning of each lesson. See soccer unit for types of small equipment that should be available prior to the beginning of each lesson.

**Level III**  **Unit 5:** Basketball
**Lesson 3.** Pivot and Pass
**Main Theme** Pivoting and passing
**Subtheme** Traveling

**Additional Lessons** If one or more additional lessons are required, stress passing and catching.

| Content | Teaching Strategies | References | Lesson 3a | 3b | 3c |
|---|---|---|---|---|---|
| **Entry Activity** | Practice dribbling and passing to a partner. | | | | |
| **Part 1: Introductory Activities** *(4 to 5 minutes)* <br><br> Running <br> Conditioning | 1. Run, skip, and slide in different directions. <br> 2. Travel with different parts leading—right foot, head, etc. <br> 3. Calisthenics. | Calisthenics, p. 180 | Repeat 1 and 3. | Tag games. | Design your own lessons. |
| **Part 2: Skill Development** *(20 to 35 minutes)* <br><br> Passing <br> Catching <br> Pivoting | 1. Review passing and catching. <br> 2. Demonstrate the two-hand overhead pass. <br> 3. Practice activities: Partner passing. <br> 4. Demonstrate pivoting. <br> 5. Practice pivoting: Individual; partners; group—pivot and pass, circle pass, Pig in the Middle. <br> 6. Lead-up games: <br> *Keep Away* <br> *Sideline Basketball*—Similar to regular basketball with sideline players. Sideline players are involved by passing to their teammates in the court area. All players are given the chance to participate from the sideline and to be involved actively in court play. <br> *Basketball Touch*—This game develops passing, catching, and guarding skills. Court players move ball around floor by passing. The object of the game is to complete a pass to your own goalie. Opposing team tries to intercept passes to prevent scoring. | Passing, p. 383 <br> Pivoting, p. 388 <br><br><br><br> Lead-up, p. 390 <br> Keep Away, p. 397 <br> Sideline Basketball, p. 397 <br> Basketball Touch, p. 397 | Review passing and pivoting. <br><br><br><br><br><br> Lead-up. | Leave out. <br><br><br><br><br><br> Lead-up. | |
| **Part 3: Closure** *(1 to 2 minutes)* <br><br> Passing <br> Pivoting | Review pivot foot. | | | | |

**Level** III **Unit 2:** Touch Football
**Lesson 4.** Punt and Catch
**Main Theme** Punt and catch

**Additional Lessons** If one or more additional lessons are desired, concentrate on the basic skills of punting and catching.

| Content | Teaching Strategies | References | Lesson 4a | 4b | 4c |
|---|---|---|---|---|---|
| **Entry Activity** | Place a variety of small equipment and footballs in four containers. Free play with equipment and balls. | | | | |
| **Part 1: Introductory Activities**<br>*(4 to 5 minutes)*<br><br>Running<br>Conditioning exercises | 1. Walk, jog, run—continue pattern established in lesson 2.<br>2. Calisthenics—increase repetitions by one. | Calisthenics, p. 180 | Design your own lessons. | Design your own lessons. | Design your own lessons. |
| **Part 2: Skill Development**<br>*(20 to 35 Minutes)*<br><br>Punting<br>Catching | *Partner activities:*<br>1. Review forward pass and catch—one stationary, one on the move.<br>2. Explain and demonstrate punting.<br>3. Practice activities. Partners punting and catching. Vary distances and kick slightly to right, then left side of partner.<br><br>*Group activities:*<br>1. Lead-up games:<br>*Punt and Catch*—Develops skills of punting and catching. Develops movement concepts of moving into space, changing direction and speed. Ball is punted back and forth from team to team over neutral zone. Punted ball must be caught by opposing team. If ball is not caught, kicking team is awarded a point. | Punting, p. 357<br>Practice activities, p. 358<br><br><br>Lead-up games, p. 358<br>Punt and Catch, p. 360 | | | |

| | | | |
|---|---|---|---|
| | *Punt Back*—Develops punting, catching, speed, change of direction, and moving into space. The object of the game is to put the ball over the opponent's goal line.<br>Play above games with three or four on each team. Stress shorter kicks, but more accuracy. | Punt Back, p. 360 | |

| Content | Teaching Strategies |
|---|---|
| **Part 3: Closure**<br>*(1 to 2 minutes)*<br><br>Punting | Discuss the key points of punting. Contact the ball as the leg begins its upward movement. Stress follow-through action. Keep eyes on ball until it is kicked. Drop rather than throw the ball to kicking foot. |

**Level** III    **Unit 2:** Touch Football
**Lesson 5.** Hike and Stance
**Main Theme** Hike and stance

| Content | Teaching Strategies | References | Lesson 5a | 5b | 5c |
|---|---|---|---|---|---|
| **Entry Activity** | Place footballs in one container. Free practice with footballs. | | | | |
| **Part 1: Introductory Activities**<br>*(4 to 5 minutes)* | 1. Introduce continuous running.<br>2. Continue calisthenics or football obstacle course. | Calisthenics,<br>p. 180 | Design your own lessons. | Design your own lessons. | Design your own lessons. |
| **Part 2: Skill Development**<br>*(20 to 25 minutes)* | *Partner activities:*<br>1. Review lateral pass.<br>2. Explain, demonstrate, and practice centering ball and two types of stances.<br><br>*Group activities:*<br>1. Practice pass and defend—require receiver and defender to assume correct stance for each respective position; rotate players after each play.<br>2. Inventive games: Present challenges involving two to ten players, stressing centering, passing, and catching.<br>3. Lead-up games:<br>*Keep Away and Score*—Passing, catching, and moving into space are developed. Team with ball attempts to score touchdown by running, passing, and catching. Opposing team tries to intercept ball. When tagged with ball, opposing team takes over possession.<br>*Grab It*—Running, changing direction, speed, and tagging skills are utilized. Players wear football tags / flags. Players protect own flags from being stolen while stealing others. | Centering ball,<br>p. 355<br><br><br><br><br><br>Inventive<br>games,<br>pp. 215, 254,<br>294<br>Lead-up<br>games, p. 358<br>Keep Away<br>and Score,<br>p. 361<br>Grab It, p. 361 | | | |
| **Part 3: Closure**<br>*(1 to 3 minutes)* | Discuss when to use 3- and 4-point stance. | | | | |

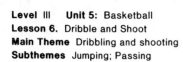

**Level** III  **Unit 5:** Basketball
**Lesson 6.** Dribble and Shoot
**Main Theme** Dribbling and shooting
**Subthemes** Jumping; Passing

**Additional Lessons** If additional lessons are required, stress the one-hand set and lay-up shot.

| Content | Teaching Strategies | References | Lesson 6a | 6b | 6c |
|---|---|---|---|---|---|
| **Entry Activity** | Practice dribbling, passing, and shooting. | | | | |
| **Part 1: Introductory Activities** *(4 to 5 minutes)* <br><br> Running <br> Conditioning | 1. Running, jumping, and leaping. <br> 2. Play a shadow game. <br> 3. Individual dribbling around two small pieces of equipment. | | Repeat 2 and 3. | Tag games, p. 286 | Design your own lesson. |
| **Part 2: Skill Development** *(20 to 35 minutes)* <br><br> Lay-up shot <br> One-hand set shot | 1. Review one-hand push (set) shot. <br> 2. Demonstrate lay-up shot. <br> 3. Practice activities: Dribble and shoot; lay-up shooting; developing inventive practice activities involving dribble, pass, and lay-up shooting, substituting target on wall, basket on chair, etc., for hoop. <br> 4. Inventive games with five or six players (three vs. two or three vs. three). Example: "In groups of six, make up a game that has two chairs, two hula hoops, one ball, with everyone always moving." <br> 5. Lead-up games: <br> *Sideline Basketball* <br> *Basketball Snatch Ball*—This game develops the skills of dribbling and shooting. On signal, one player from each team runs out to the center, picks up a ball, dribbles to designated basket, and shoots until a basket is made. After making a basket, the player dribbles back and replaces the ball. First player to make a basket and return the ball scores a point for his or her team. | Practice activities, p. 390 <br><br><br><br> Lead-up games, p. 390 <br><br><br> Sideline Basketball, p. 397 Basketball Snatch Ball, p. 398 | Leave out. <br><br><br><br> Lead-up games. | Leave out. <br><br><br><br> Lead-up games. | |
| **Part 3: Closure** *(1 to 2 minutes)* <br><br> Lay-up shot | Stress the important key points of the lay-up: proper takeoff foot / opposite shooting hand; reaching up toward the basket and releasing the ball off fingertips; lay the ball against the backboard. | | | | |

**Level** III    **Unit 5:** Basketball
**Lesson 7.** Check and Pass
**Main Theme** Checking and passing
**Subtheme** Change of speed

**Additional Lessons** If one or more additional lessons are required, stress passing and checking.

| Content | Teaching Strategies | References | Lesson 7a | 7b | 7c |
|---|---|---|---|---|---|
| **Entry Activity** | Practice passing and catching. | | | | |
| **Part 1: Introductory Activities** *(4 to 5 minutes)*<br><br>Running<br>Conditioning | 1. Traveling with change of direction, level, and speed.<br>2. Play a shadow game around small equipment scattered on the floor. | Shadow game (p. 35 of this guide) | Tag games, p. 286 | Repeat 1 and 2. | Design your own lessons. |
| **Part 2: Skill Development** *(20 to 35 minutes)*<br><br>Passing<br>Checking | 1. Review two-hand chest pass, bounce pass, and baseball pass.<br>2. Demonstrate checking skill.<br>3. Practice activities:<br>  a. One-on-One: Defensive player moves body into position to stop the offensive player.<br>  b. Pass, Post, and Shoot: The post player and offensive player may pass ball back and forth until the offensive player makes the decision to move toward the basket and attempt a shot. The defensive player tries to prevent the offensive player from maneuvering past him or her. | Passing, p. 383 | Leave out. | Leave out. | Arrange players as shown in diagram.<br><br><br><br>X Defensive player<br>⊗ Post player<br>○ Offensive player |
| | 4. Inventive games involving seven or eight players (three vs. four or four vs. four). Example: "Design a game in your group of eight that involves dribbling, checking, and passing. You may use four pieces of small equipment." | Lead-up games, p. 390 | Lead-up games. | Lead-up games. | |
| **Part 3: Closure** *(1 to 2 minutes)*<br><br>Passing<br>Checking | Review the rules and skill of checking. | | | | |
| **Level III**<br>**Unit 5:** Basketball<br>**Lesson 8.** Evaluation | This lesson and additional lessons if needed should be used to administer the skill tests used at the beginning of this unit. | | | | |

Administer the skill tests used at the beginning of this unit (p. 110 of this guide).

# Game Activities
## Developmental Level III
## Unit 6: Softball

## Expected Learning Outcomes

### Psychomotor Skills

1. Ability to throw a ball with an overhand, side arm and underhand throwing action
2. Ability to catch a softball from below and above the waist while stationary and while on the move
3. Ability to field a grounder
4. Ability to hit a ball using a field swing, bunt, or fungo hitting action
5. Ability to play all infield and outfield positions

### Cognitive and Affective Knowledge and Skills

1. Understanding of one's level of ability prior to and after a unit of softball
2. Understanding of the basic rules and regulations of softball
3. Understanding of the basic batting and fielding strategies of softball
4. Respect and appreciation for referees
5. Appreciation of individual differences of other players
6. Understanding and appreciation of good sportsmanship, team loyalty, and fair play
7. Ability to design, modify, or create practice activities and inventive games involving softball skills

## Softball Skill Test

The general level of skill of each respective class can be determined through two evaluation techniques. The first is to have the children play one or more softball-type lead-up games and to observe and record individual and general levels of skill and playing ability. This general overview provides a basis for the selection and emphasis of skills, practice activities, and lead-up games.

The following lead-up games can be used to provide a general overview of the class' general level of skill and playing ability.

| Games | Page in text |
|---|---|
| Six-Player Softball | 414 |
| One Old Cat | 415 |
| Tee Ball | 416 |

An observation sheet, such as the one shown below, can be used to record performance on specific skills as well as to note general weaknesses or problems common to most children.

### Class Observation Sheet—Softball

| Skills | Level of Ability | | Comments |
|---|---|---|---|
| | High | Low | |
| Throwing | | | |
| Pitching | | | |
| Catching | | | |
| Fielding | | | |
| Batting | | | |
| Positional play | | | |

A standardized or teacher-made test is the second technique used to assess a class' level of skill and playing ability. In the majority of classroom situations, a teacher-made test outline is normally used for this purpose. It is strongly recommended that teachers use a test similar to the one shown in the accompanying reference and modify this test to meet the level of skill, need, and interest of each respective class.

| Softball Skill Test | Page in text |
|---|---|
| Accuracy Throw | 419 |
| Distance Throw | 419 |
| Fielding | 419 |
| Subjective Evaluation | 420 |

**Softball Skill Test**

| Name | Accuracy Throw (total pts.) | Distance Throw (total pts.) | Fielding (total pts.) | Subjective Evaluation (50 pts.) | Total Score | Grade |
|------|------|------|------|------|------|------|
| 1 | | | | | | |
| 2 | | Rank total scores for the class, than convert to letter grades or ratings (superior, good, etc.) | | | | |
| 3 | | | | | | |
| 4 | | | | | | |

**Additional Lessons** The amount that can actually be covered in this lesson will depend upon time allotment, skill level, and general behavior of the class. If the teacher feels more time is necessary to cover skills or to establish more efficient procedures and class tone, develop one or more lessons.

| Content | Teaching Strategies | References | Lesson 2a | 2b | 2c |
|---|---|---|---|---|---|
| **Entry Activity** | Practice throwing and catching. | | | | |
| **Part 1: Introductory Activities** (*4 to 5 minutes*) Conditioning Running | 1. Walk, jog, run. 2. Calisthenics. | Calisthenics, p. 180 Jogging, p. 191 | Repeat 1 and 2. | | Design your own lessons. |
| **Part 2: Skill Development** (*20 to 35 minutes*) Throwing Catching | 1. Explanation and demonstration of overhand throwing skills and underhand and overhand catching skills. 2. Practice activities  a. Partner activities: Both stationary; one partner stationary and other moving; pitcher/catcher.  b. Develop challenges that involve overhand throwing, catching, and a variety of small equipment. 3. Inventive games involving six players. Use similar challenges used in skill development. Example: "In your group of six, can you make up a throwing and catching game using one traffic cone and two hoops?" 4. Lead-up games: *Six-Player Softball*—This game is similar to softball with several modifications. Some of these modifications are: three bases, six innings, four outs per inning, and a batter is out after two strikes. *Danish Rounders*—This game develops throwing, catching, and baserunning skills. One team is at bat and the other is in the field. The batter tries to hit a pitched ball with his or her hand. Whether ball is hit or not, the batter runs to first base and farther if possible. Fielding team tries to return the ball to the pitcher who touches his or her own base. If at any time a base runner is off base and the ball is "downed" by the pitcher, the base runner is out. Any number of batting players may be on any base at the same time, and on any strike or hit may run to the next base or remain where they are. A point is scored when a player reaches home plate. | Throwing, p. 404 Practice activities, p. 411  Lead-up games, p. 411  Six-Player Softball, p. 414  Danish Rounders, p. 415 | Introduce side-arm throw.  Lead-up games. | Leave out.  Lead-up games. | Fielder |
| **Part 3: Closure** (*1 to 2 minutes*) | Explain and illustrate the importance of a good follow-through in a throwing activity. | | | | |

*Note:* Entry activities should be provided at the beginning of each lesson. Have balls, bats, and if possible, mats available at the beginning of each lesson.

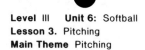

**Level** III   **Unit 6:** Softball
**Lesson 3.** Pitching
**Main Theme** Pitching
**Subthemes** Traveling and catching; Running

**Additional Lessons** If one or more additional lessons are required, stress pitching.

| Content | Teaching Strategies | References | Lesson 3a | 3b | 3c |
|---|---|---|---|---|---|
| **Entry Activity** | | | | | |
| **Part 1: Introductory Activities**<br>*(4 to 5 minutes)*<br><br>Running<br>Conditioning | 1. Walk, jog, run.<br>2. Calisthenics. Continue above sequence. | Calisthenics, p. 180 | Design your own lessons. | Design your own lessons. | Design your own lessons. |
| **Part 2: Skill Development**<br>*(20 to 35 minutes)*<br><br>Pitching | 1. Demonstrate pitching skill.<br>2. Practice activities<br>  a. Partner activities: Throw and catch; pitcher/catcher; practice hitting target.<br>3. Inventive games involving eight players. Stress pitching in your challenges.<br>4. Lead-up games:<br>*Overtake the Ball*—This game develops throwing and catching skills. Players on two teams are placed in alternate positions forming a circle. One player from each team stands in the center of the circle. On signal, players in center toss ball to one of their teammates who toss the ball back. This continues around the circle until all members have been thrown to and the ball is returned to the player in the center. The team that tosses the ball completely around the circle first scores a point.<br>*One Old Cat*—This game develops hitting, catching, and throwing skills as well as speed, change of direction, and hitting/moving in space. There are two teams with one team at bat and the other in the field. There are only two bases (first/home). A batter must make a complete trip—scoring a run or recording an out. A batter is out if tagged with the ball before reaching home or if a fielder catches a fly ball. | Pitching, p. 406<br><br><br>Lead-up games, p. 411<br>Overtake the Ball, p. 417<br><br><br><br><br><br><br>One Old Cat, p. 415 | Leave out.<br><br><br><br>Lead-up games. | Leave out.<br><br><br><br>Lead-up games. | |
| **Part 3: Closure**<br>*(1 to 2 minutes)*<br><br>Pitching | Review the pitching zone and pitching strategies. | | | | |

**Level III    Unit 6:** Softball
**Lesson 4.** Batting
**Main Theme** Batting
**Subthemes** Throwing and catching

**Additional Lessons** If additional lessons are required, stress batting.

| Content | Teaching Strategies | References | Lesson 4a | 4b | 4c |
|---|---|---|---|---|---|
| **Entry Activity** | Practice throwing and catching. | | | | |
| **Part 1: Introductory Activities** *(4 to 5 minutes)* <br><br> Running <br> Conditioning | 1. Continue, shortening walking and jogging time, plus calisthenics. <br> 2. Develop an outdoor obstacle course. | Obstacle course, p. 190 | Repeat 1 and 2. | Repeat 1 and 2. | Design your own lesson. |
| **Part 2: Skill Development** *(20 to 35 minutes)* <br><br> Batting | 1. Review throwing and catching. Partner activities. Inventive practice activities with partner and small equipment. <br> 2. Demonstrate batting grips and swinging movements. <br> 3. Practice activities <br>   a. Partner activities: One pitches and the other hits back a fly or grounder. <br>   b. Small group activities: In threes, "Make up a drill involving a hit, a pitch, a run, and two pieces of small equipment"; in groups of five or six, "Pepper" (p. 414). This drill develops hitting, catching, and throwing skills. <br> 4. Lead-up games: <br> *Long Ball*—This game has two teams with one team at bat and the other in the field. There are only two bases in this game. Any hit is good and there are no fouls. The batter may stop on first base and any number of runners may be on base at the same time. Batters are out when touched off base with the ball or if a fly ball is caught. One point is awarded for each run. <br> *T-Ball*—This game is similar to softball, with the exception that batters hit off a tee. Since there is no pitcher, a runner must stay on base until the ball is hit by a teammate. Batters could self-toss and hit (fungo-style) if so desired. | Throwing, p. 404 <br> Practice activities, p. 411 <br><br><br><br><br><br> Lead-up games, p. 411 <br> Long Ball, p. 416 <br><br><br><br><br> T-Ball, p. 416 | Repeat 2 and 3. <br><br><br><br><br><br><br><br> Lead-up games. | Leave out. <br><br><br><br><br><br><br><br> Lead-up games. | |
| **Part 3: Closure** *(1 to 2 minutes)* <br><br> Batting | Discuss the importance of a good stance, keeping an eye on the ball, and follow-through action. | | | | |

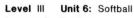

**Level** III    **Unit 6:** Softball
**Lesson 5.** Fielding
**Main Theme** Batting
**Subthemes** Sidearm; Throwing; Catching

**Additional Lessons** If additional lessons are required, stress fielding.

| Content | Teaching Strategies | References | Lesson 5a | 5b | 5c |
|---|---|---|---|---|---|
| **Entry Activity** | Practice throwing and catching. | | | | |
| **Part 1: Introductory Activities** (4 to 5 minutes) | 1. Continue with walk, jog, run activity, plus calisthenics. 2. Continue with obstacle course. Shorten time, change equipment, add equipment. | Obstacle course, p. 190 | | | Design your own lessons. |
| Running Conditioning | | | | | |
| **Part 2: Skill Development** (20 to 35 minutes) | 1. Demonstrate fielding grounders.   a. Partner activities: One partner throws or rolls ball along the ground to partner. Partner fields ball and throws back.   b. Small group activities: In threes or fours, develop drill involving fielding, throwing, and running. | Fielding, p. 406 | Repeat 1. | Repeat 1 (no calisthenics) and 2. | |
| Fielding Side-arm throw | 2. Practice activities: In partners, one partner throws or rolls ball along the ground to partner. Partner fields ball and throws back, using sidearm throw. In threes or fours, develop drill involving fielding and a sidearm throw. | | | | |
| | 3. Lead-up games: Allow groups to modify games and to add new rules as they desire. *Six-Player Softball* *Flies and Grounders*—This game develops catching, fielding, and batting skills. A batter hits the ball off a tee or fungo-style to field players. A field player "calls for the ball" and attempts to catch or field the ball. Points are received for catching and fielding successfully. The first fielder to reach 15 points becomes the new batter. *Scrub*—One player (the "scrub") stands at bat. The batter hits a pitched ball and must run to first base and back (only two bases). Batter must score a run or an out. Batter is allowed three times at bat and then becomes a fielder. Game continues until all players have played each position and have batted. | Lead-up games, p. 411 Six-Player Softball, p. 414 Flies and Grounders, p. 415 Scrub, p. 417 | Lead-up games. | Lead-up games. | |
| **Part 3: Closure** (1 to 2 minutes) | | | | | |
| Fielding | Discuss the importance of moving into position to field a ball. | | | | |

**Level** III   **Unit 6:** Softball
**Lesson 6.** Fungo Batting
**Main Theme** Batting
**Subthemes** Throwing; Grounders

**Additional Lessons** If additional lessons are required, stress hitting and fielding.

| Content | Teaching Strategies | References | Lesson 6a | 6b | 6c |
|---|---|---|---|---|---|
| **Entry Activity** | Practice grounders and throwing. | | | | |
| **Part 1: Introductory Activities** *(4 to 5 minutes)* <br><br> Running <br> Conditioning | 1. Continue with walk, jog, run activity, plus calisthenics. <br> 2. Continue with obstacle course, varying the time, equipment, and movement patterns (run, hop, leap, etc.). | Obstacle course, p. 190 | Tag games. | Tag games. | Design your own lessons. |
| **Part 2: Skill Development** *(20 to 35 minutes)* <br><br> Fungo batting <br> Fielding | 1. Review fielding grounders and sidearm throw. Repeat practice activities in above lesson. <br> 2. Demonstrate fungo batting. <br> 3. Practice activities: <br>   a. In partners: one fungo hits to partner. <br>   b. Inventive games involving fungo batting, baserunning, and fielding. <br> 4. Lead-up games: <br> *Six-Player Softball* (add one more player—7 vs. 7) <br> *Roll at the Bat*—A batter hits the ball into the field of play. If a field player catches a fly ball, he or she rolls it back and tries to hit the bat, which has been placed on the ground. A fielder becomes the new batter when he or she successfully rolls a ball back and hits the bat; when the fielder catches two fly balls; or when he or she successfully retrieves three grounders. <br> *500*—The object of this game is for each fielder to try to be the first to reach 500 points. Points are received for catching fly balls and for fielding grounders. The same number of points are deducted from a player's score if an error is committed. The first fielder to receive 500 points becomes the next batter. <br> Allow groups to modify games and add any new rule they desire. | Fungo hitting, p. 410 <br> Practice activities, p. 411 <br><br><br><br> Lead-up games, p. 411 <br> Six-Player Softball, p. 414 <br> Roll at the Bat, p. 417 <br> 500, p. 417 | Leave out. <br><br><br><br><br><br> Softball game. | Leave out. <br><br><br><br><br><br> Softball game. | |
| **Part 3: Closure** *(1 to 2 minutes)* <br><br> Hitting | Discuss fielding positions when a left- or right-handed hitter is batting. | | | | |

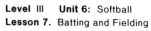

**Level III**    **Unit 6:** Softball
**Lesson 7.** Batting and Fielding
**Main Theme** Bunting
**Subthemes** Throwing; Catching

**Additional Lessons** If additional lessons are required, stress bunting and all other skills.

| Content | Teaching Strategies | References | Lesson 7a | 7b | 7c |
|---|---|---|---|---|---|
| **Entry Activity** | Practice grounders and throwing. | | | | |
| **Part 1: Introductory Activities** (*4 to 5 minutes*) | 1. Continue with walk, jog, run activities, plus calisthenics. <br> 2. Continue with obstacle course varying challenges. | Obstacle course, p. 190 | Repeat 1 and 2. | Tag games. | Design your own lessons. |
| Running <br> Conditioning | | | | | |
| **Part 2: Skill Development** (*20 to 35 minutes*) <br><br> Bunting and all skills | 1. Demonstrate bunting. <br> 2. Arrange class into four stations. Remain with station 3 to give assistance in partners practicing bunting. Rotate groups every three to six minutes. | Bunting, p. 410 | Leave out. | Leave out. | |
| | Softball Game. | Softball, p. 418 | Softball games. | Softball games. | |
| **Part 3: Closure** (*1 to 2 minutes*) | | | | | |
| Bunting | Discuss the strategy of bunting. | | | | |

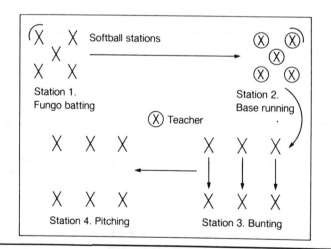

**Level** III   **Unit 6:** Softball
**Lesson 8.** All Skills
**Main Theme** All skills
**Subtheme** Positioning play

**Additional Lessons** If additional lessons are required, stress skills according to revealed needs and interests of the class.

| Content | Teaching Strategies | References | Lesson 8a | 8b | 8c |
|---|---|---|---|---|---|
| **Entry Activity** | Practice throwing and catching. | | | | |
| **Part 1: Introductory Activities**<br>*(4 to 5 minutes)*<br><br>Running<br>Conditioning | 1. Continue with walk, jog, run activities, plus calisthenics, or<br>2. Continue with obstacle course varying challenges. | | Design your own lessons. | Design your own lessons. | Design your own lessons. |
| **Part 2: Skill Development**<br>*(20 to 35 minutes)*<br><br>All Skills | 1. Repeat station work activities of previous lesson.<br>2. Play regulation softball, modifying or adding rules according to interest of the class. | Softball,<br>p. 418 | | | |
| **Part 3: Closure**<br>*(1 to 2 minutes)* | Discuss softball unit. What the children enjoyed and what they disliked. | | | | |
| **Level III**   **Unit 6:** Softball<br>**Lesson 9.** Evaluation | This lesson and additional lessons if needed should be used to administer the skill test used at the beginning of this unit. | | | | |

Administer the skill tests used at the beginning of this unit (p. 118 of this guide).

# Game Activities
## Developmental Level III
## Unit 7: Track and Field

### Expected Learning Outcomes

**Psychomotor Skills**

1. Ability to perform standing and sprinting starts
2. Ability to perform sprints, relays, and distance running skills
3. Ability to perform standing broad jump, long jump, triple jump, and high jump skills
4. Ability to perform shot put skill

**Cognitive and Affective Knowledge and Skills**

1. Understanding of one's level of ability prior to and after a unit of track and field
2. Understanding of basic training procedures for running and field events
3. Appreciation of the individual differences of other children
4. Appreciation of good sportsmanship and fair play

**Level III    Unit 7:** Track and Field
**Lesson 1.**  Sprints
**Main Theme**  Sprints
**Subthemes**  Shot put; Broad jump; High jump

| Content | Teaching Strategies | References | Lesson 1a | 1b | 1c |
|---|---|---|---|---|---|
| **Part 1: Introductory Activities** *(4 to 5 minutes)* | 1. Walk, jog, run.<br>2. Calisthenics. | Calisthenics, p. 180 | Repeat 1 and 2. | Repeat 1 and 2. | |
| Conditioning | | | | | |
| **Part 2: Skill Development** *(20 to 35 minutes)*<br><br>Sprints<br>Shot put<br>Standing broad jump<br>High jump | *Part A: Class Activity* (approx. five mins.)<br>Arrange class in a long line across the field.<br>  1. Demonstrate sprint start and sprinting form to class. Use students to demonstrate.<br>  2. Practice activities: Individual start and sprint according to teacher's commands ("on your mark . . . set . . . go"); start and baton pass.<br>*Part B: Station Work* (approx. five mins. at each station)<br>Divide class into three groups and assign to stations for approximately five minutes. Teacher remains with shot put throughout part B.<br>Group A: *Standing Broad Jump:* Working in partners with one jumping, the other marking the landing (p. 426).<br>Group B: *Shot Put:* Teacher explains and demonstrates (use student if desired) shot put skill plus safety precautions. Individual practice (p. 432).<br>Group C: *High Jump:* Individual practice—scissors, high jumping skill (p. 429).<br>*Note:* After approximately five minutes, blow whistle and have groups rotate clockwise to next station. | Starts, p. 424<br>Practice activities, p. 432<br>Station work, p. 423 | Repeat rotation with teacher shifting to the high jump. | Repeat rotation with teacher shifting to the standing broad jump. | |
| **Part 3: Closure** *(1 to 2 minutes)*<br><br>Starting positions | Discuss and illustrate the main difference between the starting position for sprint and for distance runs. | | | | |

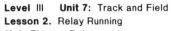

**Level** III **Unit 7:** Track and Field
**Lesson 2.** Relay Running
**Main Theme** Relay running
**Subthemes** Jumping; Shot put

**Additional Lessons** Additional lessons should be used to practice each skill on a rotational basis.

| Content | Teaching Strategies | References | Lesson 2a | 2b | 2c |
|---|---|---|---|---|---|
| **Part 1: Introductory Activities** *(4 to 5 minutes)* | 1. Continue walk, jog, run.<br>2. Continue calisthenics. | Calisthenics, p. 180 | Repeat 1 and 2. | Repeat 1 and 2. | Repeat 1 and 2. |
| Conditioning | | | | | |
| **Part 2: Skill Development** *(20 to 35 minutes)*<br><br>Baton passing<br>Standing broad jump<br>Sprints<br>Shot put<br>Long jump | *Part A: Class Activity* (approx. five min.)<br>Arrange class in a long double line across the field.<br>  1. Demonstrate baton pass.<br>  2. Practice activities: baton passing.<br>*Part B: Station Work* (approx. five min. at each station)<br>Divide class into four groups and assign to stations for approximately five minutes. Teacher remains with long jump. Explanation and demonstration of this skill to each group.<br>Group A: *Standing Broad Jump:* Working in partners with one jumping, the other marking the landing.<br>Group B: *Sprints:* Work in partners, one calling signals ("on your mark . . . set . . . go"), the other practices starts and twenty- to thirty-yard sprints.<br>Group C: *Shot Put:* In partners, one puts shot from circle, partner marks spot, picks up shot, returns to circle, and takes his or her turn. Other partner shifts to waiting spot in field. (Safety: Waiting spot should be a reasonable distance from landing area.)<br>Group D: *Long Jump:* Teacher explains and demonstrates (use student if desired) long jump approach, takeoff, and landing (p. 426).<br>After five minutes, rotate groups clockwise. | Passing, p. 425<br>Practice activities, p. 432 | Repeat rotation with teacher shifting to shot put. | Repeat rotation with teacher shifting to sprints. | Repeat rotation with teacher shifting to standing broad jump. |
| **Part 3: Closure** *(1 to 2 minutes)* | Discuss the importance of good timing on the part of the passer and the receiver of the baton. | | | | |

**Level** III    **Unit 7:** Track and Field
**Lesson 3.** Triple Jump
**Main Theme** Triple jump
**Subthemes** Sprinting; Jumping; Shot put

**Additional Lessons** Continue pattern as illustrated in previous lesson.

| Content | Teaching Strategies | References | Lesson 3a | 3b | 3c |
|---|---|---|---|---|---|
| **Part 1: Introductory Activities** <br> *(4 to 5 minutes)* <br><br> Conditioning | 1. Introduce interval training (check distance). <br> 2. Continue with calisthenics, adding one or two repetitions to each exercise. | Interval training, p. 433 | Repeat 1 and 2. | Repeat 1 and 2. | Design your own lessons. |
| **Part 2: Skill Development** <br> *(20 to 35 minutes)* <br><br> Triple jump <br> Long jump <br> Sprints <br> Shot put <br> High jump | *Part A: Class Activity* (approx. five min.) <br> Arrange class in a long line across the field. <br> 1. Demonstrate the triple jump: hop, step, and jump (Use students to demonstrate.) <br> 2. Practice activities <br> *Part B: Station Work:* (approx. five min. at each station rotating A to D, D to A, etc.) <br> Use the same groups from previous lesson and assign as follows: <br> Group A: *Long Jump* and *Triple Jump:* Work in partners, one jumps, the other checks takeoff and marks landing. <br> Group B: *Sprints:* Work in partners, one calling signals, the other practicing starts and thirty- to forty-yard dashes. <br> Group C: *Shot Put:* One puts the shot while other marks and returns shot to circle. <br> Group D: *High Jump:* Teacher explains and demonstrates straddle style of jumping to each group as they rotate to this station. | Triple jump, p. 431 | Repeat rotation, teacher shifts to another station. | Repeat rotation, teacher shifts to another station. | |

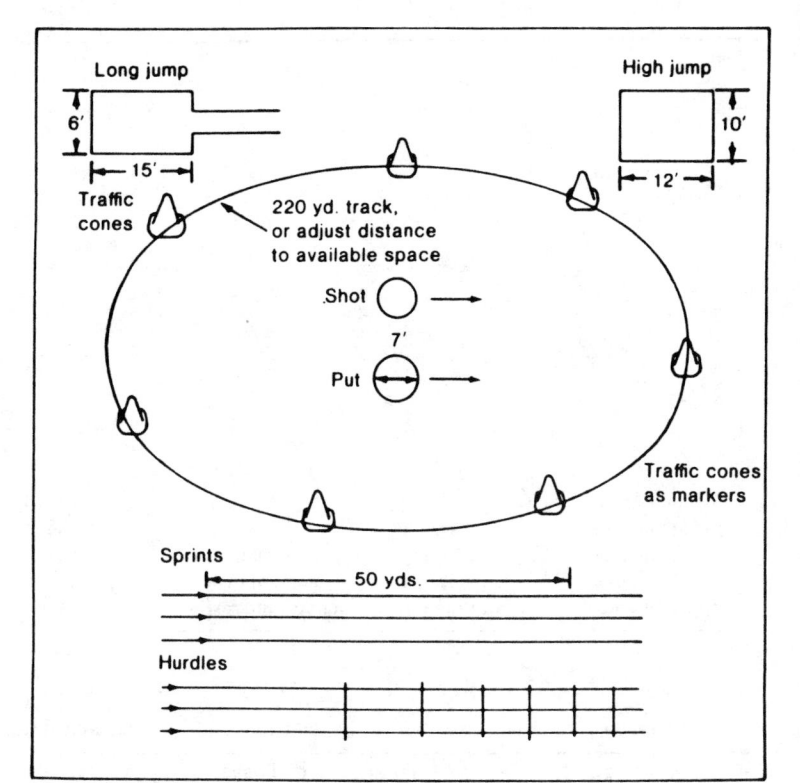

**Track and Field Circuit**

**Part 3: Closure**
*(1 to 2 minutes)*

Discuss the importance of a good takeoff (takeoff foot hitting the same mark on each takeoff attempt).

**Level** III **Unit 7:** Track and Field
**Lesson 4.** Hurdles
**Main Theme** Hurdling
**Subthemes** Jumping; Running; Shot Put

**Additional Lessons** Continue pattern as illustrated in previous lesson.

| Content | Teaching Strategies | References | Lesson 4a | 4b | 4c |
|---|---|---|---|---|---|
| **Part 1: Introductory Activities**<br>*(4 to 5 minutes)*<br><br>Conditioning | 1. Continue with interval training.<br>2. Continue with calisthenics adding one or two repetitions to each exercise. | | Repeat 1 and 2. | Repeat 1 and 2. | Design your own lessons. |
| **Part 2: Skill Development**<br>*(20 to 35 minutes)*<br><br>Hurdles<br>Long jump<br>Shot put<br>Triple jump<br>High jump | *Part A: Class Activity* (approx. five min.)<br>1. Demonstrate and practice each phase of hurdle event in the sequence described on page 428.<br>*Part B: Station Work* (approx. five min. at each station, rotating from A to D, D to A, etc.) Divide class into four groups and assign stations.<br>Assign above groups as follows:<br>Group A: *Long Jump:* Work in partners—one jumps, the other checks takeoff and marks landing.<br>Group B: *Shot Put:* One puts the shot, while the other marks and returns the shot to the circle.<br>Group C: *Triple Jump:* In partners, one performs triple jump, partner checks takeoff, current movements, and distance.<br>Group D: *High Jump:* Work in groups—two perform placing stick on bars. Keep bar at minimum height to accommodate all jumpers. | Hurdles, p. 428 | Repeat rotation with teacher shifting to another station. | Repeat rotation with teacher shifting to another station. | |
| **Part 3: Closure**<br>*(1 to 2 minutes)*<br><br>Hurdles | Discuss and illustrate the importance of good leg action as the performer crosses the hurdle. | | | | |

**Lesson III    Unit 7:** Track and Field
**Lesson 5.**  All Skills

| Content | Teaching Strategies | References | Lesson 5a | 5b | 5c |
|---|---|---|---|---|---|
| **Part 1: Introductory Activities**<br>*(4 to 5 minutes)*<br><br>Conditioning | Allow students the choice of<br>1. walk, jog, run.<br>2. interval training.<br>3. continuous running.<br>4. calisthenics. | Walk, jog, run,<br>p. 191<br>Interval<br>training, p. 433<br>Continuous<br>running, p. 433<br>Calisthenics,<br>p. 180 | | | |
| **Part 2: Skill Development**<br>*(20 to 35 minutes)*<br><br>All Skills | *Note:* Allow students to choose *three* of the following events to concentrate on<br>during this part of the lesson.<br>*Track Events*<br>1. Sprints 50 to 100 yards.<br>2. Middle distance runs 220 and 440 yard runs.<br>3. One-mile run. (Teacher works with these children.)<br>4. Hurdles.<br>*Field Events*<br>1. Standing broad jump.<br>2. Long jump.<br>3. High jump.<br>4. Triple jump.<br>5. Shot put. | Cross-country,<br>p. 436 | Repeat lesson. | Repeat lesson. | Repeat lesson. |
| **Part 3: Closure**<br>*(1 to 2 minutes)*<br><br>Cross-country running | Emphasize value of cross-country running as an enjoyable activity that helps<br>maintain optimum levels of cardiorespiratory fitness. | | | | |

**Level III    Unit 7:** Track and Field
**Lesson 6.**  Evaluation

Evaluation, p. 439
Evaluation in track and field activities is quite difficult and sometimes hard on the
less-gifted performer. As suggested in the text, have each child keep his or her
own evaluation form. The form would include initial and sequential records of the
performer's performance of each event and thus a personal assessment.

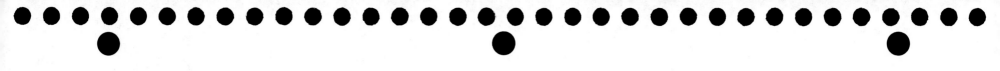

# Gymnastic Activities

# Gymnastic Activities
## Developmental Level I
## Unit 1: Gymnastics—
## Movement Patterns

### Expected Learning Outcomes

**Psychomotor Skills**

1. Traveling and stopping
2. Change of direction
3. Balancing on different parts of the body
4. Balancing small equipment on different parts of the body
5. Performing stretch, curl, wide, narrow, and twisted shapes
6. Performing simple sequences of movement skills
7. Rolling skills—log, side, forward, diagonal roll
8. Change of level
9. Flow—ability to perform two or more basic movement skills in a sequential order
10. Animal movements, agility, and balance stunts

**Cognitive and Affective Knowledge and Skills**

1. Understand the basic movement terminology
2. Understand the meaning of "sequence" development
3. Know the names of different parts of the body
4. Ability to work with a partner in the development of movement
5. Appreciation of the individual strengths and weaknesses of self and of others in the class
6. Understanding and ability to share space and equipment with others in the instructional space

Evaluative Techniques: See chapter 9 for observational methods and evaluative tools to assess structured or movement education skills and concepts.

**Level** I  **Unit 1:** Gymnastics—Movement Patterns
**Lesson 1.** Balance
**Main Theme** Balancing
**Subthemes** Traveling; Safety skills
**Equipment** Class set of beanbags

**Additional Lessons** In virtually every Level I classroom situation, few teachers will ever completely cover all that is contained in this lesson. This lesson may be expanded to two or more lessons to allow each teacher to complete, review, or expand on different ideas contained in this first lesson.

| Content | Teaching Strategies | References | Lesson 1a | 1b | 1c |
|---|---|---|---|---|---|
| **Entry Activity** | Place beanbags in four containers. Free play with equipment. | | Repeat previous. | Repeat previous. | Repeat previous. |
| **Part 1: Introductory Activities** (5 to 10 minutes)<br><br>Traveling<br>—in different ways<br>—in different directions<br>Safety skills—controlled stopping | The first few lessons may take maximum time. Ask children to put equipment away and find a space. Pose the following challenges:<br>1. "Walk very quickly in any direction, but do not touch anyone." Check for spacing and general behavior. Teacher keeps shifting his or her own location in the instructional area.<br>2. "Now, see if you can run in any direction, but when I say 'freeze,' stop and touch the floor with your fingertips."<br>3. Repeat 2 with children hopping, skipping, or while performing an animal walk movement (lame puppy, etc.). | Teaching gymnastic activities, p. 442<br>Lame puppy, p. 463 | Repeat 1 and 2. | Repeat 1 and 2 adding change of direction to challenge. | Repeat 1 and 2 adding change of level to challenge. |
| **Part 2: Skill Development** (10 to 20 minutes)<br><br>Balancing on different parts of the body | Ask children to return to their section places ("section places" should have been learned in the first games unit, p. 23). Pose the following challenges to encourage each child to answer the challenge in his own way. Begin with structure and gradually shift to giving children more freedom and scope in answering the question.<br>1. "Can you balance (or use words "take the weight") on your seat?" Wait a few moments, then, "on your knees, side." Continue naming parts.<br>2. "Can you show me how you can balance on three parts of your body?" "Three different body parts?" | Balance or weight bearing, pp. 37, 496 | Repeat 1 and 2. | Repeat 2 and 3. | Repeat 2 adding "on two and four parts." |
| Balancing with small equipment—beanbags | From their scattered positions on the floor, "Go to the nearest box, get one beanbag, then find a new space . . . off you go!"<br>3. "How many different parts of your body can you balance the beanbag on?"<br>4. "See if you can balance the beanbag on your foot, shoulder, knee." Continue calling out different parts.<br>5. "Can you balance the beanbag on your foot while moving across the floor?" Continue calling out different body parts. | Beanbag activities, p. 506 | Repeat 3 and 4. | Repeat 3 and 4. | Repeat 3 and 4 with a wand or hoop. |
| **Part 3: Closure** (1 to 3 minutes)<br><br>Balancing on different parts of the body | Discuss importance of safety skills and meaning of balance or weight bearing. | | | | |

**Level I    Unit 1:** Gymnastics—Movement Patterns
**Lesson 2.** Transfer of Weight
**Main Theme** Transfer of weight
**Subthemes** Traveling; Safety skills
**Equipment** Variety of small equipment and small and large tumbling mats

**Additional Lessons** Additional lessons should stress transferring body weight from one part to another. Strong emphasis should be given to moving safely and rolling skills.

| Content | Teaching Strategies | References | Lesson 2a | 2b | 2c |
|---|---|---|---|---|---|
| **Entry Activity** | Place a variety of small equipment in the four containers. Free play with equipment. | Use of time before a lesson, p. 106 | Repeat previous. | Repeat previous. | Repeat previous. |
| **Part 1: Introductory Activities** (5 to 10 minutes)  Traveling —in different directions | Equipment away and return to own space. Explain importance of running safely and watching out for others, etc., then beginning sequence of tasks. "Begin walking anywhere and when I call out a new way to move, quickly shift to the new way . . . 'go' (wait a few seconds), sideways, forward, backward," continue pattern. Watch for good movements and spacing. Select one or two to demonstrate. Give praise to each performer. Continue pattern. | | Repeat run and changing directions. | Play Nine Lives (p. 30 of this guide). | Repeat run and changing directions. |
| **Part 2: Skill Development** (10 to 20 minutes)  Safety skills —log roll  Transfer of weight —from parts to parts | Safety Skills 1. Explain and demonstrate the log roll (use children to demonstrate). 2. Practice—on mat or rug, individual rolling toward right and left sides and experiment by changing arm position. Transfer of Weight 3. "Try and balance on your seat, then log roll all the way around and back to balancing on your seat." 4. "Find a way to balance on three parts, then log roll and end up balancing on three new parts." 5. "Find a way to balance on one body part, then log roll and end up balancing on three body parts." Continue challenges involving balancing, transferring weight by rolling, then back to balancing. | Log roll, p. 469 Transfer of weight, pp. 37, 496 | Repeat 1 and 2. | Repeat 2 and 3. | Leave out. |
| Transfer of weight —with small equipment | Ask children to select a beanbag, hoop, individual rope, or wand. 6. "See if you can place your equipment on any part of your body and perform a wicket walk or a tightrope walk," etc. 7. Invent a new stunt with your equipment. Have one or two demonstrate. Choose a variety—not always the best or most unique. 8. "Place your equipment on the floor and show me three ways you can cross over it." 9. "Can you cross over your equipment without using your feet?" Continue challenges stressing a transfer of weight. | Wicket walk, p. 462 Tightrope walk, p. 479 Transfer of weight with small equipment, pp. 496, 505 | Repeat 6 and 7. | Repeat 8 and 9. | Repeat any of 6 to 9 or design new challenges. |
| **Part 3: Closure** (1 to 2 minutes)  Transfer of weight | Discuss transfer of weight: the ability to shift from one balanced position to another. | | | | |

**Level I     Unit 1:** Gymnastics—Movement Patterns
**Lesson 3.** Shapes
**Main Theme** Stretch and curl shapes
**Subtheme** Rolling
**Equipment** Large and/or small mats; Class set of individual ropes (or wands)

**Additional Lessons** Additional lessons should stress stretch and curl shapes combined with a transfer of weight.

| Content | Teaching Strategies | References | Lesson 3a | 3b | 3c |
|---|---|---|---|---|---|
| **Entry Activity** | Place a variety of small equipment in the four containers. Free play with equipment. | | Repeat previous. | Repeat previous. | Repeat previous. |
| **Part 1: Introductory Activities** (*5 to 8 minutes*)<br><br>Traveling<br>—in different directions<br>—in different speeds | Equipment away and find your own space.<br>1. "Run, and every time you change direction also change your speed."<br>2. Scatter individual and/or large mats around instructional area. Ask class to show you a log roll toward right and left sides.<br>3. "Now, show me how you can log roll in any direction, but when you get too close to another player, stand up and walk to a new free space and continue your log rolls. Keep moving until I say stop." | | Repeat 1 to 3. | Play Tails (p. 31 of this guide). | Repeat 1 and 3. Ask children to use a log roll first, then next time a side roll. |
| **Part 2: Skill Development** (*10 to 20 minutes*)<br><br>Safety skills<br>—side roll<br>Shapes<br>—stretch and curl | 1. Explain and demonstrate the side roll.<br>2. Practice on mat or rug.<br>Introduce stretch and curl shapes. Ask children to find a new space. Pose the following challenges:<br>3. "Show me how high you can stretch. Can you touch the ceiling?"<br>4. "Stretch to the side, under your legs." Continue pattern.<br>5. "Can you stretch very tall, then curl up like a very small ball?" | Shapes, pp. 37, 448<br>Side roll, p. 449 | Repeat 5 adding, "Can you make a new shape?" "See if you can make a stretch, then a curled shape." | Leave out. | Repeat 5 of lesson 3a and add one or two challenges involving balance challenges from lesson 1. |
| Shapes with small equipment | Ask children (each section place) to go to their box to get a rope then find a new space and sit down.<br>6. "Place your rope on the floor any way you like, then make a shape over your rope."<br>7. "Can you make a stretch shape over your rope?"<br>8. "Can you make the same shape again, change to a small ball shape, and roll away from your rope?"<br>9. "Make a circle with your rope. Curled up like a ball, can you bounce in and out of your circle?" Continue challenges, stressing curled and stretched shapes. | Inventive challenges with small equipment, p. 509 | Repeat 6 to 9 with a beanbag or hoop. | Repeat 6 to 9 with a beanbag or hoop. | Repeat 6 to 9 from lesson 3b. |
| **Part 3: Closure** (*1 to 2 minutes*)<br><br>Shapes | Discuss and show illustrations of stretch and curl shapes. | | | | |

**Level I  Unit 1:** Gymnastics—Movement Patterns
**Lesson 4.** Shapes
**Main Theme** Stretch and curl shapes
**Subtheme** Rolling
**Equipment** One set for each "section" (about 8) of individual ropes, hoops, beanbags, and wands; Large and small mats

**Additional Lessons** Additional lessons should stress wide and narrow shapes combined with stretch and curl and rolling skills. Use rotation system to encourage children to explore other ideas with their new equipment.

| Content | Teaching Strategies | References | Lesson 4a | 4b | 4c |
|---|---|---|---|---|---|
| **Entry Activity** | Place a variety of small equipment in the four containers. Free play with equipment. | | Repeat previous. | Repeat previous. | Repeat previous. |
| **Part 1: Introductory Activities** (5 to 7 minutes)<br><br>Traveling<br>—in different directions<br>—in different way<br>Safety skills<br>—diagonal roll<br>—run, jump, land, and roll | Equipment away and find a space.<br>1. Run, jump, land, and continue pattern.<br>2. Travel anywhere on "hands and feet," wait a few moments, "on one foot," "on two feet and one hand." Continue pattern.<br>3. Scatter individual and/or large mats. "Run, jump, land, and roll across mat." (Use log or side roll.)<br>4. Explain and demonstrate diagonal roll.<br>5. Individual practice. | Diagonal roll, p. 452 | Repeat 3 using log or side roll. | Play Tails (p. 31 of this guide). | Repeat 2 and 3. |
| **Part 2: Skill Development** (10 to 20 minutes)<br><br>Shapes<br>—stretch and curl<br>—wide and narrow | When children are in their own spaces:<br>1. Introduce sequence. "Can you think up three shapes that you can perform one right after the other? We will call this a sequence." Wait a few minutes, then select one or two for demonstrations.<br>2. "Can you make a wide shape . . . now shift to a very thin shape?"<br>3. "Let's combine stretch and curl with wide and narrow shapes . . . first make a curled shape . . . now change to a wide shape." Continue pattern, gradually building sequence to three or four stages. | Sequence of shapes, p. 37 | Repeat 1. | Repeat 3. | Leave out. |
| | Divide class into four groups.<br>Give group A, hoops; B, individual ropes; C, beanbags; and D, wands. Assign each group to a corner of the gymnasium. Present the following challenges:<br>4. "Make up a sequence of shapes over your piece of equipment. Practice this sequence for a few minutes." Check for quality of movements and general working tone of class.<br>5. Introduce rotation stations. "Think up your favorite wide or thin shape. When I say 'one,' everyone makes their favorite shape over their equipment. When I say 'two,' everyone shift to the next station (show A moving to B and B moving to C), and make the same shape over a new piece of equipment." Ready. . ."one." Wait a few minutes then call "two" etc., to last station. | Hoops, p. 522<br>Individual ropes, p. 509<br>Beanbags, p. 506<br>Station work, pp. 253, 447 | Repeat 4 and 5. | Repeat 4 and change the challenge to involve balancing over equipment on one, two, or three parts. | Repeat 4 of lesson 4b. |
| **Part 3: Closure** (1 to 2 minutes)<br><br>Shapes | Discuss meaning of sequence. | | | | |

Level I    Unit 1: Gymnastics—Movement Patterns
Lesson 5. Shapes
**Main Theme** Twisted shapes
**Subthemes** Traveling; Safety skills
**Equipment** Variety of small equipment; Two types of large apparatus

**Additional Lessons** Each child has now acquired several safety skills and has a basic idea of the meaning and use of such movement skills as balance, shape, and transfer of weight. The scope and variety of each child's movement patterns should reflect these newly acquired movement skills.

| Content | Teaching Strategies | References | Lesson 5a | 5b | 5c |
|---|---|---|---|---|---|
| **Entry Activity** | Place a variety of small equipment in the four containers. | | Repeat previous. | Repeat previous. | Repeat previous. |
| **Part 1: Introductory Activities** (5 to 7 minutes)<br><br>Traveling<br>—in different directions<br>—at different speeds<br>Safety skills<br>—log, side, and diagonal roll | Equipment away and scatter small and large mats in the instructional area. Run, jump, land, touch floor with fingers, and roll. Challenge children to try to make a half turn in the air, land, and perform a backward diagonal roll. Continue pattern. | Diagonal roll, p. 452 | Repeat introductory activities. | Play Nine Lives (p. 30 of this guide). | Design your own lesson. |
| **Part 2: Skill Development** (10 to 20 minutes)<br><br>Shapes<br>—stretch and curl<br>—wide and narrow<br>—twisted<br>Shapes with small equipment and large apparatus | 1. Introduce twisted shapes. "Place your feet as far apart as possible. Can you keep your feet on the floor and twist your body to the side? Can you twist between your legs, twist just your head?" Continue pattern.<br>2. "Invent a sequence that has a curl, twist, and a wide shape."<br>*Station work:* Divide class into four groups.<br>Ask children to move to designated stations. Introduce large apparatus and methods of carrying heavy apparatus. Set up equipment, apparatus and arrange stations A, B, C, and D. Set two challenges, one for small equipment and one for large apparatus.<br>*Small Equipment:* "Make up a sequence with your equipment that has a balance, a roll, and a twist."<br>*Large Apparatus:* "Practice balancing on, and crossing over or under the apparatus." Allow a few minutes of practice at each station, then call "change" or "rotate." (A moves to B, B moves to C, etc.) Watch for general safety on apparatus; using top, side, and ends of large apparatus; no line-ups, i.e., approaching apparatus from various angles or moving to different positions rather than waiting behind someone for a "turn."<br>*Note:* Substitute equipment and apparatus according to what is available in your school. | Twisted shapes, p. 37<br><br>Carrying large apparatus, p. 536<br>Station work, pp. 506, 536<br>Hoops, p. 522<br>Individual ropes, p. 509 | Repeat 1 and 2.<br><br>Continue same format as lesson 5. | Leave out.<br><br>Continue same format as lesson 5 and add to or change the two challenges. | |
| **Part 3: Closure** (1 to 2 minutes)<br><br>Twisted shapes | Discuss moving safely and quickly to next station. | | | | |

139

**Level I   Unit 1:** Gymnastics—Movement Patterns
**Lesson 6.** Speed
**Main Theme** Quick and slow
**Subthemes** Rolling; Transfer of weight
**Equipment** Variety of small equipment; Large and small mats; Two types of apparatus

**Additional Lessons** More instructional time is now being given to apparatus activities and less time to introductory activities and stunts and movement skills. Supplementary lessons should adhere to this changing emphasis and change the type and arrangement of small equipment and large apparatus.

| Content | Teaching Strategies | References | Lesson 6a | 6b | 6c |
|---|---|---|---|---|---|
| **Entry Activity** | Place a variety of small equipment in the four containers. Free play with equipment. | | Repeat previous. | Repeat previous. | Repeat previous. |
| **Part 1: Introductory Activities**<br>*(5 to 8 minutes)*<br><br>Traveling<br>—in different directions<br>—in different ways<br>Safety skills<br>—log, side, diagonal, and forward roll<br>—run, jump, land, roll | Equipment away and scatter small and large mats in the instructional area.<br>1. "Run, jump, land, touch floor with fingertips, and roll." Challenge children to try to make a half turn in the air, land, and perform a backward diagonal roll. Continue pattern.<br>2. Explain and demonstrate forward roll.<br>3. Individual practice. | Forward roll, p. 451 | Repeat 1 and 2. | Play Nine Lives (p. 30 of this guide). | Repeat 1. |
| **Part 2: Skill Development**<br>*(10 to 20 minutes)*<br><br>Speed<br>—quick and slow<br>Transfer of weight | Present several challenges involving transferring weight from patches (any wide surface of body such as back, seat) to points (any narrow surface such as toes, knees, fingertips).<br>—from a patch quickly to three points to a new patch<br>—from seat and slowly to two points<br>—from a patch quickly to four points slowly to a new patch. Continue challenges. | Transfer of weight, pp. 37, 496 | Repeat lesson 6. | Leave out. | Repeat lesson 6. |
| Transfer of weight with small equipment and large apparatus<br>Quick and slow<br>—on or with small equipment or large apparatus | *Station work:*<br>Arrange equipment and apparatus as shown in lesson 5. Assign section places and new challenges as follows:<br>*Small Equipment:* "Can you make up a new sequence with your equipment that shows transferring from patches to points and quick and slow?"<br>*Large Apparatus:* "Can you move from a patch on the floor to balancing on points on the apparatus and back to a new patch on the floor? Practice your sequence and when you are ready, move as quickly as you can from patch to points to patches." Rotate groups and repeat challenges. | Large apparatus, p. 535 | Continue same format as lesson 6. | Continue same format as lesson 6. | Continue same format as lesson 6 and add to challenges. |

**Part 3: Closure**
*(1 to 2 minutes)*

Quick and slow          Discuss and illustrate different ways of moving quickly and slowly.

**Level I    Unit 1:** Gymnastics—Movement Patterns
**Lesson 7.** Force
**Main Theme** Strong and light
**Subtheme** Traveling
**Equipment** Variety of small equipment; Large and small mats; Two types of large apparatus

**Additional Lessons** If a variety of large indoor or outdoor apparatus is available, develop challenges to complement new apparatus; however, stress forceful movements such as jumping or leaping on or off apparatus and contrasting light movements while on the floor or on apparatus.

| Content | Teaching Strategies | References | Lesson 7a | 7b | 7c |
|---|---|---|---|---|---|
| **Entry Activity** | Place small equipment in the four containers. Free play with small equipment. | | Repeat previous. | Repeat previous. | Repeat previous. |
| **Part 1: Introductory Activities** *(5 minutes)* | Run, jump over equipment, land, change directions, and continue pattern. | Shadow game (p. 35 of this guide). | Repeat introductory activities. | Play shadow game (p. 35 of this guide). | Design your own lesson. |
| Traveling —in different directions | | | | | |
| **Part 2: Skill Development** *(10 to 20 minutes)* | Ask the children to find a piece of small equipment. Pose the following challenges: | Transfer of weight, pp. 37, 496 | Repeat 1 and 2. | Leave out. | |
| Force and transfer of weight —using feet —using hands | 1. "Show me how many different ways you can cross over your equipment." Watch for those using their hands and use for demonstration. 2. "Can you cross over sideways, backward, making a twisted shape in the air?" Add other challenges. 3. "Now, using all the space and all the equipment, run and jump over a piece of equipment, cross over the next piece with your hands, and the next with your feet." Continue pattern around equipment. | | | | |
| Force and transfer of weight on small and large apparatus | *Station work:* Arrange equipment and apparatus as shown in lesson 5. Assign section places and new challenges as follows: *Small Equipment:* "Can you make a sequence of crossing over your equipment just using your hands?" *Large Apparatus:* "See if you can find two or three ways of jumping on to your apparatus and jumping off and landing gently on your feet." Rotate groups and repeat challenges. | Transfer of weight with small equipment, pp. 496, 506 | Continue same format as lesson 7. | Continue same format as lesson 7 and add to or modify challenges. | |

| Content | Teaching Strategies |
|---|---|
| **Part 3: Closure** *(1 to 2 minutes)* | |
| Strong and light | Discuss and illustrate meaning of force: the effect one body has on another; the effort or tension involved in a movement. |

141

**Level I    Unit 1:** Gymnastics—Movement Patterns
**Lesson 8.** Levels
**Main Theme** High, medium, and low
**Subtheme:** Transfer of weight
**Equipment** Class set of individual ropes; Eight hoops and eight wands; Large apparatus as listed or available

**Additional Lessons** Additional lessons should stress levels and one or more movement skills performed within the second or third part of the lesson.

| Content | Teaching Strategies | References | Lesson 8a | 8b | 8c |
|---|---|---|---|---|---|
| **Entry Activity** | Place a variety of small equipment in the four containers. Free play with equipment. | | Repeat previous. | Repeat previous. | Repeat previous. |
| **Part 1: Introductory Activities** (*4 to 5 minutes*)<br><br>Traveling<br>—in different directions<br>Levels<br>—high and low | 1. "Run and make yourself as tall as you can . . . keep running, but move as low as you can . . . alternate high and low."<br>2. "Run again, but when I call 'freeze,' (or 'stop'), make your shoulder the highest part of you." Repeat and change parts such as elbow, nose, etc.<br>3. "Next, run, but this time when I call 'stop,' you choose your own part that will end up being the highest." | Levels, space, awareness, pp. 39, 496, 500 | Repeat 1 and 2. | Play Tails (p. 31 of this guide). | Design your own lesson. |
| **Part 2: Skill Development** (*10 to 20 minutes*)<br><br>Traveling<br>Transfer of weight<br>Change of level and transfer of weight on large apparatus<br>Shape with small equipment | Ask children to select their own rope and find a space.<br>1. "Place the rope on floor and see if you can tie a knot with your feet."<br>2. "Make a straight line with your rope. Now show me how many different ways you can travel up and down your rope."<br>3. Develop other challenges involving transfer of weight or shapes.<br>*Station work:*<br>Arrange apparatus and equipment as indicated below. Assign groups of children and challenges to stations as indicated.<br>Section A: *Agility Apparatus.* "Move from low to very high and travel on different parts of your body."<br>Section B: *Hoops.* "Can you make up a sequence of shapes with your hoop with each shape at a different level?"<br>Section C: *Boxes and Benches.* "Can you travel in different ways on the boxes or benches?"<br>Section D: *Wands.* "Make up a sequence of shapes with your wand always the highest part." | Individual ropes, p. 508<br><br><br><br>Agility apparatus, p. 446<br>Wands, p. 524 | Leave out.<br><br><br><br>Continue same format as lesson 8. | Leave out.<br><br><br><br>Continue same format as lesson 8 and add to or change challenges. | |

| Station A<br>Agility Apparatus<br>(or substitute apparatus) | Station B<br>Hoops |
|---|---|
| Station D<br>Wands | |
| | Station C<br>Box and Benches |

**Part 3: Closure**
(*1 to 2 minutes*)

Levels    Discuss and illustrate various examples of levels on the floor or on equipment.

142

**Level I     Unit 1:** Gymnastics—Movement Patterns
**Lesson 9.** Flow
**Main Theme** Flow
**Subtheme** Traveling
**Equipment** Variety of small equipment; Bench, agility apparatus, or other available apparatus

**Additional Lessons** Additional lessons should stress flow and two or more movement skills.

| Content | Teaching Strategies | References | Lesson 9a | 9b | 9c |
|---|---|---|---|---|---|
| **Entry Activity** | Place a variety of small equipment in the four containers. Free play with equipment. | | Repeat previous. | Repeat previous. | Repeat previous. |
| **Part 1: Introductory Activities** *(4 to 5 minutes)* <br><br> Traveling <br>—in different directions <br>—in different pathways <br>Rolling | Equipment away and find a space "Run, skip, slide, or gallop in a circle pattern—zigzag or any pattern you like." | | Repeat 1. | Play Nine Lives (p. 30 of this guide). | Design your own lesson. |
| **Part 2: Skill Development** *(10 to 20 minutes)* <br><br> Balance and transfer of weight <br><br><br> Flow with small equipment and large apparatus | 1. "Can you roll and find a balance position, roll to a new balance position?" Continue pattern. <br> 2. "Select a piece of equipment and make up your own sequence of three shapes on your equipment." <br> 3. "Develop a series of challenges involving balance, transfer of weight, shape, speed, or levels." Allow adequate time for practice of sequence. <br> *Station work:* <br> Arrange apparatus and equipment as indicated below. Assign a group of children to each station and allow each group to arrange the apparatus or equipment any way they want. Once the apparatus is arranged, ask them to develop their own sequence. <br> Section A: Hoops and traffic cones <br> Section B: Benches and mats <br> Section C: Agility apparatus <br> Section D: Chairs and mats <br> Allow a few minutes for students to develop their sequence. Select one or two for demonstration, then rotate groups. As groups approach the new apparatus or equipment, allow them to rearrange apparatus or equipment as they desire. | Flow, pp. 41, 498 <br> Shapes, pp. 37, 497 <br><br><br><br><br><br> Sequences, p. 446 | Repeat 3. <br><br><br><br><br><br><br><br><br><br> Continue same format as lesson 9. | Leave out. <br><br><br><br><br><br><br><br><br><br> Continue same format as lesson 9a and add to challenges. | |
| **Part 3: Closure** *(1 to 2 minutes)* <br><br> Flow | Discuss meaning of flow: how a movement or series of movements is linked (bound and free). | | | | |

# Gymnastic Activities
## Developmental Level I
## Unit 2: Gymnastics—
## Transfer of Weight

### Expected Learning Outcomes

**Psychomotor Skills**

1. Traveling and stopping
2. Balancing on different parts of the body
3. Rolling skills—log, side, forward, and diagonal roll
4. Transfer of weight
5. Change of direction
6. Change of speed
7. Flow: ability to perform three or more movement skills with ease and efficiency

**Cognitive and Affective Knowledge and Skills**

1. Understanding movement terminology
2. Understanding the meaning of sequence
3. Expanded understanding of the meaning of transfer of weight
4. Understanding and ability to develop partner sequences stressing transfer of weight
5. Appreciation of others' strengths and weaknesses
6. Ability to share ideas, equipment, and space

**Level** I  **Unit 2:** Gymnastics—Transfer of Weight
**Lesson 1.** Rolling and Balancing
**Main Theme** Transfer of weight
**Subtheme** Balance
**Equipment** Class set of beanbags and chairs

**Additional Lessons** Additional lessons should continue to stress the main theme of transfer of weight. Each lesson below adds one new subtheme throughout each part of the lesson.

| Content | Teaching Strategies | References | Lesson 1a | 1b | 1c |
|---|---|---|---|---|---|
| **Entry Activity** | Place a variety of small equipment in containers. Free play with equipment. | | Repeat previous. | Repeat previous. | Repeat previous. |
| **Part 1: Introductory Activities** (*4 to 6 minutes*) | 1. Traveling and stopping—run, skip, slide, hop. 2. Run and stop on different parts of body, on one foot, seat; continue pattern. | | Repeat 1 adding change of speed. | Repeat 2 adding a change of direction. | Repeat 2 adding a change of level while running. |
| Traveling and stopping Balancing | | | | | |
| **Part 2: Skill Development** (*10 to 20 minutes*) | 1. "Balance on seat, roll sideways using log or side roll, and balance on seat again." 2. "Backward diagonal roll to a balance on parts, to a side roll." | Transfer of weight, pp. 37, 496 | Repeat 1 and 2 adding a change of speed. | Repeat 3 adding a change of direction. | Repeat 3 adding a change of level with each new balance position. |
| Transfer of weight | 3. "Balance on parts of body (two hands and one foot), roll to balancing on new parts (knees and elbows)." 4. Design other challenges involving the main theme of transfer of weight. | | | | |
| | 5. "Place beanbag on head (or another part) and balance on different parts—on one foot, on seat and one hand, etc." 6. "Keep beanbag on head, shift from balancing on one part (seat), to another part (stomach)." 7. Beanbag on floor. Pose challenges involving one or more parts on beanbag with one or more parts on floor. | Beanbag activities, p. 506 | Repeat 5 and 6 adding a change of speed. | Repeat 7 adding a change of direction. | Repeat 7 adding a change of level. |
| Balance and transfer of weight with small equipment | 8. Design other challenges involving balance and transfer of weight. Other small equipment could be used as well (wands, hoops, etc.) | | | | |
| **Part 3: Closure** (*1 to 2 minutes*) | | | | | |
| Transfer of weight | Ask for suggestions to build a sequence of movements involving different ways of transferring weight (e.g., from seat to stomach, from a patch to a patch). | | | | |

**Level I** **Unit 2:** Gymnastics—Transfer of Weight
**Lesson 2.** Patches to Points
**Main Theme** Transfer of weight
**Subthemes** Balancing; Change of direction
**Equipment** Class set of individual ropes; Available large apparatus

**Additional Lessons** Lesson 2 continues the main theme of transfer of weight. The three accompanying supplementary lessons continue this emphasis and add one subtheme throughout each lesson.

| Content | Teaching Strategies | References | Lesson 2a | 2b | 2c |
|---|---|---|---|---|---|
| **Entry Activities** | Place a class set of individual ropes in the containers. Free play with ropes. | | Repeat with beanbags. | Repeat with hoops. | Repeat with balls. |
| **Part 1: Introductory Activities** *(4 to 6 minutes)*<br><br>Traveling on parts of body<br>Change of direction | 1. "Run and stop on different parts of the body."<br>2. "Traveling on different parts of body—moving on seat and hands, on stomach," etc.<br>3. "Move forward, sideways, or backward without using feet." | | Repeat 1 and 3. | Repeat 3 adding stretch and curl shapes to challenge. | Repeat 3 adding your own subtheme. |
| **Part 2: Skill Development** *(10 to 20 minutes)*<br><br>Transfer of weight | 1. *Patch to patch:* "Balance on a patch (large surface like seat), roll to balancing on a new patch." Add a change of direction between each patch.<br>2. *Patch to point:* "Balance on a patch, roll to taking weight on points (a small surface)."<br>3. *Patch to point to patch:* "Balance on a patch, shift to balancing on points, then shift to balancing on a new patch." Design other challenges. | | Repeat 2 and 3 adding a change of direction. | Repeat 3 adding stretch and curl shapes to challenge. | Repeat 3 adding your own subtheme. |
| | *Station work:* Divide the class into four groups.<br>The following task can be applied to any of the suggested apparatus at each station.<br>1. "Travel across or along the apparatus on one patch and two points."<br>2. "Travel across or over your apparatus moving from a patch to pois to a patch."<br> | Large apparatus, p. 535 | Repeat 1 adding a change of direction. | Repeat 1 adding stretch and curl shapes to challenge. | Repeat 1 adding your own subtheme. |
| Transfer of weight on and over large apparatus | 3. "Travel over apparatus on points and patches and change direction or level or speed (teacher's choice)." Rotate groups and repeat challenges. | | | | |

| Station A | Station B |
|---|---|
| Agility Apparatus (or substitute apparatus) | Hoops |
| Station D | |
| Wands | |
| | Station C |
| | Box and Benches |

**Part 3: Closure**
*(1 to 2 minutes)*

Transfer of weight

Ask for suggestions to build a sequence of patches and points across a balance bench (or any other large apparatus).

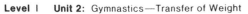

**Level** I   **Unit 2:** Gymnastics—Transfer of Weight
**Lesson 3.** Points to Points
**Main Theme** Transfer of weight
**Subtheme** Balancing
**Equipment** Class set of hoops; Available large apparatus

**Additional Lessons** Additional lessons shown below continue the main theme and stress one subtheme in each succeeding lesson.

| Content | Teaching Strategies | References | Lesson 3a | 3b | 3c |
|---|---|---|---|---|---|
| **Entry Activity** | Place enough hoops for the entire class in the four corners of the gymnasium. Free play with hoops. | | | | |
| **Part 1: Introductory Activities**<br><br>Traveling on parts of the body<br>Change of direction | 1. "Run and stop on different parts of the body."<br>2. "Traveling on different parts and in different directions."<br>3. Play Nine Lives. | Nine Lives (p. 30 of this guide). | Repeat 2 and 3. | Play Tails (p. 31 of this guide). | Design your own lesson. |
| **Part 2: Skill Development**<br>(*10 to 20 minutes*)<br><br>Transfer of weight | 1. *Point to Point:* "Balance on points, change to new points." Continue pattern.<br>2. "Make a bridge any way you like."<br>3. "Make a new bridge, different from the one you just made."<br>4. "Get a hoop and find a new space. See if you can make a sequence balancing on points inside your hoop. Change to a new balance on points outside your hoop." Continue pattern. | Hoop activities, p. 522 | Repeat 3 adding a change in level. | Leave out. | |
| Transfer of weight on or over apparatus | *Station work:*<br>The following tasks can be applied to any of the suggested apparatus.<br>1. "Find different ways of getting on and off apparatus."<br>2. "Travel over or along apparatus on points."<br>3. "Make up a sequence that has a transfer of weight from point to point and change of direction or level."<br>4. Develop other challenges that permit each child to use all apparatus. | Large apparatus, p. 535 | Repeat 2 adding a change of level. | Repeat 3. | |

| Station A<br>Agility Apparatus<br>(or substitute apparatus) | Station B<br>Hoops |
|---|---|
| Station D<br>Wands | |
| | Station C<br>Box and Benches |

| **Part 3: Closure**<br>(*1 to 2 minutes*) | Have one or two children explain (not illustrate) their sequences. | | | | |

147

# Gymnastic Activities
## Development Level II
## Unit 1: Gymnastics—
## Level 1

**Expected Learning Outcomes**

**Psychomotor Skills**

1. Running, jumping, landing, and rolling
2. Changing direction, pathway, and level
3. Balancing on different parts of the body
4. Performing stretch, curl, wide, narrow, and twisted shapes
5. Performing movement sequences involving two or more elements
6. Ability to perform two or more movement skills
7. Ability to safely move on, over, or through gymnastic apparatus
8. Ability to perform matching and contrasting sequences with a partner
9. Ability to perform structured gymnastic skills

**Cognitive and Affective Knowledge and Skills**

1. Understanding of Laban's movement vocabulary
2. Understanding of and ability to design movement sequences involving self, a partner, and/or small and large equipment
3. Appreciation of individual differences existing within the class
4. Ability to work cooperatively with a partner and within small and large groups

Evaluative Techniques: See chapter 9 for observational methods and evaluative tools to assess structure and movement education skills and concepts.

**Level II** **Unit 1:** Gymnastics—Level 1
**Lesson 1.** Balance
**Main Theme** Balancing
**Subthemes** Traveling and stopping
**Equipment** Mats and individual ropes

**Additional Lessons** This lesson assumes that the class has completed the first games unit for this age level, and so they are used to more exploratory methods of teaching. The following lesson outline illustrates how this lesson may be expanded to two or more lessons.

| Content | Teaching Strategies | References | Lesson 1a | 1b | 1c |
|---|---|---|---|---|---|
| **Entry Activity** | Place a variety of small equipment in four containers. Free practice with equipment. | | Repeat previous. | Repeat previous. | Repeat previous. |
| **Part 1: Introductory Activities** *(5 to 10 minutes)* | Ask children to put equipment away and find a space. If children do not move quickly or bunch up, repeat procedure until performance is adequate. When ready, pose the following tasks. | Teaching strategies, p. 124 | Repeat 1 to 3. | Repeat 3 changing number of parts as children stop and balance. | Play Nine Lives (p. 30 of this guide). |
| Traveling—in different directions | 1. "Let me see you travel (run, walk, skip, slide) in any direction and without touching any other player . . . away you go." | | | | |
| Safety skills—controlled stopping on parts of body | 2. "Next, just run, and when I call stop, slow right down and touch the floor with your fingertips." | | | | |
| | 3. After children have stopped, explain that the next time you call "stop" they must come to a slow stop and end up balancing on three parts of their body. | | | | |
| **Part 2: Skill Development** *(20 to 35 minutes)* | Children are still in scattered formation. | Balance or weight bearing, p. 496 | Repeat 1 and continue challenge on "knees and | Leave out. | Repeat 1 and 2 and change parts of body for |
| Balancing on different parts of body | 1. "Can you balance on one leg and two hands?"<br>2. "Try balancing on knees and fingertips."<br>3. "Can you invent your own balance stunt?" Select one or two to demonstrate.<br>4. "Can you perform the following balance stunts?" (Have a child demonstrate a frog stand, knee dip, V-sit, and thread the needle.) | Balance stunts, p. 478 | elbows, seat and toes," etc.<br><br>Review 4. | | each challenge. |
| | Ask children to get an individual rope and find a space. | Rope activities, p. 509 | Repeat 5 adding other challenges such as "two parts on floor, two parts on the rope." | Repeat 5 and 6 and change rope to a traffic cone or hoop. | Repeat 5 and 6 with new equipment. |
| Balance stunts with individual ropes | 5. "Can you balance on one part on the rope and on three parts on the floor?" Select one or two for demonstration.<br>6. "Change the position of your rope and design your own balance position with parts on the rope and parts on the floor."<br>7. "Tie the rope ends together and hold the rope with one hand and under one foot. Now, can you find three balance positions while holding the rope between these two parts of your body?" | | | | |
| **Part 3: Closure** *(1 to 2 minutes)* | | Chapter 5, p. 75 | | | |
| Balance | Discuss how many different parts of the body one can balance on. Also, what makes a good balance position: wide base of support; low to the ground; line of gravity running through middle of base of support. | | | | |

Level II   Unit 1: Gymnastics—Level 1
Lesson 2.   Transfer of Weight
Main Theme   Transfer of weight
Subthemes   Safety skills
Equipment   Large and small mats; Class set of individual ropes

**Additional Lessons** One of the main reasons for expanding this lesson is to ensure that the level of safety skills is sufficient to move on to more advanced movement challenges.

| Content | Teaching Strategies | References | Lesson 2a | 2b | 2c |
|---|---|---|---|---|---|
| **Entry Activity** | Place individual ropes in the four containers. Free practice with equipment. | | Repeat previous. | Repeat previous. | Repeat previous. |
| **Part 1: Introductory Activities** (5 to 8 minutes)<br><br>Traveling<br>—in different directions<br>—on different parts<br>Safety skills<br>—log and side rolls | Individual ropes away, then place large and small mats in a scattered pattern around instructional area. Present the following challenges:<br>1. "Run, jump over mats, land, and continue pattern."<br>2. "Demonstrate and practice log and side roll." | Log roll, p. 469<br>Side roll, p. 449<br>Forward roll, p. 450 | Repeat 1 to 3 and demonstrate and practice forward roll. | Repeat 1 to 3. | Repeat 1 to 3. |
| **Part 2: Skill Development** (20 to 35 minutes)<br><br>Balance on different parts of body<br>Transfer of weight | Leave mats on floor and find a space on the bare floor. Keep off mats!<br>1. "See if you can balance on one leg, lower your body, side roll, and finish balancing on the same leg."<br>2. "Balance (or take the weight) on your seat, shift to balancing on knees and hands."<br>3. "Make up your own routine in which you take the weight on one or more parts of your body, then roll or shift to take the weight on another part of your body."<br>4. "Can you make up a routine that includes a one-leg balance, a roll, and a frog stand?" | Transfer of weight, pp. 37, 496 | Repeat 3. | Leave out. | Repeat 1 and 2. |
| Transfer of weight with individual ropes | Ask children to select an individual rope and find a space.<br>5. "Show me how many different ways you can skip with your rope." (Watch for level of abilities.)<br>6. Demonstrate and practice two-foot basic skills.<br>7. "Make up a routine that involves jumping over the rope while it is on the floor and skipping with it." | Two-foot basic skills, p. 511<br>Alternate step, p. 512 | Repeat 5 and 6. | Repeat 5 and 6 and introduce alternate step. | Repeat 5 and 6. |
| **Part 3: Closure** (1 to 2 minutes) | Discuss importance of transferring weight by rolling on wide or flat surfaces of body rather than on pointed parts such as elbows, head, or knees. | | | | |

**Level** III **Unit 5:** Basketball
**Lesson 4.** Dribble and Pass
**Main Theme** Dribbling and passing
**Subthemes** Traveling; Pathways; Change of speed

**Additional Lessons** If additional lessons are required, stress passing and dribbling.

| Content | Teaching Strategies | References | Lesson 4a | 4b | 4c |
|---|---|---|---|---|---|
| Entry Activity | Practice dribbling and passing the ball. | | | | |
| Part 1: Introductory Activities | 1. Run and change direction and speed.<br>2. Run, jump, and land, change direction and speed.<br>3. Travel on different parts of the body—two hands, one foot, crab walk, etc.<br>4. Tag game. | Tag games, pp. 273, 286 | Shadow game (p. 35 of this guide). | | Design your own lessons. |
| Part 2: Skill Development<br>(20 to 35 minutes)<br><br>Bounce pass<br>Dribbling<br>Catching | 1. Review passing and catching.<br>2. Demonstrate bounce pass and dribbling.<br>3. Practice activities: Individual—dribbling activities; partner—Follow the Leader, Dribble and Pass. | Passing, p. 383<br>Dribbling, p. 385<br>Practice activities, p. 390<br>Inventive games, pp. 215, 254, 294 | Repeat 1 and 3.<br><br><br><br><br><br>Lead-up games. | Repeat 3.<br><br><br><br><br><br>Lead-up games. | |
| | 4. Inventive games with three players. Example: "In groups of three, make up a game with one ball, one hoop, a dribble, and a pass."<br>5. Lead-up games:<br>*Five Passes*<br>*Captain Basketball*—This game utilizes the skills of passing, catching, guarding, and dribbling. The object of this game is for the guards to get the ball to any of their forward players. Forward players are confined to a designated circle/hoop. Forwards receiving the ball try to get it to their "captain." | Lead-up games, p. 390<br>Five Passes, p. 397<br>Captain Basketball, p. 398 | | | |

| Part 3: Closure<br>(1 to 2 minutes)<br><br>Dribbling | Reinforce the importance of "pushing" rather than slapping the ball toward the ground when dribbling. | | | | |

**Level** III    **Unit 5:** Basketball
**Lesson 5.** Pass and Shoot.
**Main Theme** Passing and shooting
**Subthemes** Traveling; Change of direction

**Additional Lessons** If one or more lessons are required, stress shooting skills.

| Content | Teaching Strategies | References | Lesson 5a | 5b | 5c |
|---|---|---|---|---|---|
| **Entry Activity** | Practice shooting or dribbling. | | | | |
| **Part 1: Introductory Activities**<br>*(4 to 5 minutes)*<br><br>Running<br>Conditioning | 1. Running and sliding with a change of speed and direction.<br>2. Individual dribbling by command—forward, side, kneeling, etc.<br>3. By teacher's signal (pointing). | Practice activities, p. 390 | Repeat 1 and 2. | Tag games, p. 260 | Design your own lesson. |
| **Part 2: Skill Development**<br>*(20 to 35 minutes)*<br><br>Set shot | 1. Demonstrate one-hand set shot.<br>2. Practice shooting: Individual—toward wall, into containers placed on chairs; partners—repeat taking turns with one shooting, one returning shots. | Shooting, p. 385<br>Practice activities, p. 390 | Repeat 2. | Leave out. | |
| | 3. Inventive games with three or four players (two vs. one or two vs. two).<br>4. Lead-up games:<br>*Bucket Ball*—This game develops passing, catching, dribbling, shooting, and guarding skills. General rules of basketball are followed; however, baskets on the floor or hoops suspended from the ceiling are used as goals.<br>*Twenty-One*—Shooting and catching skills are developed in this game. A combination of free throws and field shots are used to score twenty-one points. Player 1 shoots from the free throw line. One point is awarded for each successful basket. Other players stand wherever they wish in the playing area. Player 1 shoots until missing, when any player who can get possession may try for a field goal. A field goal scores two points. If the field goal fails, any player who can gain possession tries for a field goal. Once a field goal is made, Player 2 takes a turn at the free throw line.<br>*Basketball*—This is one of the most popular team sports for upper elementary students. The regulation game of basketball should be played several times during a unit of instruction. | Lead-up games, p. 390<br>Bucket Ball, p. 396<br>Twenty-One p. 398<br><br><br><br><br><br><br>Basketball, p. 399 | Lead-up games. | Lead-up games. | |

Positions:

**Part 3: Closure**

Set Shot
Free Throw

Discuss the importance of releasing the ball off fingertips and the follow-through action in the direction of the basket.

**Level** II **Unit 1:** Gymnastics—Level 1
**Lesson 3.** Shapes
**Main Theme** Stretch and curl
**Subthemes** Traveling; Safety skills
**Equipment** Large and small mats; Hoops, wands, individual ropes

**Additional Lessons** It is suggested that one or two additional lessons be given before progressing to lesson 4.

| Content | Teaching Strategies | References | Lesson 3a | 3b | 3c |
|---|---|---|---|---|---|
| **Entry Activity** | Place a variety of small equipment in the four containers. Free practice with equipment. | | Repeat previous. | Repeat previous. | Repeat previous. |
| **Part 1: Introductory Activities**<br>*(5 to 8 minutes)*<br><br>Traveling—in different directions<br>Safety skills<br>Shapes—stretch | Put small equipment away, then place small and large mats in a scattered pattern around the instructional area. Pose the following challenges:<br>1. "Run, jump, land, and roll."<br>2. "Run, leap, and stretch high, land, and roll."<br>3. "Run, jump, curl (or tuck), land, and roll."<br>4. "Travel on all fours forward, backward, sideways, continue pattern." Return mats and find a new space. | Diagonal roll, p. 452 | Repeat 1 and 2, then introduce diagonal roll. | Repeat 1 to 3 with diagonal roll. | Play Nine Lives. (p. 30 of this guide) |
| **Part 2: Skill Development**<br>*(20 to 35 minutes)*<br><br>Shapes—stretch, curl<br>Level—high, medium, low | Review or introduce stretch and curl shapes. Pose the following challenges:<br>1. "Place feet about shoulder-width apart, then stretch arms up as high as you can, stretch to the side, between your legs." Continue pattern.<br>2. "On your back, stretch out as far as you can . . . fingers and toes."<br>3. "From a stretch on your back, curl up to a tight ball. Stretch back out."<br>4. "Can you curl up on your side (or any other flat part of body) then stretch out on your stomach? Continue changing position from both stretch and curl."<br>5. With a partner, "Stand side by side and develop a matching sequence of stretch and curl shapes." | Stretch and curl shapes, pp. 37, 497<br>Levels, p. 39<br>Matching sequences, p. 446 | Repeat 4. | Leave out. | Leave out. |
| Small equipment—balance, roll, stretch, and curl shapes<br>Large mats—jump and curl shapes then rolling | *Station work:*<br>Ask children to return to section places. Explain station work, then assign children to stations. Have task cards available at each station.<br>*Station A:* Children set up equipment as shown on task card. "Make up a matching sequence that has a balance, a roll, and a stretch over the wand, then a jump over the hoop."<br><br>Mat → Wand → Hoop →<br><br>*Station B:* Children set up equipment as shown on task card. "Design a follow the leader routine that has a jump over a cone, a stretch over a rope, and a curl on a mat."<br><br>Cone → Rope → Chair<br><br>*Station C:* Children set up equipment as they wish. "Make up a sequence that shows stretch and curl shapes and a change in direction." (Use three available pieces of equipment.)<br>*Station D:* Children set up mats as they wish. "Design a matching sequence of stretch and curl shapes and two different rolls." (Use two or three mats.) Rotate groups and repeat challenges. | Station work, pp. 253, 447<br>Task cards, p. 112<br>Small equipment, p. 506 | Rotate groups and repeat. | Rotate groups and repeat. | Rotate groups and repeat. |
| **Part 3: Closure**<br>*(1 to 2 minutes)*<br><br>Shapes | Discuss using words "routine" and "sequence" to mean the same thing. | | | | |

**Level II   Unit 1:** Gymnastics—Level 1
**Lesson 4.** Shapes
**Main Theme** Wide, narrow, and twisted shapes
**Subtheme** Traveling
**Equipment** Mats and a variety of small equipment

**Additional Lessons** One or two additional lessons may be required to develop an understanding of various types of shapes.

| Content | Teaching Strategies | References | Lesson 4a | 4b | 4c |
|---|---|---|---|---|---|
| **Entry Activity** | Place a variety of small equipment in the four containers. Free practice with equipment. | | Repeat previous. | Repeat previous. | Repeat previous. |
| **Part 1: Introductory Activities**<br>*(5 to 6 minutes)*<br><br>Traveling—in different directions, on different levels<br>Shapes—stretch, curl, wide, narrow, and twisted | Pose the following challenges:<br>1. "Travel in three different ways with three changes in direction." Continue pattern.<br>2. "Run, jump, or leap; make stretch or curl shapes; land and continue pattern."<br>3. "Repeat making a wide, narrow, or twisted shape; land and continue pattern." | | Repeat 2 adding rolling. | Repeat 3. | Design your own lesson. |
| **Part 2: Skill Development**<br>*(20 to 35 minutes)*<br><br>Shapes—stretch and curl, wide and narrow, twisted<br><br><br><br><br><br><br><br><br><br><br><br>Small equipment—shapes, balance, change of level, change of direction | *Individual activities:*<br>1. Review stretch and curl shapes. "Make a stretched shape, curl up on your back, then find another stretched shape."<br>2. Introduce wide and narrow shapes. "Stand up and make your arms and legs as wide apart as possible. Now make your body as thin as you can."<br>3. "Can you find a new position and make one part of your body wide and the other part thin?"<br>4. "Shift to balancing on your back and make a wide shape."<br>5. Introduce twisted shapes. "Keep your feet on the floor then twist your body to the side, under your legs, as high as you can."<br>6. "Can you make up a routine that includes a single-leg balance, a roll, and two shapes?"<br>*Partner activities:*<br>1. "See if you can make up a matching sequence of shapes using two individual ropes."<br>2. "Invent your own matching sequence of balance stunts and shapes and show a change of level and direction. You may use two pieces of small equipment if you like." | Wide, narrow, twisted shapes, pp. 37, 497<br>Single-leg balance, p. 487<br><br><br><br><br><br><br><br>Matching challenges, p. 517<br>Stunts, p. 445 | Repeat 2 and 3.<br><br><br><br><br><br><br><br><br><br>Design new matching challenges. | Repeat 4 and 5.<br><br><br><br><br><br><br><br><br><br>Design new matching challenges. | |
| **Part 3: Closure**<br>*(1 to 2 minutes)* | Discuss what kinds of shapes are represented in stunts such as single-leg balance, frog stand, or side roll. | | | | |

**Level** II   **Unit 1:** Gymnastics—Level 1
**Lesson 5.** Speed
**Main theme** Quick and slow
**Subtheme** Transfer of weight
**Equipment** Large mats, individual ropes, traffic cones, balance bench and beam

**Additional Lessons** Additional lessons may be required to complete the rotating in lesson 5. Substitute equipment where necessary.

| Content | Teaching Strategies | References | Lesson 5a | 5b | 5c |
|---|---|---|---|---|---|
| **Entry Activity** | Place individual ropes in the four containers. Free practice with equipment. | | Repeat previous. | Repeat previous. | Repeat previous. |
| **Part 1: Introductory Activities** *(5 to 6 minutes)*<br><br>Traveling—in different directions | Ask class to put individual ropes away, then find a space. Present the following activities:<br>1. Play Nine Lives.<br>2. Play a tag game. | Tag games, p. 261 | Play a tag game. | Play Nine Lives. (p. 30 of this guide) | Design your own lesson. |
| **Part 2: Skill Development** *(20 to 35 minutes)*<br><br>Balance—on different parts<br>Transfer of weight<br>Speed—quick and slow | 1. Review taking weight on different parts. "Can you show me a sequence where you balance on your hands, seat, and back?" Repeat sequence and add one roll.<br>2. "Invent a routine that shifts your balance from three to two to four parts of your body."<br>3. "Repeat above sequence, moving slowly from three to two points, quickly from two to four, then slowly back to your three-point balance."<br>4. "Can you make up a series of rolls and show a change of speed and direction between each roll?"<br>*Note:* As soon as students understand the meaning of shapes, weight bearing, and transfer of weight, begin to combine two or more elements such as, "Take the weight on three parts and make a twisted shape, then shift to balancing on two parts with the body curled." This extends a child's movement vocabulary, rather than limiting a sequence to combining individual elements such as from shape to balance to shape. Also, draw from the agility and balance stunts and incorporate these into movement challenges. | Quick and slow, pp. 40, 498<br>Agility stunts, p. 460<br>Balance stunts, p. 478 | Repeat 1 and 2. | Repeat 4. | |
| Change of speed on or over apparatus | *Station work:*<br>Assign class to the following stations. Have task cards available at each station. Students moving from station B have a choice of shifting to station C1 or C2.<br>*Station A:* "Make up a routine that includes a change of direction, level, and speed" (large mats).<br>*Station B:* "Design a sequence that includes moving quickly on the floor and slowly on the beams or benches."<br>*Stations C and D:* "Plan a sequence that includes a jump, leap, shape, and quick and slow" (four individual ropes and four traffic cones). Students may arrange their own equipment. Rotate groups and repeat challenges. | Station work, pp. 253, 447<br>Large apparatus, p. 535 | Rotate groups and repeat challenge. | Rotate groups and repeat challenge. | |

| | | | | | |
|---|---|---|---|---|---|
| **Part 3: Closure** *(1 to 2 minutes)* | Discuss and illustrate moving individual parts of the body in a quick or slow motion. | | | | |

**Level** II    **Unit 1:** Gymnastics—Level 1
**Lesson 6.** Flight
**Main Theme** Flight
**Equipment** Balance bench or beam, chairs, traffic cones, vaulting box

**Additional Lessons** If additional lessons are planned, the following suggestions will help provide variety and maintain interest. (a) Change the challenge at each station. (b) Allow children to design their own challenges at each station as well as rearrange apparatus to complement their own routines.

| Content | Teaching Strategies | References | Lesson 6a | 6b | 6c |
|---|---|---|---|---|---|
| **Entry Activity** | Place a variety of small equipment in four containers. Free practice with equipment. | | Repeat previous. | Repeat previous. | Repeat previous. |
| **Part 1: Introductory Activities**<br>*(5 to 6 minutes)*<br><br>Traveling and landing<br>Change of direction | Leave small equipment scattered around instructional area. Present the following tasks:<br>  1. "Play a tag game, but do not cross over any equipment—always travel around or dodge equipment."<br>  2. "Run, leap, or jump over equipment."<br>  3. "Run, leap, or jump with *hands* stretching up as high as possible, land and continue pattern."<br>  4. "Find a piece of equipment. See how many ways you can find to cross your apparatus." | Force, p. 41 | Repeat 1 to 3. | Repeat 3 and 4. | Design your own lesson. |
| **Part 2: Skill Development**<br>*(20 to 35 minutes)*<br><br>Agility stunts—heel slap, rabbit jump, knee jump, flight | *Individual activities:*<br>Equipment away and find a space. When children are in their own spaces, present the following challenges:<br>  1. Review or introduce heel slap, rabbit jump, and knee jump.<br>  2. "Make up a sequence with the heel slap, rabbit jump, and a roll."<br>*Partner activities:*<br>  3. Explain, demonstrate, and practice leap frog.<br>  4. One partner crouches on floor. Standing partner runs and jumps over crouched partner. Rotate positions after each of the following tasks: Increase height of crouched partner; make shape over partner; make one-half turn in air over partner; use hands on crouched partner to vault over, gradually increasing height of legs. | Heel click, p. 473<br>Rabbit jump, p. 466<br>Knee jump, p. 464<br>Leap frog, p. 464 | Repeat 1 and 2. | Repeat 3 and 4. | |
| Balance, shapes and flight over apparatus | *Station work:*<br>Assign class to the following stations. Have task cards available at each station.<br>*Station A:* "In partners, make up a sequence that shows flight over bean bags or hoops."<br>*Station B:* "In partners, with one on the floor and one on the bench, make up a matching sequence of shapes."<br>*Station C:* "In partners and with two traffic cones, invent a sequence that includes flight."<br>*Station D:* "In partners, with one on the floor and one on the box, keep in contact with your partner and make up three different balance positions." Rotate groups and repeat challenges. | Small equipment, p. 505<br>Large apparatus, p. 535 | Rotate groups and repeat challenges. | Rotate groups and repeat challenges. | |
| **Part 3: Closure**<br>*(1 to 2 minutes)*<br><br>Strong and light movements | Discuss the meaning of strong and light movements. | | | | |

**Level II   Unit 1:** Gymnastics—Level 1
**Lesson 7.** Climbing
**Main Theme** Transfer of weight
**Subtheme** Balancing
**Equipment** Box, climbing rope, wall climbing, or agility apparatus; Large and small mats and individual ropes

**Additional Lessons** Additional lessons will be dictated by the type and amount of large apparatus. Use outdoor apparatus if available to complement the lesson.

| Content | Teaching Strategies | References | Lesson 7a | 7b | 7c |
|---|---|---|---|---|---|
| **Entry Activity** | Place small and large mats in a scattered pattern around the instructional area. Practice individual or partner balance stunts. | | Repeat previous. | Repeat previous. | Repeat previous. |
| **Part 1: Introductory Activities** *(4 to 5 minutes)*<br><br>Traveling<br>Shapes<br>Safety and skills | Leave mats scattered around instructional area. Present the following challenges:<br>1. "Run, jump, land, and roll."<br>2. "Run, jump, make one-half turn in the air, land, and roll" (diagonal or backward).<br>3. "Run, jump, make shape, land, and roll." | Backward roll, p. 454 | Repeat 1 to 3. | Play a tag game. | Design your own lesson. |
| **Part 2: Skill Development** *(20 to 35 minutes)*<br><br>Balance—headstand, single leg balance<br>Transfer of weight<br>Agility stunts—wheelbarrow | *Individual activities:*<br>Leave mats on the floor and allow children to use mats when performing the following tasks.<br>1. Explain, demonstrate, and practice single-leg balance and headstand.<br>2. "Begin with the single-leg balance, transfer weight to a three-point balance, transfer again to a new three-point balance."<br>*Partner activities:*<br>3. Explain, demonstrate, and practice a wheelbarrow.<br>4. "Can you make up new stunts with your partner that require balance and a transfer of weight?" | Single leg balance, p. 487<br>Headstand, p. 484<br>Wheelbarrow, p. 465<br>Stunts, p. 445 | Repeat 1 to 4 or introduce new stunts. | Repeat 1 to 4 or introduce new stunts. | |
| Small equipment—balance, transfer of weight, change of level, change of direction<br>Large apparatus—climbing skills, transfer of weight | *Station work:*<br>Assign class to the following stations. Have task cards available at each station.<br>*Station A:* Teacher remains at this station. Explain, demonstrate, and practice climbing skill and spotting techniques (climbing rope).<br>*Station B:* "Make up a partner routine that shows balance, transfer of weight, and a change in speed" (box).<br>*Station C:* "Design a sequence that has a hang, a pull, and a transfer of weight" (wall apparatus).<br>*Station D:* "Leave the individual ropes on the floor in any pattern you like, then make up a routine that has a skipping step, a change in level, and a change in direction." Rotate groups and repeat challenges.<br>*Note:* Substitute apparatus and challenges where necessary. | Rope climbing, p. 542<br>Outdoor apparatus, p. 554 | Rotate groups and repeat challenges. | Rotate groups and repeat challenges. | |
| **Part 3: Closure** *(1 to 2 minutes)*<br><br>Climbing | Stress the importance of always having a minimum of three points of contact when performing a climbing movement. | | | | |

**Level** II **Unit 1:** Gymnastics—Level 1
**Lesson 8.** Swinging
**Main Theme** Swinging
**Subthemes** Relationships
**Equipment** Large and small mats, climbing ropes, balance bench, wands, horizontal bar, individual ropes

**Additional Lessons** Additional lessons should emphasize stunts, movement skills, and swinging activities.

| Content | Teaching Strategies | References | Lesson 8a | 8b | 8c |
|---|---|---|---|---|---|
| **Entry Activity** | Place a variety of small equipment in the four containers. Free practice with equipment. | | Repeat previous. | Repeat previous. | Repeat previous. |
| **Part 1: Introductory Activities** (*5 to 6 minutes*)<br><br>Traveling<br>Animal walks | Ask class to put equipment away and find a space. Present the following challenges:<br>1. Play Nine Lives.<br>2. Animal walks—begin with a seal walk, lame puppy, bear walk, rabbit jump, etc. | Agility Stunts, p. 460 | Repeat 1 and 2. | Play a tag game. | Design your own lesson. |
| **Part 2: Skill Development** (*20 to 35 minutes*)<br><br>Balance—knee stand, side stand | *Individual activities:*<br>Place small and large mats around instructional area. Present following tasks.<br>*Partner activities:*<br>1. Explain, demonstrate and practice knee dip and frog stand.<br>2. "Make up a matching routine that includes a frog stand, a roll, and a new balance stunt."<br>3. "Invent a balance stunt where one foot and one hand of each partner is touching the floor." | Knee dip, p. 488<br>Frog stand, p. 483 | Repeat 3. | Repeat 3 or design a new challenge. | |
| Small equipment—balance, shapes, skipping<br>Large apparatus—swinging skill, shapes | *Station work:*<br>Present the following challenges (use task cards if desired) or modify them to accommodate local conditions.<br>*Climbing ropes:* Teacher remains at this station. Explain, demonstrate, and practice swinging skills. Swing and make shapes; swing from bench across to another bench; swing, land on mat, and roll." (Station A)<br>*Wands:* In partners. Both hold the opposite ends of two wands and without losing contact, make up a matching sequence of balance and shapes. (Station B)<br>*Horizontal bar:* Design a sequence that includes a swing, a shape, and a climbing skill. (Station C)<br>*Individual ropes:* "In partners, make up a rope skipping routine with one rope." (Station D)<br>*Note:* If the class is reasonably well skilled and enjoys creating their own routines, allow each group an opportunity to design their own individual or partner sequences at each station. Rotate groups and repeat challenges. | | Rotate groups and repeat challenges. | Rotate groups and repeat challenges. | |
| **Part 3: Closure** (*1 to 2 minutes*)<br><br>Swinging | Stress the importance of developing arm and shoulder girdle strength in order to perform many swinging skills. | | | | |

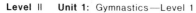

**Level II    Unit 1:** Gymnastics—Level 1
**Lesson 9.** Flow
**Main Theme** Flow
**Subthemes** Balance; Shapes; Levels
**Equipment** Climbing ropes, box, bench, beams

**Additional Lessons** The tasks in parts 2 and 3 of this lesson should extend over three lessons to allow partners to pra ctice and refine their sequences. Equally important is the allowance of time for each pair to demonstrate their sequence to the class.

| Content | Teaching Strategies | References | Lesson 9a | 9b | 9c |
|---|---|---|---|---|---|
| **Entry Activity** | Place a variety of small equipment in four containers. Free practice with equipment. | | Repeat previous. | Repeat previous. | Repeat previous. |
| **Part 1: Introductory Activities** *(4 to 5 minutes)* | Equipment away and mats optional. Present the following challenges: <br> 1. "Travel in different pathways—circle, square, zigzag, etc." <br> 2. "Find a balance position, roll to a new balance position, and continue pattern." <br> 3. "Run, jump, make shapes, land, and roll to a balance position and continue pattern." | Flow, pp. 41, 498 | Repeat 1 to 3. | Repeat 3. | Design your own lesson. |
| Traveling—pathways <br> Balance <br> Safety skills | | | | | |
| **Part 2: Skill Development** *(20 to 35 minutes)* | Put mats away. Present following challenges. "Select one of the following tasks (task cards) then find a space and practice your sequence." <br> *Task no. 1: Transfer of weight:* "Make up a sequence that shows a transfer of weight and three levels." <br> *Task no. 2: Shapes:* "Design a sequence that has a stretch, curl, and twisted shape, a change in direction, and a change in speed." <br> *Task no. 3: Levels:* "Invent a sequence of movements and shapes that is performed standing and on your back." <br> *Task no. 4: Balance:* "Create four different balance positions and roll from one to the other." <br> *Task no. 5:* "Make up your own sequence of movements." <br> *Note:* Allow sufficient time for practice, refinement, and student demonstrations. | Task cards, p. 112 | Rotate groups and repeat challenge. | Rotate groups and repeat challenge. | |
| Transfer of weight <br> Shapes <br> Levels <br> Balance | | | | | |
| Sequence with partner using small and large equipment | Arrange class into partners. Explain they may use any three pieces of equipment and share the large apparatus listed below. The task for all sets of partners is to design their own sequence and to explain and demonstrate their sequence to the class. <br> 1. *Small equipment:* Place where available space permits. <br> 2. *Large apparatus:* <br>     Station A: Climbing ropes <br>     Station B: Boxes and benches <br>     Station C: Benches and beams | Small equipment, p. 506 <br> Large apparatus, p. 535 | Rotate groups and repeat challenge. | Rotate groups and repeat challenge. | |
| **Part 3: Closure** *(1 to 2 minutes)* | | | | | |
| Flow | Discuss the meaning of quality (not quantity) of a movement or sequence of movements. | | | | |

# Gymnastic Activities
## Developmental Level II
## Unit 2: Gymnastics—
## Partner Relationships

**Expected Learning Outcomes**

**Psychomotor Skills**

1. Performing stretch, curl, wide, narrow, and twisted shapes
2. Changing direction, pathway, and level
3. Performing matching sequences
4. Performing partner sequences involving following and leading, supporting, adapting, and contrasting
5. Ability to move with concern for safety of self and partner
6. Ability to incorporate structured skills in partner movement sequences

**Cognitive and Affective Knowledge and Skills**

1. Understanding of Laban's movement terminology
2. Understanding of relationships with partner, small equipment, and large apparatus
3. Ability to work cooperatively with a partner
4. Appreciation of the individual differences of other students
5. Ability to cooperatively design partner sequences

**Level** II **Unit 2:** Gymnastics—Partner Relationships
**Lesson 1.** Matching and Mirroring
**Main Theme** Matching movements
**Subthemes** Traveling; Shapes; Balance
**Equipment** Hoops, individual ropes, benches, box, ladder, climbing ropes, or agility apparatus

**Additional Lessons** Each additional lesson should concentrate on parts 2 and 3 of this lesson. Special emphasis should be given to quality of performance; allow time for practice and polishing sequences.

| Content | Teaching Strategies | References | Lesson 1a | 1b | 1c |
|---|---|---|---|---|---|
| **Entry Activity** | Place hoops and individual ropes in containers. Free practice with equipment. | | Repeat previous. | Repeat previous. | Repeat previous. |
| **Part 1: Introductory Activities** *(3 to 5 minutes)* | 1. "Run, jump, land." <br> 2. "Run, jump, make stretch, curled, or twisted shapes, land, and continue pattern." | | Repeat 1 and 2. | Play Nine Lives (p. 30 of this guide). | Play Tails (p. 31 of this guide). |
| Traveling <br> Shapes | | | | | |
| **Part 2: Skill Development** *(20 to 35 minutes)* | *Individual activities:* <br> 1. "Make up a sequence of stretch, curl, and twisted shapes." <br> 2. "Make up a sequence of stretch, curl, or twisted shapes, hop to a new space, and repeat sequence of shapes." <br> *Partner activities:* <br> 3. "Teach each other your sequence." <br> 4. "Make up a new sequence together." <br> 5. "Make up a routine of balance and agility stunts." | Matching movements, p. 446 Balance and agility stunts, pp. 460, 478 | Repeat 3. | Repeat 3. | Repeat 3 and add to or change the challenge. |
| Shapes <br> Matching movements | | | | | |
| | *Station work:* <br> *Hoops:* "Make up a sequence of matching shapes using two hoops" (or any other small equipment). <br> *Individual ropes:* "Make up a sequence of balance stunts with an individual rope" (or other small equipment). <br> *Benches, box, ladder, climbing ropes or agility apparatus:* The following challenges can be applied to any of this apparatus. <br> 1. "Design a matching sequence with one on and one off the apparatus." <br> 2. "Make up a sequence moving side by side across or along the apparatus." <br> Rotate groups and repeat challenges. | Matching movements, pp. 517, 523 Large apparatus, p. 535 | Rotate groups and repeat challenges. | Rotate groups and repeat challenges. | Rotate groups and repeat challenges. |
| Shapes <br> Balance <br> Relationships | | | | | |
| **Part 3: Closure** *(1 to 2 minutes)* | | | | | |
| Relationships | Stress value of both partners sharing in the planning of each matching sequence. | | | | |

**Level II    Unit 2:** Gymnastics—Partner Relationships
**Lesson 2.** Following
**Main Theme** Copying partner
**Subthemes** Change of direction; Shapes; Balance; Transfer of weight
**Equipment** Bench, box, climbing ropes, or agility apparatus

**Additional Lessons** Each additional lesson should concentrate on parts 2 and 3 of this lesson. Special emphasis should be on quality of performance; allow time to practice and polish sequences.

| Content | Teaching Strategies | References | Lesson 2a | 2b | 2c |
|---|---|---|---|---|---|
| **Entry Activity** | Place individual ropes in containers. Free practice with ropes. | | Repeat previous. | Repeat previous. | Repeat previous. |
| **Part 1: Introductory Activities** (3 to 5 minutes) | 1. "Traveling and stopping on different parts." <br> 2. "Run, jump, make a shape, land, and continue." | | Repeat 1 and 2. | Play Nine Lives (p. 30 of this guide). | Design your own lesson. |
| Traveling <br> Safety Skills <br> Shapes | | | | | |
| **Part 2: Skill Development** (20 to 35 minutes) | *Partner activities:* <br> 1. "With one partner behind the other, develop a matching sequence of shapes showing a change of direction." <br> 2. "With one partner following, develop a sequence that shows a transfer of weight and rolling." <br> 3. "With one partner following, develop a routine of balance and rolling stunts." | Matching sequences, p. 446 | Repeat 1 and 2 adding to challenges. | Repeat 1 and 2 and add a new challenge. | |
| Shapes <br> Change of direction <br> Transfer of weight <br> Relationships | | | | | |
| | *Station work:* <br> *Individual ropes:* "One partner behind the other with both holding rope in right hands. Keep rope tense at all times, and develop a sequence of movements involving shape, balance, and speed." <br> *Benches, boxes, ladders, climbing ropes, or agility apparatus:* The following tasks can be applied to any of this apparatus. <br> 1. "Make up a sequence with one behind the other and show a change in direction and level." <br> 2. "With one behind the other, travel on the same three parts of the body and cross over four different types of apparatus." <br> Rotate groups and repeat challenges. | Matching sequences, p. 517 Large apparatus, p. 535 | Rotate groups and repeat challenges. | Rotate groups and repeat challenges. | |
| Shapes <br> Balance <br> Speed <br> Direction <br> Level <br> Transfer of weight <br> Relationships | | | | | |
| **Part 3: Closure** (1 to 2 minutes) | | | | | |
| Relationships | Discuss the importance of timing and flow when working together in the execution of two or more movements. | | | | |

**Level** II **Unit 2:** Gymnastics—Partner Relationships
**Lesson 3.** Adapting
**Main Theme** Adapting to partner's space and movement patterns
**Subthemes** Traveling; Change of direction; Transfer of weight
**Equipment** Bands, individual ropes, hoops, large apparatus

**Additional Lessons** This lesson could be expanded to several more interesting and challenging lessons. Lesson 3a will illustrate how to plan additional challenges.

| Content | Teaching Strategies | References | Lesson 3a | 3b | 3c |
|---|---|---|---|---|---|
| **Entry Activity** | Place hoops, individual ropes, and bands in containers. Free practice with equipment. | | Repeat previous. | Repeat previous. | Repeat previous. |
| **Part 1: Introductory Activities**<br>*(3 to 5 minutes)*<br><br>Traveling<br>Safety skills<br>Shapes | 1. Traveling and stopping on different parts.<br>2. Run, jump, make shape, land, and roll.<br>3. Play Tails. | Tails (p. 31 of this guide) | Repeat 1 and 2. | Design your own lesson. | Design your own lesson. |
| **Part 2: Skill Development**<br>*(20 to 35 minutes)*<br><br>Balance<br>Change of direction<br>Transfer of weight | *Partner activities:*<br>One partner makes a tunnel by spreading legs, the other crawls through. Continue making tunnels from many different positions and using different parts of body (for example, on back through one leg and two arms). Change around after each new position. | | Repeat challenge adding one more "player" to each group. New player makes holes. | | |
| Balance<br>Change of direction<br>Transfer of weight | *Station work:*<br>*Bands or individual ropes with ends tied:* One partner holds rope with both hands to form large tunnel. One partner crawls through. Change positions and make different tunnel with alternate player holding and crawling after each new position.<br>*Hoops:* One player holds one hoop while the other player crawls through. Shift position of body and position of hoop each time. Repeat above with player holding two hoops in different positions. One player rolls hoop and other moves through hoop.<br>*Large apparatus:* One player makes tunnel with parts of his body and side, end or top of apparatus. Partner crawls through tunnels. | | Repeat challenge adding one or two "players" to each challenge. | | |
| **Part 3: Closure**<br>*(1 to 2 minutes)*<br><br>Relationships | Ask children what would happen if you posed the same challenge, but with three children . . . four . . . plus equipment. | | | | |

**Level** II **Unit 2:** Gymnastics—Partner Relationships
**Lesson 4.** Supporting
**Main Theme** Lifting, carrying, and supporting partner
**Subthemes** Traveling; Balancing; Transfer of weight
**Equipment** Small equipment, benches, boxes, ladders, climbing rope, and agility apparatus

**Additional Lessons** This lesson is similar to the previous lesson. Lesson 4a again provides an example of one or more supplementary lessons stressing supporting and quality of performance.

| Content | Teaching Strategies | References | Lesson 4a | 4b | 4c |
|---|---|---|---|---|---|
| **Entry Activity** | Place a variety of small equipment in the containers. Free practice with equipment. | | Repeat previous. | Repeat previous. | Repeat previous. |
| **Part 1: Introductory Activities** *(3 to 5 minutes)* <br><br> Traveling <br> Animal movements | 1. Traveling on different body parts and in different directions. <br> 2. Traveling in animal walk movements—crab, lame puppy, seal walk, measuring worm, etc. | Agility Stunts, p. 460 | Repeat 1 and 2. | Design your own lesson. | Design your own lesson. |
| **Part 2: Skill Development** *(20 to 35 minutes)* <br><br><br><br><br><br> Balance <br> Levels <br> Relationships | *Partner activities:* <br> 1. "One partner crouches and balances on all fours. Other partner tries to balance on partner." <br> 2. "Discover three other ways to balance on your partner." <br> 3. "Make a statue with your partner. Both must be joined by knees touching." <br> 4. "Make a statue with your partner. Name various body parts that must be touching." Continue pattern. <br> 5. "Make a statue with one partner's hands the lowest part of statue while the other partner's hands are the highest." | Relationships, pp. 41, 500 | Repeat any one of 1 to 5 or change the challenge. | | |
| Balance <br> Transfer of weight <br> Relationships | *Station work:* <br> *Benches, boxes, ladders, climbing ropes, and agility apparatus:* The following challenges can be applied to any of this apparatus. <br> 1. "One partner on floor and the other on the apparatus. Both must be joined in some way. Find three other ways of balancing and joining different parts." <br> 2. "Make three statues on the side or top of your apparatus." <br> 3. "Design a sequence of statues that begins on one side of the apparatus and shifts onto and over the apparatus." Rotate groups and repeat challenges. | Benches, p. 544 | Rotate groups and repeat the challenge. | | |
| **Part 3: Closure** *(1 to 2 minutes)* <br><br> Relationships | <br><br> Discuss what makes a solid and safe balance position: wide base of support; low to the ground; have center of gravity near the middle of the base of support. | Principles of balance, p. 76 | | | |

**Level** II   **Unit 2:** Gymnastics—Partner Relationships
**Lesson 5.** Contrasting
**Main Theme** Contrasting movements
**Subthemes** Traveling; Transfer of weight; Shapes
**Equipment** Benches, boxes, beans, hoops, braids, individual ropes

**Additional Lessons** This last lesson in unit 2 could also continue for several additional lessons. Develop additional lessons on basis of student interest.

| Content | Teaching Strategies | References | Lesson 5a | 5b | 5c |
|---|---|---|---|---|---|
| **Entry Activity** | Place small equipment in containers. Free practice with equipment. | | Repeat previous. | Repeat previous. | Repeat previous. |
| **Part 1: Introductory Activities** *(3 to 5 minutes)*<br><br>Traveling<br>Transfer of weight | 1. Traveling in different directions with a change of speed.<br>2. Alternating traveling on hands, then feet, then hands, etc. | | Repeat 1. | Design your own lesson. | Design your own lesson. |
| **Part 2: Skill Development** *(20 to 35 minutes)*<br><br>Shapes<br>Weight bearing<br>Near and far<br>High and low | *Partner activities:*<br>1. "Partners facing, one make a curled shape, the other a stretched shape. Continue making a sequence of contrasting stretch and curled shapes."<br>2. "Make up a contrasting sequence of shapes and include near and far."<br>3. "Make a contrasting sequence of balance positions and include high and low." | | Repeat any of 1 to 3 or change challenges. | | |
| Balance<br>Strength<br>High and Low | *Station work:*<br>*Hoops, braids, or individual ropes:*<br>Present the same challenges for any of the above equipment.<br>1. "Develop a contrasting sequence of balance stunts using your equipment" (each partner has the same equipment).<br>2. "Use one piece of equipment between two partners and make up a contrasting sequence showing push and pull, and high and low."<br>*Benches, boxes, and beams:*<br>3. "Design your own sequence that shows contrasting shapes or movement skills." Rotate groups and repeat challenges. | Contrasting shapes, pp. 37, 497 | Rotate groups and repeat challenges. | | |
| **Part 3: Closure** *(1 to 2 minutes)*<br><br>Relationships | Discuss importance and value of working together in planning and executing partner sequences. | | | | |

# Gymnastic Activities
## Developmental Level III
## Unit 1: Gymnastics—
## Level 1

**Expected Learning Outcomes**

**Psychomotor Skills**

1. Ability to perform a variety of balance and agility stunts
2. Ability to perform stretch, curl, wide, narrow, and twisted shapes
3. Ability to perform extended movement sequences involving traditional stunts, and movement skills involving small and large apparatus
4. Ability to perform matching sequences of movement skills with a partner
5. Ability to perform a variety of traditional skills with small equipment and large apparatus

**Cognitive and Affective Knowledge and Skills**

1. Understanding of Laban's movement terminology
2. Understanding of relationships with partner, small and large apparatus
3. Ability to work cooperatively with a partner
4. Appreciation of individual differences of other students
5. Ability to design individual and partner movement sequences

Evaluative Techniques: See chapter 9 for observational methods and evaluation tools to assess structured or movement education skills and concepts.

**Level III Unit 1:** Gymnastics—Level 1
**Lesson 1.** Balance
**Main Theme** Balance
**Subthemes** Traveling; Rope skipping
**Equipment** Class set of individual ropes

**Additional Lessons** The following lesson outline will illustrate how the main theme and subthemes may be continued for two or more lessons before progressing to lesson 2.

| Content | Teaching Strategies | References | Lesson 1a | 1b | 1c |
|---|---|---|---|---|---|
| **Entry Activity** | *Note:* Leave this prelesson activity out of the first lesson. Explain that small equipment will be placed in containers at the start of each lesson. In lesson 2 and all subsequent lessons, students may enter the gymnasium as soon as they are changed and choose a piece of equipment to practice any stunt or movement pattern as they wait for the lesson to begin. | Free play activities, p. 106 | Free practice with small equipment. | Repeat previous. | Repeat previous. |
| **Part 1: Introductory Activities** (5 to 10 minutes)  Traveling Change of direction | Present the following challenges:  1. "Run in different directions." As they begin to run, call out "backward, forward, sideways," etc.  2. "Travel and touch the floor." Explain that as they travel and see an open space they should bend down, touch the floor with both hands (indicates good body control), and continue this pattern.  3. Tag game: Go for It—On signal, each team sends first player in line to pick up a stick from the center. After picking up a stick players run counterclockwise around the outside of all three teams and return to the back of their line to receive a point. There are only three sticks in the center. The player who was unable to pick up a stick tries to tag the other players before they return to their team. Players tagged lose their point. Play continues until all have had a turn. | Tag game, p. 261 | Repeat 1, 2 and 3. | Play a vigorous tag game. | Repeat 1 and 2 and play a shadow game (p. 35 of this guide). |
| **Part 2: Skill Development** (20 to 35 minutes)  Balance stunts—knee dip, the bridge | Have students find their own space.  *Balance Stunts*  1. Explain, demonstrate (use students wherever possible to demonstrate stunts), and practice the knee dip and the bridge. Use mats if desired.  2. Ask class, "Can you change the knee dip or the bridge stunt to make either stunt a little more difficult to perform?" Select one or two children to demonstrate and continue, allowing other students to try different modifications.  3. "Can you combine a knee dip, a roll, and another knee dip?" | Knee dip, p. 488 Bridge, p. 485 Balance stunts, p. 478 | Review knee dip, bridge, and introduce a new balance stunt. | Leave out. | Review balance stunts. |

165

| Content | Teaching Strategies | References | Lesson 1a | 1b | 1c |
|---|---|---|---|---|---|
| Individual ropes, two-foot basic step, alternate step | 4. Ask class to select a rope and find a space. Explain how to determine the proper length for each performer, then allow children to exchange ropes for correct lengths. Explain, demonstrate, and practice the two-foot basic step and the alternate step. After several minutes of practice, "Make up a routine of your two-foot basic and alternate step and add a sideways swinging movement with your rope." | Two-foot basic step, p. 511 Alternate step, p. 512 | Review two-foot basic and alternate step. Introduce a new rope skipping skill. | Review rope skipping skills. Develop continuous routine using two or more skills. | Review rope skipping skills. Develop continuous routine using three skills. |

**Part 3: Closure**
*(1 to 2 minutes)*

Safety — Explain that the children will be given more freedom in designing their routines. Stress the importance of watching out for their own safety as well as the safety of all members of the class.

**Level III    Unit 1:** Gymnastics—Level 1
**Lesson 2.** Transfer of Weight
**Main Theme** Transfer of weight
**Subthemes** Balancing; Agility stunts
**Equipment** Class set of individual ropes

**Additional Lessons** The following lesson outline illustrates how a teacher might continue the lesson emphasis and substitute other small equipment for variety and interest.

| Content | Teaching Strategies | References | Lesson 2a | 2b | 2c |
|---|---|---|---|---|---|
| **Entry Activity** | Place individual ropes (color code for length) in gymnasium. Free practice with ropes. | | Repeat previous. | Add additional equipment and repeat previous. | Repeat previous. |
| **Part 1: Introductory Activities** *(5 to 8 minutes)* | Ropes away and scatter large and small mats around instructional area. Allow students to use bare feet if their skill level is adequate and school policy permits. Pose the following tasks: | Diagonal roll, p. 452 | Repeat 1 to 3. | Play Crab Walk Tag. | Design your own lesson. |
| Traveling in different directions Landing and rolling | 1. "Run in different directions, jump, land, and roll." 2. Individual practice of diagonal roll across mats. 3. Run, jump, and make a half turn in air, land, diagonal roll, and continue pattern. | | | | |
| **Part 2: Skill Development** *(20 to 35 minutes)* | *Balance Stunts* | Knee dip, p. 488 | Repeat 3 and 4. | Repeat 4 and add a new challenge. | |
| Balance stunts rolling the log Transfer of weight | 1. Review the bridge and knee dip stunts with students performing at least one modification of each stunt. 2. Explain, demonstrate, and practice V-sit, and headstand. Once acquired, challenge class to modifications of stunt. 3. "Make up a routine beginning with the knee dip, shift to a roll, and finish with the V-sit." Allow time to practice. Select one or two for demonstrations. 4. "Add one modification to each stunt and repeat your routine." | Bridge, and Headstand, pp. 484, 485 V-sit, p. 485 Routines, p. 446 | | | |
| Individual ropes—one-foot hop, rocker step | *Individual ropes:* Ask children to select a rope and find a space. 5. Review rope skipping. 6. Explain, demonstrate, and practice the foot hop and rocker step. 7. Ask class to place a rope on the floor in any design and challenge them to develop a routine using two-foot basic, alternate, hop, and rocker steps. | Alternate step, p. 512 One-foot hop, p. 514 Rocker step, p. 515 | Introduce new steps, repeat 7. | Introduce wand activities. | |
| **Part 3: Closure** *(1 to 2 minutes)* | | | | | |
| Designing a routine | Discuss how each performer made up his or her own routine. | | | | |

**Level III    Unit 1:** Gymnastics—Level 1
**Lesson 3.** Balance and Vaulting
**Main Theme** Balance and vaulting
**Subthemes** Traveling; Rolling
**Equipment** Cones, hoops, benches, and vaulting box

**Additional Lessons** Teachers must be able to use alternate equipment or apparatus that is available in their own schools. If a second or third lesson is needed to complete the rotation, begin lesson 3a with the same introductory activities, then move directly to part 3 and continue with rotation.

| Content | Teaching Strategies | References | Lesson 3a | 3b | 3c |
|---|---|---|---|---|---|
| **Entry Activity** | Place cones and hoops in container. Free play with equipment. | | Repeat previous. | Repeat previous. | Repeat previous. |
| **Part 1: Introductory Activities** *(5 to 8 minutes)* <br><br> Traveling—in different directions, on different parts <br> · Landing and rolling | Leave small equipment scattered over instructional area. Pose following challenges: <br> 1. "Run, jump over equipment, land, change direction, and continue." <br> 2. "Run, jump over equipment, land, roll, change direction, and continue pattern." Use mats if desired or required. <br> 3. Have each child stand beside a small piece of equipment. "Show me how many ways you can cross your equipment." Wait a few moments, then, "Now, using hands only, crossing sideways," etc. <br> Put small equipment away and scatter large and small mats around instructional area. | Rolling and landing, p. 541 <br> Tag games, p. 261 | Repeat 1 to 3. | Repeat 1 to 3. | Play a tag game. |
| **Part 2: Skill Development** *(20 to 35 minutes)* <br><br> Tumbling stunts—judo, forward, side, backward, and diagonal rolls <br> Balance—side stand, table | *Part A: Class Activity* <br> *Tumbling stunt* <br> 1. Explain, demonstrate, and practice judo roll. <br> 2. Organize class into five or six children per large mat. Instruct each group to be constantly on the move and performing a log, side, forward, diagonal, or judo roll across the mat according to individual choice and available space on the mat. <br> *Balance stunts/Partner stunts* <br> 3. Explain, demonstrate, and practice the side stand and table. <br> 4. Pose challenge, "See if you can invent a new balance stunt with your partner." | Judo roll, p. 455 <br> Side stand, p. 488 <br> Table, p. 489 <br> Balance stunts, p. 478 <br> Routines, p. 446 | Leave out. | Leave out. | Leave out. |
| Cones—vaulting, traveling <br> Hoops—vaulting, directions <br> Benches—vaulting, landing, and rolling <br> Box—vaulting, balancing | *Part B: Station Work* <br> Arrange class and equipment according to available space. Present the following tasks to each respective group and allow three to five minutes of practice before rotating each group clockwise to the next station. <br> *Benches:* "Develop three ways of getting on the benches. Leap off, land, and roll after each approach onto the bench." (Station A) <br> *Hoops:* "Make up a routine of crossing your hoop that includes forward, sideways, and backward." (Station B) <br> *Boxes:* "Design a routine that includes vaulting onto apparatus, a balance position on top, and a leap off, landing and rolling to a new balance position." (Station C) | | Rotate groups and repeat challenges. | Rotate groups and repeat challenges. | Rotate groups and repeat challenges. |

| Content | Teaching Strategies | References | Lesson 3a | 3b | 3c |
|---|---|---|---|---|---|
| | *Cones:* "Invent a routine that includes a leap, jump, and hop over the cone." (Station D) | | | | |
| | Teaching suggestions: Write out these challenges on task cards and leave at each station. Design other task cards for the above stations as well as for other substitute equipment or apparatus. | | | | |

**Part 3: Closure**
*(1 to 2 minutes)*

| Content | Teaching Strategies | References | Lesson 3a | 3b | 3c |
|---|---|---|---|---|---|
| Task cards | Discuss the use of task cards. Ask class if they could design challenges for task cards to be used in the next lesson. | | | | |

Level III    Unit 1: Gymnastics—Level 1
Lesson 4.  Shape and Agility
Main Theme  Shape and agility
Subthemes  Traveling; Landing and rolling
Equipment  Variety of small equipment, springboard, mats, vaulting box, and agility apparatus

**Additional Lessons** Instruct students who were *last* working on a station to set it up in the next lesson. To save time as well as to provide additional challenges, write out two additional task cards for each station. If students have completed the first challenge, allow them to select a new task card for the same apparatus.

| Content | Teaching Strategies | References | Lesson 4a | 4b | 4c |
|---|---|---|---|---|---|
| **Entry Activities** | Place a variety of small equipment in four containers. Free practice with equipment. | | Repeat previous. | Repeat previous. | Repeat previous. |
| **Part 1: Introductory Activities** (*5 to 7 minutes*)<br><br>Traveling—in different directions, on different parts<br>Shapes—twisted, narrow, curved | Scatter large and small mats around the instructional area. Pose the following challenges:<br>1. "Run, jump, land, change direction, and continue."<br>2. "Run, jump, make tucked shape in air, land, and continue." Teacher calls out new shapes as children are traveling—"straddle, twisted, narrow, curved," and so on.<br>3. "Travel on two hands and one foot, all fours, one foot." Continue changing points of contact.<br>Teaching suggestion: If 1 to 3 are presented reasonably fast, changing points of contact, etc., children will experience a strenuous warm-up period. | Landing and rolling, p. 541 | Repeat 1 to 3. | Repeat 1 to 3. | Design your own lesson. |
| **Part 2: Skill Development** (*20 to 35 minutes*)<br><br>Tumbling—side, forward, diagonal, or shoulder roll<br>Shapes—stretch, curl, and twisted | *Part A: Class Activity*<br>Ask class to find a space on the floor or mat. Pose following tasks:<br>1. "Stretch out on floor or mat and see if you can keep rolling, but shift from stretched shape to a side roll, to a judo roll, to a diagonal roll."<br>2. "Start with your stretch shape, roll to a twisted shape."<br>3. "Begin in a curled or tucked position, roll to a twisted shape, roll again to a different curled shape."<br>4. "Start in a standing position with arms extended, make a diagonal roll and end in a tucked or curled shape."<br>5. "Make up your own routine or sequence."<br>*Note:* Begin to use "sequence" as part of teaching vocabulary. | Shapes, p. 497 | Leave out. | Leave out. | |
| Springboard and mats—take-off, shapes, landing<br>Agility apparatus—shapes, traveling<br>Boxes | *Part B: Station Work:*<br>Arrange the class and apparatus according to available space. Substitute small equipment or other appropriate large apparatus where necessary. Present the following challenges verbally or by task cards to each group. Allow three to five minutes, then rotate groups clockwise to the next station.<br>*Springboard and mats:* Teacher remains at this station to explain and demonstrate takeoff skill. Students perform shapes in air, land, and roll. Spotting positions are also taught at this station. (Station A) | Takeoff skill, p. 545<br>Agility apparatus, p. 553<br>Benches or beams, p. 536<br>Box, p. 544 | Rotate groups and repeat challenges. | Rotate groups and repeat challenges. | |

170

| Content | Teaching Strategies | References | Lesson 4a | 4b | 4c |
|---------|--------------------|-----------|-----------|-----|-----|
| | *Agility apparatus:* Find three different locations on the apparatus and make a twisted, curled, and stretched shape at each location. (Station B) | | | | |
| | *Boxes:* Make up a sequence that includes a vault onto apparatus, shape, flight off, land, and roll. (Station C) | | | | |
| | *Benches or beams:* Design a routine that includes a squat mount, a twisted shape, and a dismount. (Station D) | | | | |

**Part 3: Closure**
*(1 to 2 minutes)*

| | | | | | |
|---------|--------------------|-----------|-----------|-----|-----|
| Shapes | Discuss what shapes are represented in agility skills, such as judo roll or squat mount. | | | | |

**Level** III **Unit 1:** Gymnastics—Level 1
**Lesson 5.** Climbing and Balancing
**Main Theme** Climbing and balancing
**Subthemes** Agility; Traveling
**Equipment** Large and small mats, individual ropes, climbing ropes, and horizontal bar

**Additional Lessons** The following outline will illustrate how a teacher might extend the lesson into two or more lessons.

| Content | Teaching Strategies | References | Lesson 5a | 5b | 5c |
|---|---|---|---|---|---|
| **Entry Activity** | Scatter large and small mats around instructional area. Practice individual balance stunts. | | Repeat previous. | Repeat previous. | Repeat previous. |
| **Part 1: Introductory Activities** *(5 to 7 minutes)* <br><br> Traveling—in different directions, at different speeds | Leave mats scattered around floor. Pose the following tasks. <br> 1. "Run, and each time you change direction, change your speed." <br> 2. "Run, jump, make a half turn in the air, land, and diagonal roll." <br> 3. "Play Crab Tag," played the same as simple tag except a player in a crab walk position is "safe." | Tag games, p. 261 | Repeat previous. | Play a tag game. | Repeat 1 to 3. |
| **Part 2: Skill Development** *(20 to 35 minutes)* | *Part A: Class Activity* <br> Ask class to find a space on the mats or floor. <br> *Balance Stunts* <br> 1. Explain, demonstrate, practice V-sit, and review headstand. <br> 2. Explain, demonstrate, and practice knee-shoulder stand. <br> 3. Pose challenge, "See if you can add a twist to the knee-shoulder stand." Or, "Can you modify this stunt?" | V-sit, p. 485 <br> Headstand, p. 484 <br> Knee-shoulder stand, p. 490 | Leave out. | Leave out. | Leave out. |
| Chairs—balance <br> Individual ropes—skipping, change of direction <br> Climbing ropes—climbing <br> Horizontal bar—pull-ups | *Part B: Station Work* <br> Arrange class and apparatus according to the space available. Although the actual layout of equipment and apparatus will depend upon where fixed apparatus (climbing ropes) are located, any rotation should move from large to small equipment and from an emphasis on one element (balance) to a different element (agility). Present the following tasks (verbally or by task cards) to each group and rotate groups clockwise every five minutes. <br> *Benches:* "Make up a sequence that involves balancing on the floor, on the chair, then on the floor." (Station A) <br> *Individual ropes:* "Design a routine that involves a rocker, an alternate and hopping step, and three changes in direction." (Station B) <br> *Climbing ropes:* Teacher remains at this station to explain and demonstrate climbing skill. Children practice skills and spotting techniques. (Station C) <br> *Horizontal bar:* Individual practice of pull-ups, roll over bar, and Skin the Snake. (Station D) <br> *Teaching suggestion:* With large classes, increase the number of stations and reduce the number assigned to each station. Also, when substituting other equipment or apparatus, attempt to design challenges that emphasize balance or climbing. | Benches, p. 536 <br> Individual rope skills, p. 509 <br> Climbing rope skills, p. 542 <br> Horizontal bar, p. 550 | Rotate groups and repeat challenges. | Rotate groups and repeat challenges. | Keep same equipment, but change challenges for each station. |
| **Part 3: Closure** *(1 to 2 minutes)* <br><br> Climbing skills | Explain and illustrate the importance of maintaining a three-foot contact when climbing a rope. | | | | |

172

**Level** III **Unit 1:** Gymnastics—Level 1
**Lesson 6.** Speed and Transfer of Weight
**Main Theme** Speed and transfer of weight
**Subthemes** Balance; Shapes
**Equipment** Large and small mats, chairs, wands, long ropes; Benches and balance beam

**Additional Lessons** If additional lessons are desired, follow the outline shown below.

| Content | Teaching Strategies | References | Lesson 6a | 6b | 6c |
|---|---|---|---|---|---|
| **Entry Activity** | Scatter large and small mats around instructional area. Practice balance and agility stunts. | | Repeat previous. | Repeat previous. | Repeat previous. |
| **Part 1: Introductory Activities** (*5 to 7 minutes*)<br><br>Traveling—in different directions, in different ways<br>Speed—quick and slow<br>Shapes | Leave mats scattered around instructional area. Pose the following challenges.<br>1. "Travel using run, skip, or slide and roll across mats."<br>2. "Run, jump, make shapes, land, and roll across mats."<br>3. "Play shadow tag, but do not touch or cross over any mats."<br>Find partner. On signal, one tries to keep the other from touching him or her. If tagged, change positions and continue. | Shadow game, (p. 35 of this guide) | Repeat 1 to 3. | Repeat 3. | Design your own lesson. |
| **Part 2: Skill Development** (*20 to 35 minutes*)<br><br>Balance—V-sit, dip<br>Agility (transfer of weight)—<br>egg roll, backward extension | *Part A: Class Activity*<br>1. Review V-sit and headstand.<br>2. Explain, demonstrate, and practice egg roll and backward extension.<br>3. "Make up a sequence that includes a headstand, a roll, and a balance position."<br>4. Repeat 3 with a change of speed between each stunt.<br>5. "Make up a sequence that has a transfer of weight and a change of speed."<br>6. "In partners, design a matching sequence that has a headstand, a backward extension (or backward diagonal roll), and one other stunt." | V-sit, p. 485<br>Headstand, p. 484<br>Backward extension, p. 456<br>Egg roll, p. 452 | Repeat 3 and 4. | Repeat 5 and 6. | |
| Chairs—transfer of weight<br>Wands—Thread the Needle, transfer of weight, change of speed<br>Long ropes—rope jumping | *Part B: Station Work*<br>Arrange class and apparatus according to available space. Present the following tasks and rotate clockwise after every four or five minutes.<br>*Vaulting box:* "Place the vaulting box in any position you like and make up a routine that shows a transfer of weight from the floor to the box and back to the floor." (Station A)<br>*Wands:* "Design a sequence that begins with Thread the Needle and shows a transfer of weight and a change of speed." (Station B)<br>*Benches and beams:* "Make up a sequence that has a squat on one leg, a swing turn, and a twisted shape." (Station C)<br>*Long ropes:* "Using a front or back door turning, design and practice three dual rope skipping stunts." Rotate new partners after one minute. (Station D) | Vaulting box, p. 544<br>Wands, p. 524<br>Benches, p. 536<br>Long rope activities, p. 521 | Rotate groups and repeat challenges. | Rotate groups and repeat challenges. | |
| **Part 3: Closure** (*1 to 2 minutes*)<br><br>Speed | Discuss and illustrate the application of quick and slow movements to a routine. | | | | |

**Level** III  **Unit 1:** Gymnastics—Level 1
**Lesson 7.** Swinging and Balancing
**Main Theme** Swinging and balancing
**Equipment** Individual ropes, large and small mats, hoops, traffic cones, horizontal bar, and climbing ropes

**Additional Lessons** In the majority of schools, large apparatus is limited. Additional lessons may be required to allow every child a sufficient exposure to this apparatus. The following illustrates the use of large apparatus; however, small equipment is substituted to provide variety.

| Content | Teaching Strategies | References | Lesson 7a | 7b | 7c |
|---|---|---|---|---|---|
| **Entry Activity** | Place individual ropes in containers. Free practice. | | Repeat previous. | Repeat previous. | Repeat previous. |
| **Part 1: Introductory Activities** (5 to 6 minutes)<br><br>Skipping—two-foot basic, alternate, rocker, hop, crosslegged, pepper | Ask children to find their own space, then pose the following challenges.<br>　1. Review the alternate step, hop, and rocker step (allow approx. one minute).<br>　2. Explain, demonstrate, and practice cross-legged and pepper skipping skills.<br>　3. Choose three rope skipping skills, begin skipping forward, change direction and skill, and continue pattern around instructional area.<br>Ropes away and bring out small and large mats. | Rope skipping, p. 509 | Repeat 3. | Play a tag game. | Design your own lesson. |
| **Part 2: Skill Development** (20 to 35 minutes)<br><br>Landing and rolling<br>Balance—forearm headstand, walk down wall | *Part A: Class Activity*<br>　1. Explain, demonstrate, and practice forearm headstand and walking down the wall.<br>　2. "Develop a routine that includes a forearm headstand and two rolls." | Forearm headstand, p. 487<br>Walking down wall, p. 485 | Leave out. | Leave out. | |
| Hoops—balance<br>Traffic cones—flight, balance, and rolling<br>Climbing ropes—climbing, swinging and landing<br>Horizontal bar—roll over barrow | *Part B: Station Work*<br>Arrange class and apparatus according to the available space. Present the following challenges and rotate clockwise after every four or five minutes.<br>*Hoops:* "Make up a sequence of three balance skills using the hoop." (Station A)<br>*Traffic cones:* "Invent a routine that shows a run, flight over traffic cone, land, roll, and balance." (Station B)<br>*Climbing ropes:* Teacher remains at this station. (Station C)<br>　1. Have children review climbing skill.<br>　2. Explain, demonstrate, and practice swinging and landing skills.<br>*Horizontal bar:* (Station D)<br>　1. Review chin-ups and Skin the Snake.<br>　2. Practice roll over barrow. | Hoops, p. 522<br>Traffic cones, p. 530<br>Climbing ropes, p. 542<br>Horizontal bars, p. 550 | Rotate groups and change cones and hoops for individual ropes and wands. | Rotate groups and repeat previous challenges. | |
| **Part 3: Closure** (1 to 2 minutes)<br><br>Swinging skills | Discuss the importance of maintaining a three-point grip through swinging movements. | | | | |

**Level** III  **Unit 1:** Gymnastics—Level 1
**Lesson 8.** Agility, Direction, and Level
**Main Theme** Agility, direction, and level
**Subtheme** Shapes
**Equipment** Individual ropes, beanbags, agility apparatus, benches, beams, springboard, and box

**Additional Lessons** Since this is nearing the end of the unit, teachers will know if additional lessons are indicated. Lack of large apparatus will normally be the restricting aspect of most lessons. Check Appendix B in the text for suggestions relating to constructing inexpensive large apparatus.

| Content | Teaching Strategies | References | Lesson 8a | 8b | 8c |
|---|---|---|---|---|---|
| **Entry Activity** | Place individual ropes in containers. Free practice with individual ropes. | | Repeat previous. | Repeat previous. | Repeat previous. |
| **Part 1: Introductory Activities** *(5 to 6 minutes)*<br><br>Traveling—on different parts<br>Rope skipping | Leave individual ropes on floor. Ropes should be in a straight line or forming an S shape. Present following challenges.<br>1. "Do not touch any rope, and move anywhere in the crab walk position."<br>2. "Find a rope. Travel up and down rope using any previously learned rope skipping step."<br>3. "Pick up rope and practice four skipping skills while traveling around the instructional area."<br>Ropes away and form large semicircle. | Rope skipping, p. 509 | Repeat 1 to 3. | Design your own lesson. | Design your own lesson. |
| **Part 2: Skill Development** *(20 to 35 minutes)*<br><br>Agility—cartwheel | *Part A: Class Activity*<br>1. Review bear dance and rolling skills.<br>2. Explain, demonstrate, and practice cartwheel. Lead-up skills: rabbit jump, mule kick.<br>3. "Make up a matching routine with your partner that includes an agility skill, a balance stunt, rolling, and a change of direction." | Bear dance, p. 470<br>Rolling<br>Mule kick, p. 457<br>Rabbit Jump, p. 466<br>Cartwheel, pp. 456, 459 | Repeat 3. | | |
| Beanbags—agility movements, change of direction<br>Agility apparatus—balance stunts, levels<br>Benches and beams—shapes, levels | *Part B: Station Work*<br>Arrange class and apparatus according to available space. Substitute small or large apparatus where necessary. Present the following challenges.<br>*Beanbags:* Each child has five beanbags. "Design a routine that stresses change of direction and agile movements, then arrange your beanbags to complement your sequence." (Station A)<br>*Agility apparatus:* "Make up a three-point balance stunt that can be performed on three different levels of the apparatus." (Station B)<br>*Benches and beams:* "In partners, design and perform a matching or contrasting routine involving shape and level." (Station C)<br>*Springboard and box:* Teacher remains at this station. (Station D)<br>1. Review takeoff from board to mat.<br>2. Explain, demonstrate, and practice squat vault. Practice lead-up skills and spotting techniques. | Beanbag activities, p. 506<br>Springboard activities, p. 544<br>Squat vaulting, p. 546<br>Spotting, p. 442 | Rotate groups and repeat challenge. | | |
| **Part 3: Closure** *(1 to 2 minutes)*<br><br>Partner Activities | Have one or two partners explain how they developed their routines. | | | | |

Level III   Unit 1: Gymnastics—Level 1
Lesson 9. Transfer of Weight and Flow
Main Theme Transfer of weight and flow
Subthemes Traveling
Equipment Individual ropes and all available large and small apparatus

Additional Lessons To contribute to quality of performance, begin each subsequent lesson with a brief warm-up, then move directly to part 2. If interest is high, allow partners to refine their sequence. Once a reasonable quality is reached, allow children to design another routine using different equipment.

| Content | Teaching Strategies | References | Lesson 9a | 9b | 9c |
|---|---|---|---|---|---|
| **Entry Activity** | Practice balance stunts while waiting for lesson to begin. | | Repeat previous. | Repeat previous. | Repeat previous. |
| **Part 1: Introductory Activities** (*5 to 6 minutes*) | On bare floor: <br> 1. Travel, changing direction, speed, and level. <br> 2. Run, jump, land, roll. <br> 3. Run, jump, land, roll to a three-point balance. <br> 4. Repeat 3 adding another roll and another new balance position. | Transfer of weight, p. 496 | Repeat 1 to 4. | Play a tag game. | Design your own lesson. |
| Traveling <br> Change of direction <br> Change of level <br> Landing and rolling | | | | | |
| **Part 2: Skill Development** (*20 to 35 minutes*) | *In partners:* Present following tasks. <br> 1. "Make up a routine with your partner that clearly shows a transfer of weight, a change of direction, and a change of speed." <br> 2. "Both must be holding one end of an individual rope. Design a routine that shows continuous contact with the rope and transferring weight." <br> 3. "Invent a contrasting sequence with your partner that has transfer of weight and flow." <br> *Note:* At this stage, children should be capable of designing relatively long and complex sequences. Challenges should be phrased to permit maximum freedom in the design and performance of each respective routine. | Partner activities, p. 500 | Leave out. | Leave out. | |
| Flow <br> Transfer of weight—change of direction, change of speed <br> Individual rope—transfer of weight | | | | | |
| Partner sequences using: <br> Chairs <br> Individual ropes <br> Benches <br> Agility apparatus <br> Horizontal bar <br> Climbing ropes | 4. Keep the same sets of partners. Explain to the class what equipment and apparatus are available. Their task is to choose the apparatus of their choice, design a new routine that stresses transferring weight and flow, set up their apparatus, and begin practicing. <br> *Note:* Since there are limited amounts of equipment and apparatus, some may have to share large apparatus or decide to move to a second choice. The challenge presented will require creativity, teamwork, and group sharing, which are important learning outcomes for all children to learn. | Transfer of weight, p. 496 | Repeat challenges. | Repeat challenges. | |
| **Part 3: Closure** (*1 to 2 minutes*) | | | | | |
| Sharing equipment | Discuss the importance of working with other sets of partners when designing, as well as executing, partner sequences. | | | | |

# Gymnastic Activities
Developmental Level III
Unit 2: Gymnastics—
Flight

## Expected Learning Outcomes

### Psychomotor Skills

1. Ability to perform flight from hands or feet off floor or apparatus
2. Ability to perform shapes while in flight
3. Ability to perform matching sequences of movements involving flight, shapes, and a transfer of weight

### Cognitive and Affective Knowledge and Skills

1. Understanding of concept and movement principles involved in flight
2. Ability to work cooperatively and creatively with a partner
3. Appreciation of strengths and weaknesses of self and other performers
4. Ability to design complex movement sequences

**Level III**  **Unit 2:** Gymnastics—Flight
**Lesson 1.** Takeoff, Land, and Roll
**Main Theme** Jumping, landing, and rolling
**Subthemes** Flight from hands; Balance
**Equipment** Springboard, box, and benches

**Additional Lessons** Additional lessons should emphasize flight, shapes, landing, and rolling.

| Content | Teaching Strategies | References | Lesson 1a | 1b | 1c |
|---|---|---|---|---|---|
| **Entry Activity** | Scatter large and small mats around instructional area. Practice with mats. | | Repeat previous. | Repeat previous. | Repeat previous. |
| **Part 1: Introductory Activities** *(3 to 5 minutes)* <br><br> Traveling <br> Flight | 1. "Run, jump, land, touch floor, and continue pattern." <br> 2. "Run, jump, land, and roll." <br> 3. Repeat 1 and 2 with a one-foot takeoff. | | Repeat 1, adding shape to challenge. | Repeat previous challenge. | Design your own lesson. |
| **Part 2: Skill Development** *(20 to 35 minutes)* <br><br> Flight <br> Shapes | *Practice activities:* <br> 1. Explain, demonstrate, and practice upswing, and jump through. <br> 2. "Design a sequence that includes an upswing, jump through, and a rolling skill." <br> 3. In partners: "Make up a matching sequence involving flight, shape, and rolling." <br> 4. Small group: Explain, demonstrate, and practice triple roll (groups of three). | Upswing, p. 472 <br> Jump through, p. 474 <br><br><br> Triple Roll, p. 456 | Repeat 2 and 3. | Leave out. | |
| Flight <br> Balance, and <br> Shape using springboard <br> and mats | Mini-tramp, springboard, beatboard, and large mats. <br> 5. Explain, demonstrate, and practice two-foot takeoff. *Boxes, benches, and beams* <br> 6. "Run, two-foot takeoff, onto apparatus, balance, leap off, land, and roll." <br> 7. Repeat 6 and add a balance stunt at end of sequence. <br> 8. Repeat 7, adding shape to the challenge. | Takeoff, p. 545 | Repeat 6 to 8. | Introduce squat or straddle vault. | |
| **Part 3: Closure** *(1 to 2 minutes)* <br><br> Flight | Discuss the importance of landing and rolling with control and a gradual slowing down of the momentum. | | | | |

**Level III    Unit 2:** Gymnastics—Flight
**Lesson 2.** Flight and Shapes
**Main Theme** Flight
**Subthemes** Shapes; Balance
**Equipment** Large and small mats, benches, box, beam, springboard

**Additional Lessons** Continue emphasis on flight, introducing specific vaulting stunts and/or more complex sequences involving flight, landing, and rolling.

| Content | Teaching Strategies | References | Lesson 2a | 2b | 2c |
|---|---|---|---|---|---|
| **Entry Activity** | Scatter large and small mats around instructional area. Free practice with mats. | | Repeat previous. | Repeat previous. | Repeat previous. |
| **Part 1: Introductory Activities** (*3 to 5 minutes*) | 1. "Run, jump, land, touch floor, and continue pattern." <br> 2. "Run, jump, land, and roll." <br> 3. "Run, jump, make shape (stretch, curl, etc.), land, and roll." <br> 4. Repeat 1, 2, and 3 with a one-foot takeoff. | Shapes, p. 497 | Repeat 1 and 2. | Design your own lesson. | Design your own lesson. |
| Traveling <br> Shapes | | | | | |
| **Part 2: Skill Development** (*20 to 35 minutes*) | 1. Review upswing (p. 472), jump through (p. 474), and cartwheel (p. 459). <br> 2. Explain, demonstrate, and practice neckspring. <br> 3. "Design a sequence involving a neckspring, a transfer of weight, and a balance position." <br> 4. Allow each child to make up his or her own sequence. | Neckspring, p. 476 <br> Balance stunts, p. 478 | Repeat 2 and 3. Design sequence including cartwheel and two other movement skills. | | |
| Transfer of weight <br> Shapes <br> Balance | | | | | |
| Flight, Shapes, and rolling using springboard and mats | *Mini-tramp, springboard, beatboard, and large mats* <br> 5. Review two-foot takeoff and landing. <br> 6. Run, take off, make shape (stretch, curl, wide, and twisted), land, and roll. <br> *Boxes, benches, and beams* <br> 7. Run, jump onto apparatus, balance, leap, make shape, land, and roll. | Takeoff, p. 545 <br> Vault, p. 545 <br> Shapes, p. 497 <br> Benches, p. 536 | Repeat 1 to 3. | | |
| **Part 3: Closure** (*1 to 2 minutes*) | | | | | |
| Flight | Discuss the importance of a consistent takeoff, that is, hitting the same spot prior to takeoff. | | | | |

**Level III    Unit 2:** Gymnastics—Flight
**Lesson 3.** Flight from Different Parts of the Body
**Main Theme** Flight
**Subthemes** Traveling; Shapes
**Equipment** Large and small mats, individual ropes, hoops, traffic cones, box, benches, or beams

**Additional Lessons** Continue the same emphasis as previous lessons. Give longer time to develop sequences and quality of movement.

| Content | Teaching Strategies | References | Lesson 3a | 3b | 3c |
|---|---|---|---|---|---|
| **Entry Activity** | Scatter large and small mats around instructional area. Free practice using mats. | | Repeat previous. | Repeat previous. | Repeat previous. |
| **Part 1: Introductory Activities** *(3 to 5 minutes)* <br><br>Flight<br>Transfer of weight<br>Shapes | 1. "Run, jump, make shape, land, and roll."<br>2. "Travel on other parts of the body, in forward and backward direction."<br>3. Crab Tag—similar to simple tag; player is safe when in crab walk position. | | Repeat 1 and 2. | Design your own lesson. | Design your own lesson. |
| **Part 2: Skill Development** *(20 to 35 minutes)* <br><br>Flight<br>Transfer of weight | 1. Review upswing, jump through, and cartwheel.<br>2. Explain, demonstrate, and practice handspring (handspring over partner—lead-up skill).<br>3. "Find three other ways of initiating flight from the body" (from seat, knees, etc.).<br>4. Allow partners to make up their own matching sequence. | Handspring over Partner, p. 549<br>Handspring, p. 549<br>Flight, p. 541 | Repeat 2 and 3. | | |
| Flight, shapes, and rolling using large appartus | *Individual ropes, hoops, or traffic cones*<br>The following tasks may be applied to all of the above equipment.<br>5. "Place equipment on floor and find three different ways of crossing over your equipment."<br>6. "Develop a routine that includes flight from hands, feet, a change of direction, and a twisted shape."<br>*Boxes, benches, and beams*<br>7. "Run, jump, or leap onto apparatus, leap off, make shape, land, and roll."<br>8. "Travel around gymnasium and cross over apparatus using hands and arms."<br>9. Make up a matching sequence with your partner involving flight, shapes, and one or more pieces of equipment. | Benches, p. 536<br>Box, p. 544 | Repeat 5 to 8. | | |
| **Part 3: Closure** *(1 to 2 minutes)* <br><br>Quality of movement | Discuss the importance of practicing the sequence to improve the quality and flow of each movement. | | | | |

**Level** III   **Unit 2:** Gymnastics—Flight
**Lesson 4.** Partners in Flight
**Main Theme** Matching movements in flight
**Subthemes** Traveling; Shapes
**Equipment** Mats, chairs, cones, hoops

**Additional Lessons** Continue same emphasis as previous lesson. Again, stress quality of performance.

| Content | Teaching Strategies | References | Lesson 4a | 4b | 4c |
|---|---|---|---|---|---|
| **Entry Activity** | Place mats, cones, chairs, and hoops in play area. Free practice with equipment. | | Repeat previous. | Repeat previous. | Repeat previous. |
| **Part 1: Introductory Activities** (*3 to 5 minutes*) | 1. "Run, changing direction, speed, and level." 2. "Travel on different parts of body." 3. Play a shadow game. Find a partner. On signal, one partner tries to tag other. If tagged, change positions and continue. | Shadow game (p. 35 of this guide) | Repeat 1 to 3. | Design your own lesson. | Design your own lesson. |
| Traveling Transfer of weight | | | | | |
| **Part 2: Skill Development** (*20 to 35 minutes*) | 1. Review cartwheel and handspring. 2. Explain, demonstrate, and practice knee handspring. 3. In partners: "One stays crouched on floor, the other runs, jumps over partner, lands, and rolls." Repeat with shape in flight. | Knee handspring, p. 474 Shapes, p. 497 | Repeat 2 and 3. | | |
| Agility stunts Shapes Flight | | | | | |
| Flight, Shapes, matching movements, landing and rolling | *Traffic cones, hoops in vertical positions.* The following tasks can be applied to the above equipment. 4. "Design a matching sequence of shapes over your equipment." 5. "Add to the above sequence by including balancing and a change of speed." *Boxes, benches, beams* 6. "Make up a sequence with your partner, one following the other, and include a leap onto apparatus, a jump, a shape in flight, landing, and rolling." 7. "Design a matching sequence using two types of apparatus and show flight." | | Rotate groups and repeat challenges. | | |
| **Part 3: Closure** (*1 to 2 minutes*) | | | | | |
| Partner activities | Discuss the importance of each person sharing in the design of the matching or contrasting sequence. | | | | |

**Level** III    **Unit 2:** Gymnastics—Flight
**Lesson 5.** Flight over Apparatus
**Main Theme** Flight over apparatus
**Subtheme** Traveling
**Equipment** Variety of small equipment; Box, benches, and beams

**Additional Lessons** By the end of lesson 5, teachers will be able to judge whether to continue the same emphasis or shift to another theme.

| Content | Teaching Strategies | References | Lesson 5a | 5b | 5c |
|---|---|---|---|---|---|
| **Entry Activity** | Place a variety of small equipment in containers. Free practice with equipment. | | Repeat previous. | Repeat previous. | Repeat previous. |
| **Part 1: Introductory Activities** <br> *(3 to 5 minutes)* <br><br> Flight <br> Change of direction | 1. "Place a variety of small equipment around instructional area. Run, jump over equipment, land, change direction, and continue." <br> 2. "Travel, alternating on hands and feet." <br> 3. Play a vigorous tag game. | Tag games, p. 261 | Design your own lesson. | Design your own lesson. | Design your own lesson. |
| **Part 2: Skill Development** <br> *(20 to 35 minutes)* <br><br> Flight <br> Transfer of weight <br><br> Shape | 1. Review cartwheel, handspring, knee handspring, neckspring, upswing, and jump through. <br> 2. "Design a sequence to include a cartwheel, a balance stunt, and a change of direction." <br> 3. "Make up your own challenge stressing flight and landing." <br><br> *Box, bench, and beam* <br> 4. Explain, demonstrate, and practice the squat and straddle vault. <br> 5. Increase height of box and add springboard or mini-tramp, then repeat squat and straddle vault. <br> 6. "Invent a vault over the box or bench." Use appropriate spotters. | Squat vault, p. 546 <br> Straddle vault, p. 547 <br> Spotting, p. 547 | | | |
| **Part 3: Closure** <br> *(1 to 2 minutes)* | Ask class to suggest other themes for future gymnastic units. | | | | |

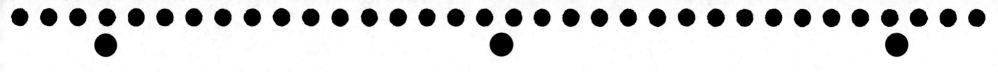

# Dance Activities

# Dance Activities
## Developmental Level I
## Unit 1: Rhythmic Movement

## Expected Learning Outcomes

**Psychomotor Skills**

1. Walking
2. Clapping and tapping
3. Change of speed
4. Change of direction
5. Running
6. Skipping
7. Change of level
8. Sliding
9. Moving in time to musical accompaniment
10. Ability to sing and move in time to musical accompaniment

**Cognitive and Affective Knowledge and Skills**

1. Ability to acquire and remember verses of singing games
2. Ability to follow simple directions
3. Ability to perform as a single performer in a large group
4. Appreciation of strengths and limitations of self and others within the class

**Level I   Unit 1:** Rhythmic Movement
**Lesson 1.** Listening and Moving
**Main Theme** Listening and moving in time to music
**Subtheme** Walk
**Equipment** Record player; Any marching tune; Class set of beanbags

**Additional Lessons** The amount of material that any class can cover in this first lesson will depend upon a number of factors—time perhaps being the most important consideration. The outline will help those teachers who wish to teach one or two extra lessons before progressing to lesson 2.

| Content | Teaching Strategies | References | Lesson 1a | 1b | 1c |
|---|---|---|---|---|---|
| **Entry Activity** | Place beanbags in four containers. Turn on brisk, walking music (any good marching music 4/4 meter) and ask children to get a beanbag and play with it in their own space. | | Repeat previous. | Repeat with new music. | Repeat with new music. |
| **Part 1: Introductory Activities** *(5 to 6 minutes)*<br><br>Walking<br>Clapping<br>Tapping | Put equipment away and ask children to find their own space and sit cross-legged on the floor. Ask class to listen very carefully to the music. (Use marching music from above.)<br>1. Clap hands with teacher in time to music.<br>2. Tap floor with teacher in time to music.<br>3. Tap knees, chest, and other parts of body in time to music.<br>4. Clap while standing.<br>5. Clap while walking on the spot.<br>6. Walk around instructional space in time to music. Teacher varies tempo from slow to fast and back to slow. | Walking skill, p. 44 | Repeat introductory activities. | Repeat introductory activities with new music. | Play Nine Lives (p. 30 of this guide)—run until music stops. |
| **Part 2: Skill Development** *(10 to 20 minutes)*<br><br>Walking<br>Clapping | 1. "Can you walk forward and backward in time to the music?" Select one or two for demonstrations.<br>2. "Now, try walking and clapping in time to the music."<br>3. Present other challenges such as "walk in a circle, walk on toes, walk on heels, walk like a giant, or walk like animals or mechanical things." Continue pattern.<br>4. "Squirrels in the Trees":<br>Ask children to find a partner and make a line facing you. Walk children into a large double circle. Children forming inside circle walk four paces toward the center. Shift three children from outer circle to inside circle.<br>  A. Call inside circle "squirrels" and outside circle "trees."<br>  B. Outside circle (trees) start clapping in time to music (same music as above), and inside circle (squirrels) join hands and walk clockwise.<br>  C. When the teacher stops the music, squirrels must quickly hide behind a tree. Any child who cannot find a tree returns to the center. Trees now become squirrels and repeat game.<br>  D. Once the children understand the game, vary the tempo and the intensity of the music.<br>  E. Change the musical accompaniment and locomotor skill to a run or a skip. | Animal movements, p. 461 | Repeat 1 and 2.<br><br><br><br><br>Repeat Squirrels in the Trees. | Repeat 2 with new music.<br><br><br><br>Repeat Squirrels in the Trees to new music. | Leave out.<br><br><br><br>Repeat Squirrels in the Trees with new music. |
| **Part 3: Closure** *(1 to 2 minutes)*<br><br>Listening and moving in time to music | Discuss and illustrate different ways of walking. | | | | |

**Level I   Unit 1:** Rhythmic Movement
**Lesson 2.** Walking
**Main Theme** Walking
**Subtheme** Change of direction
**Equipment** Record player; Musical accompaniment for selected dances; Variety of play or utility balls

**Additional Lessons** Several additional lessons may be added to allow time to introduce other singing games that stress walking, individual and group experimentation, and listening skills. Follow the same procedure suggested previously for each of the following lessons.

| Content | Teaching Strategies | References | Lesson 2a | 2b | 2c |
|---|---|---|---|---|---|
| **Entry Activity** | Place a variety of inflated balls in the four containers. Play lively 4/4 musical tunes and tell children to take a ball in their own space and practice bouncing to music. | | Repeat previous. | Repeat previous. | Repeat previous. |
| **Part 1: Introductory Activities** (4 to 5 minutes)<br><br>Walking<br>Directional movements | *Note:* Have children learn words, rhythm, phrases, and tempo of "Ring around the Rosy" (or "Did You Ever See a Lassie") before beginning lesson 2. Provide background information (pictures, slides, music, history) appropriate to age level.<br>Put equipment away and ask children to find their own space.<br>1. Play "Ring around the Rosy" and have children stand and clap hands in time to music. Add walking in place and clapping hands.<br>2. Walk around instructional area in time to music. As music is playing, add "backward, forward, in a circle, or on the spot," etc.<br>3. Add "walk on toes, lightly, like a bear," etc.<br>4. Play "Did You Ever See a Lassie" and repeat 1, 2, and 3 above. | "Ring around the Rosy," p. 588<br><br>"Did You Ever See a Lassie," p. 589 | Repeat 1 to 3. | Play Tails (p. 31 of this guide). | Play Nine Lives (p. 30 of this guide). |
| **Part 2: Skill Development** (10 to 20 minutes)<br><br>Walking<br>Nonlocomotor movements<br>Change of direction | Arrange children in a single circle, girls on boys' right and all facing the center with hands joined.<br>The following tasks can be carried out for the "Farmer in the Dell" and the "Muffin Man."<br>1. Without music, walk clockwise around the circle, then drop to a squatting position. Repeat one or two more times.<br>2. With music and singing the verse repeat above.<br>3. Repeat 2 and allow children to make up their own ending, such as "jump-up, turn around," etc. Allow one or two children to show the others their own ending.<br>4. Add clapping as they move around the circle.<br>Children of this age level enjoy variety as well as repetition within each and every lesson.<br>Repeat Squirrels in the Trees from the previous lesson adding variations in locomotor movements, new musical accompaniments, and/or special teacher signals to sharpen their listening skills. | "Farmer in the Dell," p. 586<br>"Muffin Man," p. 588<br><br><br><br><br><br><br><br>Squirrels in the Trees (p. 185 of this guide) | Leave out.<br><br><br><br><br><br><br><br><br>Repeat "Ring around the Rosy." | Introduce "Farmer in the Dell."<br><br><br><br><br><br><br><br>Repeat "Ring around the Rosy." | Introduce "Muffin Man."<br><br><br><br><br><br><br><br>Repeat "Farmer in the Dell." |

**Part 3: Closure**
*(1 to 2 minutes)*

Walking in time to musical accompaniment

Discuss and illustrate different directional movements.

**Level** I  **Unit 1:** Rhythmic Movement
**Lesson 3.** Running
**Main Theme** Running
**Subtheme** Change of direction
**Equipment** Record player; Musical accompaniment for selected dances; Variety of small equipment

**Additional Lessons** The suggestions made in the previous lesson apply to this lesson. Teachers should check the dances recommended for this age level, or if the level of ability is relatively high, choose one or two dances from the grades 2–3 list.

| Content | Teaching Strategies | References | Lesson 3a | 3b | 3c |
|---|---|---|---|---|---|
| **Entry Activity** | Place individual ropes, beanbags, and inflated balls in containers. Free play with equipment to music. | | Repeat previous. | Repeat previous. | Repeat previous. |
| **Part 1: Introductory Activities** (4 to 5 minutes)  Running | *Note:* Have children learn the words, rhythm, phrases, and tempo of "Dance of Greeting" before beginning lesson 3.  Put equipment away and ask children to find a space.  1. "Run in any direction you like, but do not touch or bump into anyone."  2. As the children are running, add "as slow as you can . . . on your toes," etc.  3. Run in time to music of "Dance of Greeting."  4. Add additional limitations such as "backward, on toes," etc. | "Danish Dance of Greeting," p. 588 | Repeat 1 to 3. | Play Nine Lives (p. 30 of this guide). | Repeat 1 to 4. |
| **Part 2: Skill Development** (10 to 20 minutes)  Running  Bow and curtsy  Change of direction | "Danish Dance of Greeting":  Arrange class into partners and in a scattered formation.  1. Begin with partners facing and without music. Demonstrate and practice clapping hands, bow and curtsey, stamping, and turning in place. Repeat with music.  2. Repeat 1 adding "Join inside hands and run to a new space and repeat the sequence."  3. Ask partners to make up their own dance. Play music and observe whether they, as partners, can work together in developing their own dance. Select one or two for demonstration.  *Note:* If this task appears to be too difficult, say "Make up your own dance with clapping, a bow and curtsy, and running in your own space." | | Repeat 1 and 2. | "Baa, Baa, Black Sheep" | Leave out. |
| Running  Bow and curtsy  Directional movements | "Baa, Baa, Black Sheep":  Arrange children into a large circle of couples with all facing the center. The girl is on the boy's right side.  1. Without music, demonstrate and practice the action to accompany the song.  2. Repeat 1 with music.  3. Without music, repeat action for song and the sixteen steps counterclockwise for the chorus.  4. Perform complete dance with musical accompaniment.  5. Ask children if they would like to change any part of the dance by adding something new or by changing any part of existing dance. | "Baa, Baa, Black Sheep," p. 585 | Repeat 4. | "Danish Dance of Greeting" | Repeat "Baa, Baa, Black Sheep" and "Muffin Man." |
| **Part 3: Closure** (1 to 2 minutes)  Running in time to musical accompaniment | Discuss and illustrate different ways of meeting and greeting. | | | | |

**Level I  Unit 1:** Rhythmic Movement
**Lesson 4.** Skipping
**Main Theme** Skipping
**Subtheme** Nonlocomotor movements
**Equipment** Record player; Musical accompaniment for the selected dances; Variety of small equipment

**Additional Lessons** If additional lessons are desired, follow the same procedure outlined in previous lessons. Do not hesitate to try the dances suggested for Level II if the level of ability and interest is sufficiently high.

| Content | Teaching Strategies | References | Lesson 4a | 4b | 4c |
|---|---|---|---|---|---|
| **Entry Activity** | Place a variety of small equipment in containers. Free play with equipment to music. | | Repeat previous. | Repeat previous. | Repeat previous. |
| **Part 1: Introductory Activities**<br>*(4 to 5 minutes)*<br><br>Skipping<br>Change of level | *Note:* Have children learn the words, rhythm, phrases, and tempo of "Loobie Loo" before beginning lesson 4.<br>Put equipment away and find a space.<br>1. Ask children to walk in any direction without touching anyone. Later add "now run . . . change to a skip."<br>2. "Try skipping and change level when I call out . . . away you go . . . low . . . very high. . ." etc. | "Loobie Loo," p. 586<br>Skipping, p. 50 | Repeat 1 and 2. | Play Tails (p. 31 of this guide). | Design your own lesson. |
| **Part 2: Skill Development**<br>*(10 to 20 minutes)*<br><br>Skipping, walking, running<br>Nonlocomotor movements<br>—shaking, etc.<br>—change of direction | Since most children of this age level know how to perform a skip, turn, shake, and other skills of this dance, they can be taught the dance "Loobie Loo" directly from the circle formation. Arrange children into a large circle facing the center with hands joined.<br>1. Without music, circle left for eight skipping steps, then back for eight skipping steps. Drop hands and face center.<br>2. Repeat 1 with music and singing chorus.<br>3. Without music, demonstrate and practice placing right hand in and shaking it, then turning body around.<br>4. Repeat 3 with music and singing verse 1.<br>5. With music, complete action, chorus, and song of first two verses.<br>*Note:* Most children from this point on can copy the teacher as she or he demonstrates the action of the next verse while the music is playing.<br>6. Ask children to add their own movements to the dance.<br>At this stage in the development of the dance unit, children should be able to review one or more dances during this part of the lesson. The following represents dances using a walk or a run.<br>1. Review "Danish Dance of Greeting."<br>2. Review "Ring around the Rosy."<br>3. Review other dances as time permits. | Supplementary dances, p. 583 | Repeat 5.<br><br><br><br><br><br><br><br><br>Review "Loobie Loo." | Leave out.<br><br><br><br><br><br><br><br><br>Review "Loobie Loo" and "Danish Dance of Greeting." | |
| **Part 3: Closure**<br>*(1 to 2 minutes)*<br><br>Skipping in time to musical accompaniment | Discuss and illustrate skipping in different directions. | | | | |

**Level I Unit 1:** Rhythmic Movement
**Lesson 5.** Sliding
**Main Theme** Sliding
**Subtheme** Change of direction
**Equipment** Record player; Musical accompaniment for selected dances; Class set of individual ropes

**Additional Lessons** If this unit has been successful, additional lessons might concentrate on two or three dances to develop more quality and perhaps for purposes of showing parents on a forthcoming visitors' day. New dances can also be selected from the supplementary list in the text.

| Content | Teaching Strategies | References | Lesson 5a | 5b | 5c |
|---|---|---|---|---|---|
| **Entry Activity** | Place individual ropes in the containers. Free practice with individual ropes. Play fast marching tune. | | Repeat previous with hoops. | Repeat previous with beanbags. | Repeat previous with ropes. |
| **Part 1: Introductory Activities**<br>(4 to 5 minutes) | *Note:* Have children learn the words, rhythm, phrases, and tempo of "Sally Go Round the Moon" before the beginning of lesson 5.<br>Put equipment away and find space.<br>1. "Travel lightly in any direction, showing a change of direction."<br>2. "Change to a slide to the side."<br>3. "Change to a gallop (a slide in a forward direction)."<br>4. "Can you travel in different directions using a slide and a gallop?" | "Sally Go Round the Moon," p. 587<br>Sliding, p. 51 | Repeat 1 to 4. | Play Nine Lives (p. 30 of this guide). | Design your own lesson. |
| **Part 2: Skill Development**<br>(10 to 20 minutes)<br><br>Sliding<br>Clapping<br>Stunts | Teaching the steps and movements of "Sally Go Round the Moon" is very similar to introducing "Loobie Loo." By this time in the unit, five- and six-year-olds should be quite capable of learning the new movements of this new dance from the basic single circle formation.<br>　Arrange children into a large single circle facing the center and with hands joined.<br>1. With music, teach slide step around circle and stop. Have all release hands and jump up and clap their hands.<br>2. Explain that the next time they stop, they should jump up and perform any stunt they wish.<br>3. Repeat full dance with music and with children singing.<br>4. Teacher or children change the nature of the stunt "just moving hands, turning in the air, making various shapes." | | Repeat 3 and 4. | Leave out. | |
| | Review one or more dances with variations in each dance provided by the teacher or suggested by the children.<br>1. Review "Loobie Loo" with a skip or slide.<br>2. Review "Danish Dance of Greeting" with a run or skip.<br>3. Review "Did You Ever See a Lassie" with a walk or skip. | Supplementary list of dances, p. 583 | Review any previous dances. | Review any previous dances. | |
| **Part 3: Closure**<br>(1 to 2 minutes)<br><br>Sliding in time to musical accompaniment | Discuss and illustrate sliding sideways and galloping forward. | | | | |

# Dance Activities
## Developmental Level I
## Unit 2: Creative Dance

## Expected Learning Outcomes

### Psychomotor Skills

1. Traveling and stopping
2. Using general and limited space
3. Moving different parts of the body in time to music
4. Performing individual and partner movement sequences
5. Moving in different directions
6. Changing speed from quick to slow
7. Performing movement skills in relationship to other persons or to equipment
8. Moving in different levels—high, medium, and low
9. Ability to make a variety of shapes—stretch, curl, wide, narrow, and twisted
10. Ability to perform strong and light movements

### Cognitive and Affective Knowledge and Skills

1. Ability to plan a creative movement response to a variety of stimuli
2. Ability to work and share creative ideas with another person
3. Appreciation of the creative talents of other performers
4. Understanding of a more extensive and descriptive movement vocabulary

**Level** I    **Unit 2:** Creative Dance
**Lesson 1.** Body Awareness
**Main Theme** Total and individual body movements
**Subtheme** Use of space
**Equipment** Tambourine or drum; Class set of beanbags

**Additional Lessons** Several additional lessons may be developed from this lesson. The following will illustrate how to extend ideas or develop new variations to the above lesson.

| Content | Teaching Strategies | References | Lesson 1a | 1b | 1c |
|---|---|---|---|---|---|
| **Entry Activity** | Place beanbags in containers. Free play with beanbags to music. | | Repeat previous. | Repeat previous. | Repeat previous. |
| **Part 1: Introductory Activities** (5 to 7 minutes)<br><br>Traveling and stopping<br>Using general space | *Note:* In previous game and gymnastic units, children have learned various aspects of space awareness (personal space, directional movement, etc.). The main focus here is to move and stop in time to the shaking and beating of a tambourine. Other instruments such as drums or sand blocks may also be used. Pose the following challenges:<br>1. "Walk very quickly anywhere you like without touching anyone . . . go!"<br>2. "When I shake the tambourine, walk anywhere, but when I tap it two times, stop and listen for the next task . . . repeat . . . shake . . . say "run" . . . tap, tap, shake . . . "hop" . . . tap, tap, shake . . . "jump." Continue pattern. | Inexpensive instruments, Appendix B, p. 636 | Repeat 1 and 2 with another instrument. | Repeat 1 and 2 adding levels. | Repeat 1 and 2 adding quick and slow. |
| **Part 2: Theme Development** (10 to 20 minutes)<br><br>Moving different parts of body in time to music | Ask children to find a new space and sit down with legs together. Continue with the following tasks.<br>1. "When I shake the tambourine, tap your toes as lightly as you can on the floor."<br>2. "Can you move them another way?"<br>3. "Could you show me another part of your body that you can move?" Select different parts—elbows, head, etc.—for demonstrations and continue pattern.<br>4. "When I start shaking the tambourine, start tapping your toes, then shake a new part, then another new part." Keep shaking long enough for children to complete their tasks. | Vocabulary, p. 615<br>Sample lesson, p. 616 | Repeat 1 and 4 with new instrument. | Repeat 1 to 4 adding levels. | Repeat 1 to 4 adding quick and slow. |
| Sequence development | 5. "When I shake the tambourine, move around in one way, but when I tap twice, freeze, turn around in your space, then move in another way." Continue pattern for three or four different locomotor movements. | Vocabulary, p. 615 | Repeat 1 to 5 with new instrument. | Repeat 1 to 5 adding levels. | Repeat 1 to 5 adding quick and slow. |
| **Part 3: Closure** (1 to 2 minutes)<br><br>Moving in time to musical accompaniment | Discuss and illustrate moving different parts of the body. | | | | |

**Level I  Unit 2:** Creative Dance
**Lesson 2.** Effort
**Main Theme**  Quick and slow
**Subtheme**  Traveling
**Equipment**  Individual ropes (15); Beanbags (15); Drum

**Additional Lessons**  When planning one or more additional lessons, continue to stress "quick and slow" as well as select subthemes from parts of lesson 1.

| Content | Teaching Strategies | References | Lesson 2a | 2b | 2c |
|---|---|---|---|---|---|
| **Entry Activity** | Place individual ropes and beanbags in containers. Free practice with equipment to music. | | Repeat previous. | Repeat previous. | Repeat previous. |
| **Part 1: Introductory Activities**<br>*(5 to 6 minutes)*<br><br>Quick and slow<br>Traveling<br>—in different directions | Put equipment away and find a space.<br>*Note:* The drum should be used in this lesson to emphasize tempo (change of speed) and to provide a variation from the instrument (tambourine) used in lesson 1.<br>1. "When I start tapping the drum, run anywhere you like, but do not touch anyone. Be ready to freeze on two loud beats of my drum. Away you go!"<br>2. "Next, I am going to beat my drum slowly, then quickly, then slowly again. See if you can run to the speed of my drum! . . . off you go!" Beat the drum slowly for eight beats, quickly for another eight beats, then slowly for the last eight beats.<br>3. Repeat 2 and ask children to change to a walk, hop, or jump. Continue pattern using a variety of other locomotor movements. | | Repeat 1 to 3. | Repeat 2 and 3. | Play Nine Lives (p. 30 of this guide). |
| **Part 2: Theme Development**<br>*(10 to 20 minutes)*<br><br>Quick and slow<br>Rising and sinking<br><br>Sequence development | Ask children to sit on the floor. Present the following challenges:<br>1. "See if you can tap your toes to the beat of my drum." Begin beating the drum very slowly, increase to fairly fast, then slow again.<br>2. "This time, when I beat the drum, reach up to the ceiling with your fingertips (or toward the wall or another child)." Vary speed of the drum beat.<br>3. Repeat 2 using elbows, knees, shoulders, or other parts of the body.<br>4. "As I beat the drum, grow very slowly up to the ceiling, then slowly all the way back to your sitting position." After one or two tries, vary the speed—slowly up and quickly down.<br>5. Everyone stand up. "This time move your feet anyway you like, but try and keep in time to my drum."<br>6. "Can you move through very wet and gluey mud?" Make the drum beats slow and sustained.<br>7. "How would you move if you were on the moon? If you were a bionic man or woman?" Continue pattern. | Vocabulary, p. 616<br><br><br>Stimuli, p. 617 | Repeat 1 and 2.<br><br><br>Repeat 4 and 5. | Repeat 3.<br><br><br>Repeat 7. | Repeat 1 and 2 with tambourine.<br><br>Repeat 7 with tambourine. |
| **Part 3: Closure**<br>*(1 to 2 minutes)*<br><br>Speed | Discuss and illustrate moving quickly and slowly in different directions. | | | | |

**Level** I　**Unit 2:** Creative Dance
**Lesson 3.** Space
**Main Theme** Near and far
**Subthemes** Traveling on different parts; Quick and slow
**Equipment** Class set of beanbags; drum; Selection of small equipment

**Additional Lessons** Additional lessons should begin with a brief introductory activity, then move to part 2. Longer and more complex sequences can be developed by this age group. It is also a time to allow children to use their creative talents in planning and practicing their own creative dances.

| Content | Teaching Strategies | References | Lesson 3a | 3b | 3c |
|---|---|---|---|---|---|
| **Entry Activity** | Place individual ropes, hoops, and beanbags in containers. Free practice with equipment to music. | | Repeat previous. | Repeat previous. | Repeat previous. |
| **Part 1: Introductory Activities**<br>*(4 to 5 minutes)*<br><br>Traveling<br>—in different directions<br>Levels<br>—low and high | Put equipment away and find a space. Use a drum, tambourine, or another percussion instrument and stress keeping in time. Vary the tempo within each challenge.<br>　1. "As soon as I begin beating my drum, start traveling in time to the drum beats and move anywhere you like." Add "travel as low as you can, as high, sideways," etc.<br>　2. "Find your own way of traveling on all fours, three parts, like a giant." Continue pattern, using different animal names. | Sound accompaniment, p. 621 | Repeat 1 and 2. | Play Nine Lives (p. 30 of this guide). | Design your own lesson. |
| **Part 2: Theme Development**<br>*(10 to 20 minutes)*<br><br>Near and far<br>Quick and slow<br>Partner sequences<br>Transfer of weight | *Individual activities:*<br>Ask children to get a beanbag and find a space. The beanbag becomes a focus for the following tasks that will stress near and far.<br>　1. "When I start shaking my tambourine, move away from the beanbag." Shake it quickly for a few seconds. "Now, show me how you can crawl (use words like slither, or, to stimulate a form of moving, slo . . . w . . . l . . . y)." Shake tambourine slowly as children return to their beanbags.<br>　2. Repeat 1 with other ways of moving such as prancing away from and galloping back to the beanbag, waddling away and marching back to, or flying away and swimming or rolling back. Continue pattern.<br><br>*Partner activities:*<br>Ask children to find a partner and a brand new space. If the children have progressed to the point where they understand the basic movement concepts and can work independently within a large group, they should be ready to work with a partner. The same challenges used for individuals can be applied to partners. To illustrate (use above musical accompaniment):<br>　1. Have one partner remain in a space while the other moves away. Partner who remains stationary moves toward his or her partner.<br>　2. Have both move away from each other then back together (prancing away—galloping back).<br>　3. Ask partners to make up a movement story of two people, animals, or mechanical things (trucks, robots, etc.) moving away from each other and coming back together. | Vocabulary, p. 615<br>Locomotor skills, p. 43<br><br><br><br><br><br><br><br>Stimuli, p. 617 | Leave out.<br><br><br><br><br><br><br><br>Repeat 1 to 3. | Leave out.<br><br><br><br><br><br><br><br>Repeat 1 to 3 adding to or changing challenges. | |
| **Part 3: Closure**<br>*(1 to 2 minutes)* | Discuss near and far, using other situations such as playground, home, and other locations familiar to this age group. | | | | |

**Level I** **Unit 2:** Creative Dance
**Lesson 4.** Relationships
**Main Theme** Relationship to teacher or to a partner
**Subtheme** Traveling
**Equipment** Tambourine, variety of small equipment; Record player, musical accompaniment for selected activities

**Additional Lessons** If additional lessons are desired, continue emphasis on relations with either the teacher or a partner.

| Content | Teaching Strategies | References | Lesson 4a | 4b | 4c |
|---|---|---|---|---|---|
| **Entry Activity** | Place a variety of small equipment in the containers. Free practice with equipment to music. | | Repeat previous. | Repeat previous. | Repeat previous. |
| **Part 1: Introductory Activities**<br>*(3 to 5 minutes)*<br><br>Traveling<br>—running<br>Shapes<br>—stretch, curl, or twisted | Children should be able to draw upon skills learned in previous gymnastic lessons. Shapes such as stretch, curl, and twisted will become subthemes in this lesson. Use an appropriate record or play a percussion instrument for each introductory activity.<br>1. Run, jump, and change direction.<br>2. Run, jump, make a shape, land, change direction. Continue pattern. | Shapes,<br>pp. 37, 615<br>Expressive words for shapes, p. 615 | Repeat 1 and 2. | Play Tails (p. 31 of this guide). | Design your own lesson. |
| **Part 2: Theme Development**<br>*(10 to 20 minutes)*<br><br>Relationships<br>—to teacher<br>—to partner<br>Traveling<br>—in different directions<br>Shapes<br>—statues<br><br><br><br><br>Relationship<br>—with a partner<br>Traveling | *Individual activities:*<br>Ask the class to move into their own space. Stand in the center of the group. Present the following challenges. Use a tambourine to accompany each challenge.<br>1. "When I shake my tambourine, creep away from me. When I change to loud beating, rush back to me." Repeat each several times.<br>2. Repeat 1 hopping away and jumping back.<br>3. Repeat 1 moving on three parts away and returning on four parts.<br>4. "Move away and when I beat three quick taps, freeze into your own statue. As I shake, move to a new space until I tap three times, signaling a new statue." Continue pattern.<br>*Partner activities:*<br>Find a partner and a new space.<br>1. "See how many ways you and your partner can move about the space." Suggest skipping, side by side, follow the leader, etc. Play a bouncy 4/4 musical accompaniment.<br>2. "Can you keep traveling together in the same way, but also show moving low to the floor and as high as you can?"<br>3. "Can you make up a sequence that has a run together, then hop away from each other?" Select one or two for demonstrations.<br>4. "Show me how you can make up a dance with your partner that has a meeting or greeting action and saying good-bye." | Words, p. 615<br>Relationships,<br>pp. 41, 581 | Repeat 2 and 3.<br><br><br><br><br><br><br><br>Repeat 1 to 3. | Leave out.<br><br><br><br><br><br><br><br>Repeat 3 to 4. | |
| **Part 3: Closure**<br>*(1 to 2 minutes)*<br><br>Shapes | Discuss how the body can make different types of shapes. | | | | |

**Level I**    **Unit 2:** Creative Dance
**Lesson 5.** Stimuli
**Main Theme** Moods
**Subtheme** Body awareness
**Equipment** Variety of small equipment; Musical accompaniment for selected dance challenges

**Additional Lessons** Numerous additional lessons can be developed around such themes as objects, stories, poems, or feelings. Teachers are encouraged to try various approaches from lesson to lesson and within each lesson.

| Content | Teaching Strategies | References | Lesson 5a | 5b | 5c |
|---|---|---|---|---|---|
| **Entry Activity** | Place a variety of small equipment in the containers. Free practice with equipment to music. | | Repeat previous. | Repeat previous. | Repeat previous. |
| **Part 1: Introductory Activities** (3 to 5 minutes)<br><br>Traveling<br>Quick and slow | The central theme of this lesson is moods. It is very important to have a discussion with the children in the classroom just prior to coming to the gymnasium. The discussion should bring out different kinds of moods and, more importantly, it should emotionally and creatively prepare children for the lesson. Without music, ask children to run to show they are very frightened, very tired, very happy, etc. Teachers should vary their voice tones and personally animate some of these expressions to stimulate children to react in particular ways. | Stimuli, p. 617<br>Strong and light, pp. 615, 617 | Repeat part 1, changing mood to strong and weak. | Design your own lesson. | Design your own lesson. |
| **Part 2: Theme Development** (10 to 20 minutes)<br><br>Traveling<br>Strong and light<br>Quick and slow | This part of the lesson should encourage children to use individual parts (fingers, legs, head) to express different moods.<br>1. Ask children to find a space and sit on the floor. "If you feel very, very happy like the day your grandpa bought you the puppy, could you sit still like you are now?" Allow time for a few comments, then ask the class to show you how they can show you a happy mood.<br>2. Continue pattern established in 1 such as, "When you are sad, do you hold your head up or down? your shoulder forward or over?" Point out other features, then say, "When I play the music, you are a very sad and tired person." Play a slow, sad musical accompaniment.<br>3. At this point, the teacher can stimulate other moods such as "being very light, lonely, angry, shaky, heavy, etc." Ask children to suggest feelings they would like to express and continue the pattern. The latter approach will, in most cases, produce very positive results as children will express feelings and ideas of immediate interest to themselves.<br>4. Ask children to find a space and sit down. Two approaches may be tried here. First select a musical accompaniment that would stimulate quick and light movement. Ask the class to express a feeling of happiness as the music plays. Stress using the whole body, just hands, fingers, toes, etc. The second approach is to play the music and ask the children to decide on the feeling the music gives each of them, then express it in any way they want. | Words, p. 615<br>Ideas, p. 614<br>Music, p. 619<br><br><br><br><br><br><br><br><br><br><br><br>Stimuli, p. 617 | Repeat part 2 changing mood to strong and weak.<br><br><br><br><br><br><br><br><br><br><br><br>Repeat 4 changing music to stress strong and weak. | | |
| **Part 3: Closure** (1 to 2 minutes)<br><br>Moods | Discuss different ways parts of the body (face, shoulders, etc.) can express happiness or some other mood. | | | | |

# Dance Activities
## Developmental Level II
## Unit 1: Folk Dance

## Expected Learning Outcomes

**Psychomotor Skills**

1. Change of direction, pathway, and level
2. Change of speed
3. Traveling in time to musical accompaniment
4. Performing a variety of nonlocomotor movements— clap, shake, twist, swing, etc.
5. Performing a variety of locomotor skills—walk, run, skip, slide
6. Ability to perform the bleking step

**Cognitive and Affective Knowledge and Skills**

1. Ability to perform independently, with a partner, or in a group
2. Appreciation of the cultural heritage of various dances
3. Appreciation of the feelings and sensitivities of others
4. Ability to lead and follow as the dance movement patterns dictate
5. Understanding of measure, accent, tempo, and phrase

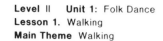

**Level** II **Unit 1:** Folk Dance
**Lesson 1.** Walking
**Main Theme** Walking
**Subthemes** Arching; Swinging
**Equipment** Record player, records, individual ropes

**Additional Lessons** During the initial lesson of this unit, several supplementary lessons are normally required to complete all aspects of each dance as well as to introduce new dances that emphasize similar locomotor skills and dance patterns.

| Content | Teaching Strategies | References | Lesson 1a | 1b | 1c |
|---|---|---|---|---|---|
| **Entry Activity** | Place individual ropes in containers. Free practice with individual ropes to music. | | Repeat previous. | Repeat previous. | Repeat previous. |
| **Part 1: Introductory Activities** *(5 to 6 minutes)* Walking Running Change of direction | *Note:* Teach children the words, rhythm, phrase, and tempo of "Shoo Fly" before the beginning of lesson 1. As soon as all children are present, "Equipment away and find a space." 1. Explain to the class that you are going to play "Shoo Fly" (or select a brisk march) in a very fast tempo. "As soon as the music starts, walk in time to the music, changing direction whenever you have an open space." 2. "In time to the music, walk on your toes, on heels, change to a light run," etc. | "Shoo Fly," p. 594 Teaching strategies, p. 577 | Repeat 1 and 2. | Repeat 1 and 2. | Repeat "Shoo Fly." |
| **Part 2: Dance Development** *(20 to 35 minutes)* Walking Shapes—arching, swinging | If the children have been taught previous game and gymnastic units, they would have become accustomed to working in partners and group activities. Thus, most children should find little difficulty in participating in the first dance of this unit. "Shoo Fly": Arrange children in a large circle with the girls on the boys' rights. Hands are joined and all facing the center of the circle. 1. Without music, demonstrate and practice the action of the song. Repeat with music, starting slowly, then increase tempo to normal speed for this dance. 2. Without music, demonstrate and practice the action of the chorus. Repeat with music. 3. With music, repeat both parts of the dance. Continue to end of music. 4. Change method of shifting to next partner. | Dance positions, p. 572 | Repeat 3 and 4. | Review "Shoo Fly." | Introduce "Paw Paw Patch," p. 595 |
| | Since this is the first dance lesson, the above activities may take up all the available time. However, if time permits, try the following additional challenges to the above dance activity. "Now, quickly organize yourselves into groups of four. Can you repeat the dance in your new group and change the pattern or skills any way you like? You must, however, keep in time to the music." Select one or two groups to demonstrate their new dance versions of "Shoo Fly." | | Repeat challenge. | Repeat challenge with new dance. | Repeat challenge with new dance. |
| **Part 3: Closure** *(1 to 4 minutes)* Walking | Have one or two groups explain how they made up a variation of "Shoo Fly." | | | | |

**Level II    Unit 1:** Folk Dance
**Lesson 2.** Walking
**Main Theme** Walking
**Subthemes** Walking; Shaking; Stamping
**Equipment** Record or tape recorder, records or tapes, small equipment listed for the intermediate grades.

**Additional Lessons** If additional lessons emphasizing running are desired, check the list of supplementary dances for this age range. Further, if the level of ability is relatively high, review chapter 30, "Rhythm and Movement" for new ideas, or check dances.

| Content | Teaching Strategies | References | Lesson 2a | 2b | 2c |
|---|---|---|---|---|---|
| **Entry Activity** | Place individual ropes, beanbags, and hoops in the containers. Free practice with equipment to music. | | Repeat previous. | Repeat previous. | Repeat previous. |
| **Part 1: Introductory Activities**<br>*(4 to 5 minutes)*<br><br>Running<br>Change of direction<br>Change of level | *Note:* Teach children the words, rhythm, phrases, and tempo of "Jolly Is the Miller" before beginning lesson 2.<br>Equipment away and find a space.<br>1. "Run and change direction and level." Play "Danish Dance of Greeting" in a fast tempo.<br>2. "Make up a sequence of running steps, moving on your toes, heels, stiff-legged, and another way you can make up." Ask one or two children to demonstrate their routines to the class. | "Jolly Is the Miller," p. 594 | Repeat 1 and 2 with new music. | Repeat 1 and 2 with new music. | Design your own lesson. |
| **Part 2: Dance Development**<br>*(20 to 35 minutes)*<br><br>Running<br>Clapping<br>Stamping<br>Turning | "Jolly Is the Miller":<br>Arrange class in a double circle facing counterclockwise. Girls are on the inside.<br>1. Without music, demonstrate and practice the action of the song. Repeat with music, starting slowly, then increasing tempo to normal speed for this dance.<br>2. Divide class into groups of four, six, or eight, and ask each group to modify the dance in any way they wish. Have groups demonstrate to the rest of the class.<br>3. Review "Shoo Fly" with and without variations.<br>4. Review "Paw Paw Patch" with and without variations. | Rhythmics in movement, p. 562 | Introduce "Glow Worm Mixer."<br><br><br><br>Review "Jolly is the Miller." | Introduce a new dance.<br><br><br><br>Review "Glow Worm Mixer." | |
| **Part 3: Closure**<br>*(1 to 2 minutes)*<br><br>Walking | Discuss and illustrate walking in time to same music but changing tempo: slow, fast, slow. | | | | |

**Main Theme** Skipping
**Subthemes** Running; Arching
**Equipment** Recorder and records or tapes

| Content | Teaching Strategies | References | Lesson 3a | 3b | 3c |
|---|---|---|---|---|---|
| **Entry Activity** | Place a variety of small equipment in the containers. Free practice with equipment to music. | | Repeat previous. | Repeat previous. | Repeat previous. |
| **Part 1: Introductory Activities** *(4 to 5 minutes)* | *Note:* Teach children the words, rhythm, phrases, and tempo of "A Hunting We Will Go" before beginning lesson 3. Ask children to put equipment away and find a space. | "A Hunting We Will Go," p. 593 | Repeat 1 and 2 with music. | Repeat 1 and 2 with "Pop Goes the Weasel" music. | Design your own lesson. |
| Skipping<br>Change of direction<br>Change of level | 1. Explain that you will turn on music for "A Hunting We Will Go." "Once the music starts, skip anywhere, changing your direction and level."<br>2. Find a partner and repeat 1 in a "follow the leader" fashion. Change positions after each performer has completed this sequence. | | | | |
| **Part 2: Dance Development** *(20 to 35 minutes)* | "A Hunting We Will Go": Divide class into two groups. Arrange groups into two parallel lines facing each other. Girls form one line; boys form the other line. | | Review "A Hunting We Will Go." | Review "A Hunting We Will Go." | |
| Walking<br>Running<br>Skipping<br>Clapping<br>Arching | 1. Without music, demonstrate and practice the action movements of the song. Repeat with music.<br>2. Without music, demonstrate and practice the action movements of the chorus.<br>3. With music, repeat both parts of the dance. Repeat dance with the new head couple.<br>4. Exchange boys from group A with the boys from group B and repeat dance.<br>5. Allow children to modify or add new parts to the dance.<br>6. Review "Jolly Is the Miller" with or without modifications.<br>7. Review "Shoo Fly" with or without variations.<br>8. Review other dances as desired. | "Jolly Is the Miller," p. 594<br>"Shoo Fly," p. 594 | Review "Jolly Is the Miller." | Review "A Hunting We Will Go." | |
| **Part 3: Closure** *(1 to 2 minutes)* | | | | | |
| Skipping | Ask children to describe and illustrate how they changed "A Hunting We Will Go." | | | | |

**Level II**    **Unit 1:** Folk Dance    **Activity** Dance
**Lesson 4.** Sliding
**Main Theme** Sliding
**Subthemes** Skipping; Running; Walking
**Equipment** Recorder and tapes or records

**Additional Lessons** If this unit has been successful, the teacher will be in search of dances that emphasize the sliding step plus partner-type activities performed within a single or double circle formation. Check the supplementary list of dances or other recommended dance references.

| Content | Teaching Strategies | References | Lesson 4a | 4b | 4c |
|---|---|---|---|---|---|
| **Entry Activity** | Place a variety of small equipment in the containers. Free practice with equipment to music. | | Repeat previous. | Repeat previous. | Repeat previous. |
| **Part 1: Introductory Activities**<br>*(4 to 5 minutes)*<br><br>Sliding<br>Running<br>Skipping | *Note:* Teach children the words, rhythm, phrases, and tempo of "Cshebogar" before beginning lesson 4.<br>Equipment away and find a space.<br>  1. Run, skip, or slide around the instructional area.<br>  2. Travel using a slide or gallop (slide in forward direction) in time to the accompanying music. Play "Cshebogar."<br>  3. "Find a partner and make up a matching sequence of slide or gallop steps, moving in time to the music." | "Cshebogar," p. 596 | Repeat 1 to 3 with "Cshebogar." | Repeat 1 to 3 with new music (for dance in part 2). | Design your own lesson. |
| **Part 2: Dance Development**<br>*(20 to 35 minutes)*<br><br>Sliding<br>Hopping<br>Running<br>Shapes<br>—butterfly dance position | "Cshebogar":<br>Arrange class into a large single circle with partners facing, both arms extended sideward, and hands joined (butterfly dance position).<br>  1. Without music, demonstrate and practice the action movements.<br>  2. Repeat with music.<br>  3. Have children design their own clapping, slapping, or shaking routines.<br>  4. Have boys turn in place at the end of the dance with girls passing under boys' arms and on to the new partner.<br>  5. Ask children for suggestions relating to changing or adding to any part of the dance.<br>By this stage in the development of the initial dance unit, children should have developed confidence and a variety of dance skills. Hence, they should be interested in reviewing the following dances and/or improvising where desired.<br>  6. Review "A Hunting We Will Go."<br>  7. Review "Paw Paw Patch."<br>  8. Review "Jolly Is the Miller."<br>  9. Review "Shoo Fly." | Dance positions, p. 572 | Repeat 3 to 5.<br><br><br><br><br><br><br><br>Review one or two previous dances. | Introduce new dance from supplementary list, p. 601.<br><br><br><br>Review one or two previous dances. | |
| **Part 3: Closure**<br>*(1 to 2 minutes)*<br><br>Sliding | Discuss why a slide and a gallop are the same movements performed in different directions. | | | | |

**Level** II  **Unit 1:** Folk Dance  **Activity** Dance
**Lesson 5.** Bleking Step
**Main Theme** Bleking step
**Subthemes** Slide; Run
**Equipment** Recorder, tapes, or records

**Additional Lessons** If the class enjoys the challenge of learning a more complex step such as the bleking step-hop movement, select a schottische or tinikling dance from the intermediate section and see how well these children manage with more complicated dances.

| Content | Teaching Strategies | References | Lesson 5a | 5b | 5c |
|---|---|---|---|---|---|
| **Entry Activity** | Place a variety of small equipment in the containers. Free play with equipment to music. | | Repeat previous. | Repeat previous. | Repeat previous. |
| **Part 1: Introductory Activities** *(4 to 5 minutes)* | Equipment away and find a space.<br>1. Begin running in a variety of directions and listen for the next command—"skip, slide, hop, hop backward, hop sideward, run," etc. | Marching music | Repeat 1 and 2 with tinikling music. | Repeat lesson 5a. | Design your own lesson. |
| Slide<br>Run<br>Hop | | | | | |
| **Part 2: Dance Development** *(20 to 35 minutes)*<br><br>Bleking step<br>Butterfly dance position | "Bleking":<br>The bleking step is perhaps the most difficult step to be learned by this age range. Begin in a scattered position and teach this step to the whole class, then in partners, and finally in a group dance setting.<br>1. Without music, demonstrate and practice the bleking step. Repeat with musical accompaniment.<br>2. Partners facing each other in butterfly dance position. Practice dance step without music. Follow with musical accompaniment. Add the turning action without, then with, musical accompaniment. Arrange class into a large circle with partners facing. Partners extend arms sideward and join hands (butterfly position).<br>3. Without music, practice action movements of measures 1–8. Repeat with music.<br>4. Without music, practice action movements of measures 9–16. Repeat with music.<br>5. With music, repeat both parts of the dance.<br>6. Allow children to modify or add variations to the above dance.<br>7. Review two or more previous dances and encourage children to improvise or change each dance to suit their own interests and creative talents. | "Bleking," p. 594<br>Dance positions, p. 572 | Introduce tinikling, p. 608<br><br><br><br><br><br><br><br><br><br><br><br><br><br><br><br>Continue tinikling or review previous dances. | Repeat lesson 5a adding new steps or patterns.<br><br><br><br><br><br><br><br><br><br><br><br><br><br>Continue tinikling or review previous dances. | |
| **Part 3: Closure** *(1 to 2 minutes)*<br><br>Bleking step | Ask children if they enjoyed modifying their dances and to suggest ideas for future folk units. | | | | |

201

# Dance Activities
## Developmental Level II
## Unit 2: Creative Dance

## Expected Learning Outcomes

### Psychomotor Skills

1. Traveling in different directions, speeds, and levels
2. Moving different parts of the body in time to musical accompaniment
3. Performing individual, partner, and group dances
4. Performing static and moving shapes individually or in relationship to a partner or group of children

### Cognitive and Affective Knowledge and Skills

1. Ability to plan a variety of creative movement responses to a variety of stimuli
2. Ability to work with and share ideas with two or more children
3. Appreciation of the creative talents of other children
4. Understanding and appreciation of the limitations, feelings, and sensitivities of others
5. Understanding of a more complex and expressive movement vocabulary

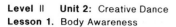

**Level** II  **Unit 2:** Creative Dance
**Lesson 1.** Body Awareness
**Main Theme** Individual parts, leading
**Subthemes** Quick and slow; Relationships—partner
**Equipment** Recorder, tape and/or records, individual ropes

**Additional Lessons** This lesson should open the door to several additional lessons. For example, the lesson could be repeated using an uneven rhythm and stressing skipping, galloping, and sliding with parts leading. The following illustrates an expansion of the main theme of this lesson.

| Content | Teaching Strategies | References | Lesson 1a | 1b | 1c |
|---|---|---|---|---|---|
| **Entry Activity** | Place individual ropes in containers. Free practice with ropes to music. | | Repeat previous. | Repeat previous. | Repeat previous. |
| **Part 1: Introductory Activities** *(5 to 6 minutes)* <br><br> Traveling—in different directions <br> Speed—quick and slow <br> Levels | *Note:* In previous game and gymnastic units children have learned various aspects of body awareness, qualities, space awareness, and relationships. Emphasis in these units was related to the utility of movement rather than on the expressive aspects. This unit will concentrate on the creative and expressive aspects through an expanded vocabulary of each movement element. Use the tambourine or drum. "Keeping in time to the beating of my tambourine (4/4 rhythm), run as lightly as you can and change direction and level." Vary the speed of the drum beats to enhance variations in movement. | Even rhythm, p. 572 <br> Uneven rhythm, p. 572 <br> Creative dance, p. 613 | Repeat introductory activity. | Repeat introductory activity. | Repeat lesson 1 using an uneven rhythmic accompaniment. |
| **Part 2: Theme Development** *(20 to 35 minutes)* <br><br> Traveling—in different directions, parts leading <br> Speed—quick and slow <br> Partner sequences | *Individual activities:* <br> Children of this age range are capable of developing movement sequences according to short phrases. Use a 4/4 meter (4 beats of the drum or 4 shakes of the tambourine) and develop two phrase sentences (tap, tap, tap, tap; tap, tap, tap, tap). <br> 1. "Make up a sequence of parts leading and a change of direction." Provide clarification, such as four running steps forward with right elbow leading, change to four jumps sideways with head leading. <br> 2. "On your tiptoes, creep slowly for three beats and freeze on the fourth beat." Beat three slow counts and call "freeze" on the fourth beat. <br><br> *Partner activities:* <br> Ask children to find a partner and a new space. <br> 1. Explain that they are to make up a dance (or sequence) in a follow-the-leader fashion. Their sequence should be built on two phrase movements such as four runs, four runs; four jumps, four jumps; four creeps, four creeps; etc. Allow time for practice before playing a 4/4 musical accompaniment (RCA Listening Activities, Vol. I. Bad Image, Hebert). After a few minutes of practice, let them listen to music to feel the beat. Repeat with children practicing their sequences. <br> 2. Continue partner activities adding, "You may change to side by side, facing, contrasting movements, or add your own ideas to your dance." | Phrases, p. 563 <br> Teaching elements of rhythm, p. 563 <br><br><br><br><br><br><br><br> Expressive words, p. 615 | Repeat 1 and 2 adding other elements, such as three runs, freeze; three creeps, freeze; three hops, freeze; three jumps, freeze. <br><br><br> Repeat 1 and 2. | Repeat previous lesson and add to challenge. "Change direction after each measure." <br><br><br><br><br> Repeat 1 and 2. | |
| **Part 3: Closure** *(1 to 2 minutes)* <br><br> Individual parts | Discuss the meaning of "phrase" or "movement" sentence. | | | | |

**Level** II **Unit 2:** Creative Dance
**Lesson 2.** Effort
**Main Theme** Quick and slow
**Subthemes** Strong and light; Shapes—twisted
**Equipment** Recorder, tapes and/or records, individual ropes

**Additional Lessons** The same situation exists with this lesson as with lesson 1. Design additional lessons stressing the four effort qualities and select 2/4 uneven musical accompaniments to encourage skipping, sliding, and galloping.

| Content | Teaching Strategies | References | Lesson 2a | 2b | 2c |
|---|---|---|---|---|---|
| **Entry Activity** | Place individual ropes and beanbags in the containers. Free practice with equipment to music. | | Repeat previous. | Repeat previous. | Repeat previous. |
| **Part 1: Introductory Activities** *(5 to 6 minutes)* <br><br> Traveling—different directions <br> Shapes—twisted <br> Speed—quick and slow | Equipment away and find a space. <br> 1. Use drum. "Run on your tiptoes, keep in time to the drum, and freeze into a twisted shape when I hit the drum with two loud bangs." Repeat several times. <br> 2. "Next time, without the drum beating, run quickly, leap into the air, and make a twisted shape, land and continue for three different shapes." <br> 3. Repeat 2, but land and slowly collapse onto the floor, then slowly back up and repeat the run and jump. | Traveling action words, p. 615 <br> Sample lesson plan, p. 617 | Repeat 1 to 3. | Repeat 1 to 3 using tambourine or other percussion instrument. | Design your own lesson. |
| **Part 2: Theme Development** *(20 to 35 minutes)* <br><br> Strength—whole and parts of body <br> Speed—quick and slow <br> Group sequence | 1. Find a new space, lie on your back with your eyes closed. Now clench one hand very tightly, relax. Continue with other hand, relax; both hands, relax; tighten one leg, relax; other leg, relax; whole body, relax. <br> 2. Clench and relax three parts in succession (example: right hand, right leg, whole body). <br> 3. Stand up and practice tightening facial muscles, hands, and stomach, and relax after each strong movement. <br> 4. Next, flick right hand sideward, upward, another way, and stop. Repeat several times. <br> 5. Make up a sequence of strong actions, quick movements, and collapsing the whole body. | Force action words, p. 615 | Repeat 3 to 5. | Repeat 3 to 5. | |
| Strength—strong and light <br> Speed—quick and slow <br> Shapes—twisted | Arrange the class into groups of three. <br> 1. "Make a group twisted shape with each person at a different level. When I beat the drum once, one person makes a slow and strong movement away from the group. Second beat number two moves and third beat number three moves. Return and repeat action." <br> 2. Ask group to practice moving strongly and slowly, then quickly and lightly back to a new twisted shape. Repeat two movements to drum or tambourine accompaniment. <br> 3. Ask groups of three to make up their own sequences that involve the combinations quick, slow, strong, and light. <br> 4. Ask children to make up their own dances to your selected musical accompaniment. | | Repeat 3 and 4. | Repeat 3 and 4 with new musical accompaniment. | |
| **Part 3: Closure** *(1 to 2 minutes)* <br><br> Strong and light | Ask children to suggest other types of musical accompaniments they would like to hear in a similar lesson (lesson 2a or 2b). | | | | |

**Level** II    **Unit 2:** Creative Dance
**Lesson 3.** Space
**Main Theme** Pathways
**Subthemes** Quick and slow; Shapes; Relationships
**Equipment** Individual ropes, recorder, and music

**Additional Lessons** By the end of the partner activities of this lesson, each teacher should have a good idea of the interest and creative ability of the class. If there is keen interest, begin with a brief introductory period, then move to the partner activities and stress similar elements.

| Content | Teaching Strategies | References | Lesson 3a | 3b | 3c |
|---|---|---|---|---|---|
| **Entry Activity** | Place individual ropes in the containers. Free practice with individual ropes. | | Repeat previous. | Repeat previous. | Repeat previous. |
| **Part 1: Introductory Activities** *(4 to 5 minutes)*<br><br>Traveling—different directions<br>Pathways<br>Speed—quick and slow | Ask children to take their individual ropes to a space and place the rope on the ground in any pattern they wish (straight, curved, etc.).<br>  1. "Travel around the space as quickly as you can. When you reach a rope, trace out its pattern and continue running."<br>  2. "Next time, travel quickly around the space and slowly when you trace out the pattern of each rope." | | Repeat 1 and 2. | Repeat 2. | Design your own lesson. |
| **Part 2: Theme Development** *(20 to 35 minutes)*<br><br>Pathways—curved, angular, zigzag, rounded<br>Levels<br>Speed—quick and slow | *Individual activities:*<br>Ask children to put away equipment and find a space. During this part of the lesson individual and partner activities will stress using pathways of movement (straight, round, curved, angular, and zigzag).<br>  1. Ask children to use their hands and trace out a curved pathway in the air, straight, round, and angular.<br>  2. "Show me how many other parts of your body you can trace out three or more different pathways."<br>  3. "Before I turn on the music, choose one or more individual parts you will trace out pathways and also think about showing three different levels." Play a musical accompaniment. | Pathways, pp. 39, 615<br>Music, p. 611 | Repeat 2 and 3. | Leave out. | |
| | *Partner activities:*<br>  1. "One partner teaches the sequence to the other, then reverse the procedure."<br>  2. "Between the two of you, make up a matching sequence, selecting parts from each other's sequence or build a brand new sequence." Allow a few minutes, then turn on music.<br>  3. "Make up a traveling sequence with your partner that includes pathways, quick and slow, and a change in level." Again, allow time for practice, then turn on the music. Choose one or two sequences for demonstration and discussion. By this stage in the creative dance unit, children should not only feel comfortable developing and performing movements, but should also feel at ease when discussing ideas, feelings, and movement patterns performed individually or in concert with others. | | Arrange in groups of three and repeat 1 to 3. | Arrange in groups of four and repeat 1 and 3. | |
| **Part 3: Closure** *(1 to 2 minutes)*<br><br>Pathways | Discuss how partners made up their matching segments. | | | | |

205

**Level** II **Unit 2:** Creative Dance
**Lesson 4.** Relationships
**Main Theme** Partners matching
**Subthemes** Shapes; Levels
**Equipment** Recorder and music, variety of small equipment

**Additional Lessons** If additional lessons are indicated, follow the pattern outlined below.

| Content | Teaching Strategies | References | Lesson 4a | 4b | 4c |
|---|---|---|---|---|---|
| **Entry Activity** | Place a variety of small equipment in the containers. Free practice with equipment to music. | | Repeat previous. | Repeat previous. | Repeat previous. |
| **Part 1: Introductory Activities** *(4 to 5 minutes)* <br><br> Traveling—flight <br> Shapes | Ask children to leave their equipment on the floor. <br> 1. "Travel and leap over equipment." <br> 2. "Travel, leap, make a shape, land, and continue." | | Repeat 1 and 2. | Repeat 1 and 2. | Design your own lesson. |
| **Part 2: Theme Development** *(20 to 35 minutes)* <br><br> Traveling <br> Levels <br> Shapes | *Partner activities:* <br> The emphasis in this part of the lesson should be directed to help each child critically observe and copy a partner's movements, moving in unison, and with both partners sharing in the dance experience. <br> 1. "With your partner, make up a sequence of traveling together, first low to the ground, then high in the air." Later add shape or a change of direction. <br> 2. "Can you add meeting and parting to the above sequence?" Select a few partners for demonstration. <br> 3. Ask children to find a new partner and a new space. "With your new partner, develop a new sequence that has part of each of your previous sequences plus a new idea to your new dance." | Words for relationships, pp. 615, 617 | Repeat 2 and 3. | Leave out. | |
| | *Group activities:* <br> Arrange class into groups of four. This is actually a continuation of partner activities. However, challenges should become more complex. More time should be allowed for groups to develop more quality of movement. <br> 1. "Make up a dance with a skip and slide, shapes, and near and far." <br> 2. Select one or two musical pieces and design five or six different task cards for the music. Allow groups to select their own task card. | Music, p. 619 | Repeat 2. | Repeat 2 rotating task cards among groups. | |
| **Part 3: Closure** *(1 to 2 minutes)* <br><br> Relationships | Discuss ease or difficulty of working in groups of four. | | | | |

**Level** II   **Unit 2:** Creative Dance
**Lesson 5.** Stimuli
**Main Theme** Partners in the forest
**Subthemes** Relationship; Traveling

| Teaching Strategies | References | Lesson 5a | 5b | 5c |
|---|---|---|---|---|
| *Note:* Since this lesson represents the closing phases of this unit, more time and effort can be devoted to this lesson. If we choose a story such as ''Partners in the Forest,'' it first requires two children to create their own story of an adventure in the forest (or swamp). The writing of this story can be a joint venture within the classroom. The teacher could indicate that a musical piece will be played during the floor practice period. Or, the teacher may allow each set to use percussion instruments to complement their dance. These details should be worked out and agreed upon by the class prior to moving to floor activities. | See text. Resource materials, p. 618 Stimuli, p. 617 | Design your own lessons. | Design your own lessons. | Design your own lessons. |

When the children come to the gymnasium, allow them to move directly into their own dance production. The teacher should visit each set of partners, assisting and encouraging where necessary.

Once children have had enough practice, allow each set to perform their dance for the class. Comments by the teacher or class should follow to show the dance was understood—some or all movements were well done, while others were in need of variation or improvement.

Other ideas that are appropriate for this age level are:
1. Interpreting poems.
2. Expressing things of nature—wind, storms, rain, etc.
3. Illustrating mechanical or animal themes.
4. Creating or expressing moods and feelings.

The success of ''Partners in the Forest'' should indicate whether one or more additional lessons are indicated. If this unit has been extended to about twelve lessons by the time you get to ''Partners in the Forest,'' even though the interest is high, perhaps it would be wise to move to another game or gymnastics unit in order to leave the dance unit with a very positive attitude. The next time you return to the creative dance area, children will be eager to continue and expand their dance experiences.

# Dance Activities
## Developmental Level III
## Unit 1: Rhythmics

**Expected Learning Outcomes**

**Psychomotor Skills**

1. Moving parts of body in time to musical accompaniment
2. Ability to move according to musical accent, tempo, and phrases
3. Ability to perform individual, partner, and group sequences involving locomotor and nonlocomotor skills with or without small equipment

**Cognitive and Affective Knowledge and Skills**

1. Understanding of rhythmic terminology
2. Ability to work with and share ideas with a partner or with a group of children
3. Appreciation of the creative talents and movement limitations of other students
4. Ability to create complex movement sequences in time to musical accompaniment

Evaluative Techniques: See chapter 9 for observational methods and evaluative tools to assess rhythmic skills and concepts.

**Lesson 1.** Underlying Beat
**Main Theme** Underlying beat
**Subtheme** Accent on first beat
**Equipment** Variety of small equipment; Recorder and tapes or records

**Additional Lessons** This lesson should normally be expanded to two or three lessons before progressing to lesson 2. The following lesson outline will therefore simply provide a guideline for one or more additional lessons.

| Content | Teaching Strategies | References | Lesson 1a | 1b | 1c |
|---|---|---|---|---|---|
| **Entry Activity** | Place a variety of small equipment in four containers. Free play with equipment to music. | | Repeat previous. | Repeat previous. | Repeat previous. |
| **Part 1: Introductory Activities** (*5 to 8 minutes*)<br><br>Moving hands and fingers in time to the underlying beat—clapping hands, slapping floor, snapping fingers | Ask students to put away equipment, find a space, and sit on the floor with their legs crossed. This is a good starting position to teach the underlying beat. Present the following challenges in a relaxed and easy manner.<br>*Without Music:*<br>1. Demonstrate clapping your hands together four times and repeat it three times (12 full beats). Ask children to copy you. Start with hands shoulder-width apart and say, "Ready—*one,* two, three, four; *one,* two," etc.<br>2. Repeat 1 with music. *<br>3. Demonstrate—clap hands four times, slap knees four times, and clap hands four times. Have children copy as you call out the count. Repeat with you only calling out "hands, knees, hands" and the four counts. Repeat with music.<br>4. Have children make up their own routine of clapping hands, slapping part of their bodies, and tapping the floor (with music).<br>*Note:* This challenge is particularly important since it is children's first opportunity to plan their own sequence. | Underlying beat, p. 562<br>Accent, p. 562<br>Measure, p. 562 | Repeat 4 with 4/4 music. | Repeat 4 with new 4/4 music. | Design your own lesson. |
| **Part 2: Skill Development** (*20 to 35 minutes*)<br><br>Matching movements in time to an underlying beat—clapping, tapping, snapping, shaking, locomotor movements, or twisting<br>Accentuating the first beat in a measure | *Partner activities:*<br>This part of the lesson is used to apply the skills learned in the previous section to partner and/or small equipment activities. Begin with partners sitting cross-legged and facing each other. Pose the following tasks.<br>*Without Music:*<br>1. "Make up a routine that includes clapping hands together in front, tapping the floor, and slapping knees." Repeat with music used in part 1.<br>2. "Develop a sequence that has clapping, tapping, shaking a part of your body, and a twisting movement." Explain four beats to a measure, accenting the first beat of each measure. Repeat with the above music.<br>3. Ask partners to stand and face each other. Ask partners to repeat 2. Later, add musical accompaniment.<br>4. Facing each other: "Design a stationary routine (stay in own space) that has marching, walking, running, hopping, and turning movements." | Routines, p. 563<br>Partners, p. 564 | Repeat 3 and 4. | Repeat 4, then add, "After you have developed your routine, you may now move anywhere in the available space." | |
| | *Group activities:*<br>5. This is basically a repeat of the above with four rather than two performers. Initially, allow "free" choice in forming groups. Later, once children feel comfortable, they may voluntarily move into mixed groups. Begin with 1 above, with four children sitting cross-legged and facing each other. Depending on enthusiasm, continue through above challenges of parts 1 and 2, modifying as necessary. | Group routines, p. 565 | Repeat 5. | Repeat 5. | |
| **Part 3: Closure** (*1-to 3 minutes*)<br><br>Underlying beat | Review underlying beat of 4/4 music. | | | | |

*Music: See chapter 29 for ideas relating to musical accompaniment. Use popular music with a good 4/4 meter.

**Level III** **Unit 1:** Rhythmics
**Lesson 2.** Accent
**Main Theme** Accenting the first beat
**Subthemes** Underlying beat; Measure
**Equipment** Variety of small equipment; Recorder, tapes, or record set

**Additional Lessons** If additional lessons are required, use the following outline.

| Content | Teaching Strategies | References | Lesson 2a | 2b | 2c |
|---|---|---|---|---|---|
| **Entry Activity** | Place a variety of small equipment in four containers. Free play with equipment to music. | | Repeat previous. | Repeat previous. | Repeat previous. |
| **Part 1: Introductory Activities** *(5 to 8 minutes)*<br><br>Locomotor movements in time to underlying beat<br>Accenting first beat of each measure | Equipment away and find a space. Present the following tasks, modifying each challenge to meet the needs, abilities, and interests of each class.<br>1. "Stay in your own space and develop a routine involving a walk, run, and a hop. Each step must be performed four times."<br>2. Repeat 1 and *accentuate* the first step of each measure.<br>3. Repeat 2 above with 4/4 musical accompaniment.<br>4. Repeat 3 above, and change direction of the first beat of each measure. | Accent, p. 562<br>4/4 rhythm, p. 562 | Repeat 4. | Repeat 4 with new musical accompaniment. | Design your own lesson. |
| **Part 2: Skill Development** *(20 to 35 minutes)*<br><br>Matching movements in time to an underlying beat<br>Accenting the first beat of each measure | *In partners*<br>Without music: "Stand side by side. Make up a new routine that has a walk, jump and hop, and a change of direction on the first beat of each measure. Do not go beyond sixteen measures." Repeat with 4/4 musical accompaniment. Pose the following challenge, then immediately turn on the 4/4 musical accompaniment. "Make up your own matching sequence of locomotor movements and show an accented movement on the first beat of each measure." Allow one or two partners to develop challenges for the class.<br>    In *small groups*, this part of the lesson is a continuation of the above involving three or more performers. By shifting to groups of four, it allows for "two boys to join up with two girls" or a similar command to maneuver boys and girls into a new group. Pose the following tasks (or write out task cards). Without music: "Begin with everyone facing the center of the group. Make up a routine that has a clap, slap, a locomotor movement on the spot, and a shaking action of the body." Allow time for practice, then play 4/4 musical accompaniment.<br>Without music: "Stand side by side or one behind the other. Design a sequence that has a walk, hop, jump, and a change in direction or level." After a few minutes, play the musical accompaniment.<br>"Make up your own matching sequence of locomotor movements and show an accented movement on the first beat of each measure."<br>"Make up a routine that begins in a cross-legged position and ends in the same position." | Matching movements, p. 564 | Repeat 1 and 2 with a new partner.<br><br><br><br>Repeat 1 to 4 in new groups of four. | Repeat 1 and 2 with new music.<br><br><br><br>Repeat 1 and 2 in new groups of four and with new music. | |
| **Part 3: Closure** *(1 to 2 minutes)*<br><br>Accent | Review accenting the first beat of the 4/4 meter. | | | | |

**Level III    Unit 1:** Rhythmics
**Lesson 3.** Even Rhythm.
**Main Theme** Moving to an even rhythm
**Subthemes** Underlying beat; Accent
**Equipment** Variety of balls, recorder, tapes or records, lummi sticks

**Additional Lessons** This lesson merits several supplementary lessons. Children of this age range enjoy lummi stick activities and can develop elaborate sequences. Use the following as a guideline.

| Content | Teaching Strategies | References | Lesson 3a | 3b | 3c |
|---|---|---|---|---|---|
| **Entry Activity** | Place a variety of small balls in the four containers. Free play with balls to music. | | Repeat previous. | Repeat previous. | Repeat previous. |
| **Part 1: Introductory Activities** (*5 to 6 minutes*)<br><br>Moving in time to a 4/4 even rhythm | Equipment away and find a space. Previous lessons have used 4/4 musical accompaniment to assist children in learning to understand and apply accent, underlying beats, and measures in their movement sequences. This lesson will help children learn to move to a 4/4 even rhythm.<br>1. "Once the 4/4 music begins, start traveling in any direction changing direction and locomotor movement on the first beat of *every measure.*" | Measure, p. 562 Underlying beat, p. 562 | Repeat 1 adding levels. | Change music and repeat 1. | Design your own lesson. |
| **Part 2: Skill Development** (*20 to 35 minutes*)<br><br>Tapping lummi sticks in time to a 4/4 even rhythm<br>Tapping and moving in time to a 4/4 even rhythm | The first few tasks should be individual challenges, starting in a cross-legged sitting position, moving to a standing position, then finally to locomotor movements while manipulating the lummi sticks.<br>*Individual tasks:*<br>1. "Make up a routine that includes tapping the floor, tapping sticks together, and tapping parts of the body." Use 4/4 even rhythm.<br>2. "Develop a standing routine, tapping the sticks in front, to the side, behind the back, and overhead." Use same record as 1.<br>*Partner tasks:*<br>3. "Ask partners to begin in a cross-legged position, tapping sticks in time to the music, and progress to standing, then to locomotor movements." | Lummi sticks, p. 567 Partner routines, p. 568 | Repeat 3. | Repeat 3 with new music. | |
| | *Group tasks:*<br>Arrange class in groups of three. At this point, challenges can include tapping, shaking, clapping, locomotor and nonlocomotor movements, plus three or more to a group. All these plus using 4/4 even rhythm. If teachers are developing rhythmic lessons for the first time, it is suggested that task cards be made to include the above tasks using the even rhythm. A few tasks are provided as examples.<br>4. "In your groups of three develop a sitting routine that includes a tap, slap, and shake." Use 4/4 music.<br>5. "In your group of three, begin in a standing position and develop a tapping sequence." | Task cards, p. 569 | Arrange in groups of four and repeat 4 and 5. | Repeat 4 and 5 in fours with new music. | |
| **Part 3: Closure** (*1 to 2 minutes*)<br><br>Even rhythm | Play three pieces of music (2/4, 3/4, 4/4) and see if children can say which meter is being used. | | | | |

211

**Level III  Unit 1:** Rhythmics
**Lesson 4.**  Uneven Rhythm
**Main Theme**  Moving to an uneven rhythm
**Subthemes**  Underlying beat; Change of direction
**Equipment**  Hoops, recorder, tapes or records

**Additional Lessons** At this stage in the rhythmic unit, children should be able to develop relatively complex and long routines. Each additional lesson should emphasize the uneven rhythm as well as stressing either the underlying beat, accent, pause, or measure.

| Content | Teaching Strategies | References | Lesson 4a | 4b | 4c |
|---|---|---|---|---|---|
| **Entry Activity** | Place hoops in the four containers. Free play with hoops to music. | | Repeat previous. | Repeat previous. | Change equipment and repeat. |
| **Part 1: Introductory Activities** *(5 to 6 minutes)* <br><br>Moving in time to a 2/4 uneven rhythm | Equipment away and find a space. The important rhythmic skill to acquire in this lesson is to move in time to an uneven rhythm. With 2/4 rhythm, the accent is on the first and third beat. Emphasis should be on the skip, slide, and gallop steps as they are performed to an uneven musical accompaniment. <br> 1. Without music, move sideways, changing direction and level. Repeat with music. <br> 2. Travel forward, keeping one foot the lead foot (gallop). <br> 3. "Design a snapping, twisting, shaking, and clapping sequence to the accompanying 2/4 musical accompaniment." | Uneven rhythm, pp. 563, 572 | Repeat 1 to 3. | Change music and repeat 3. | Design your own lesson. |
| **Part 2: Skill Development** *(20 to 35 minutes)* <br><br>Moving in time to a 2/4 uneven rhythm—while twirling or manipulating a hoop, while moving around or over the hoop | *Individual activities:* <br> Ask children to select a hoop, find a space, and wait for your first challenge. <br> *Note:*  All of the following routines may require a pause between each separate movement. <br> 1. Without music: "On how many different parts of your body can you twirl your hoop?" Look for elbows, neck, foot, and "other" parts. <br> 2. With 2/4 musical accompaniment: "See if you can twirl on one or two parts in time to the music." <br> 3. Without music: "Place the hoop on the floor and see if you can find three or more different ways of moving in and out, across, or around your hoop." <br> 4. Repeat 3 with music. <br><br> *Partner activities:* <br> 1. Put hoops on the floor and partners stand side by side next to their hoops. "Make up a matching sequence that has a clap, a shake, and moves in and out, across, or around your hoop(s)." <br> 2. Repeat adding a skip or gallop. (Play music.) <br> 3. Repeat adding a twirling action with a hoop. (Play music.) <br> 4. Design your own challenges emphasizing moving to an uneven rhythm. (Play music.) | Small equipment, p. 566 <br> Ropes, p. 566 | Repeat Partner and Group Activities | Change music and repeat Partner and group activities. | |
| | *Group activities:* <br> 1. Arrange class into groups of four. Each child has a hoop. Use task cards or develop a series of challenges similar to the above tasks, but involving four in each group. | Groups, p. 567 | Repeat 1, but as individual ropes. | Design new challenges for three in a group. | |
| **Part 3: Closure** *(1 to 2 minutes)* <br><br>Uneven rhythm | Review accenting on the first and third beat of a 2/4 meter. | | | | |

**Level** III   **Unit 1:** Rhythmics
**Lesson 5.** Tempo
**Main Theme** Moving quickly or slowly
**Subtheme** Underlying beat
**Equipment** Variety of balls, recorder, tapes, and records

**Additional Lessons** If there is sufficient interest and ability in the class, develop one or two additional lessons and increase the number within each group to five or six players. Spend a minimum of time with introductory and partner activities and allow a maximum amount of time for larger groups to develop their routines.

| Content | Teaching Strategies | References | Lesson 5a | 5b | 5c |
|---|---|---|---|---|---|
| **Entry Activity** | Place a variety of inflated balls in the four containers. Free play with balls to music. | | Change equipment and repeat previous. | Change equipment and repeat previous. | Change equipment and repeat previous. |
| **Part 1: Introductory Activities** *(4 to 5 minutes)* <br><br> Moving in time to an uneven rhythm <br><br> Moving in time to an increasing or decreasing tempo | Ask children to leave their balls on the floor. Present the following challenges. <br> 1. "Do not touch any ball as you travel around the areas . . . go." (Play 4/4 music.) <br> 2. "Change direction after jumping over a ball." (Play music.) <br> 3. "Travel sideways using a slide or crossover step." (Play music.) <br> 4. "Pick up a ball and bounce anywhere, changing direction, level, and speed." Use the same music. Begin with slow tempo and once routine is learned, begin to increase, then decrease tempo of music. | Tempo, p. 563 | Repeat 4. | Repeat 4. | Design your own lesson. |
| **Part 2: Skill Development** *(20 to 35 minutes)* <br><br> Ball bouncing and moving in time to an increasing and decreasing tempo | *Partner activities:* <br> 1. Partners stand facing each other, balls on the floor by their feet. "Make up a matching routine, without your ball, that has a clap, turn, and shake" (helps children pick up the rhythm and tempo of music). Use 4/4 music. <br> 2. Start facing each other and hold your ball with both hands. "Design a matching set of movements, but do not take your hands off your ball during the routine." Begin with a slow 4/4 musical accompaniment and gradually increase the tempo. <br> 3. "Begin standing side by side. Make up a matching routine of bouncing, traveling, and exchanging balls." Allow time for practice, then play a 4/4 musical accompaniment, gradually increasing, then decreasing speed as partners repeat their routine. <br> 4. Add change of direction, level, and other measurements such as clapping, turning, or shaking to your routine. <br> 5. Add one or two hoops to the routine. <br> 6. Design your own challenges stressing an increase or decrease in the tempo of the accompanying music. | Balls, p. 566 | Repeat 4 and 6. | Repeat 6. | |
| | *Group activities:* <br> Arrange one-half of the class into groups of three and the other half into groups of four. Use task cards or present challenges as listed below. <br> 1. Repeat 1 and 2 of part 2 in groups of three or four. <br> 2. Everyone faces the center. "Design a sequence of ball bouncing with a change in level and direction." Later add 4/4 musical accompaniment. Start with slow tempo, then change to a steady fast tempo; do not alter tempo again. <br> 3. Add hoops, pins, or traffic cones to the previous challenge. <br> 4. All performers must hold their ball with both hands throughout their routine. Design a routine similar to 2 in part 2. | Task cards, p. 569 <br> Groups, p. 566 | Repeat 1 and 2 in groups of five. | Repeat 1 and 2 in groups of six. | |
| **Part 3: Closure** *(1 to 2 minutes)* <br><br> Tempo | Discuss how tempo is used in different types of dances. | | | | |

**Level III   Unit 1** Rhythmics
**Lesson 6.** Phrase
**Main Theme** Movement ideas matching movement phrases
**Subthemes** Change of direction; Rope skipping
**Equipment** Balls, individual ropes, recorder, tapes, or records

**Additional Lessons** Additional lessons may be required to give children an opportunity to rotate the other stations to repeat the same task.

| Content | Teaching Strategies | References | Lesson 6a | 6b | 6c |
|---|---|---|---|---|---|
| **Entry Activity** | Place individual ropes in the four containers. Free practice with individual ropes to music. | | Change equipment and repeat previous. | Change equipment and repeat previous. | Repeat previous. |
| **Part 1: Introductory Activities** *(4 to 5 minutes)* <br><br> Matching movements to musical phrases <br> Locomotor skills <br> Change of direction | The routines developed by children in the previous lessons varied from two to over sixteen measures. The main focus of this lesson is to encourage children to complete a series of movements (movement phrase matches a musical phrase) before repeating them or before shifting to a new series of different movements. <br> 1. "Begin running for eight counts (2 measures), change direction, and run for another eight counts and continue." Repeat with 4/4 music. <br> 2. "Travel using a run, jump, hop, or leap, completing two measures of each step before shifting to a new step." Repeat with 4/4 music. <br> 3. "Develop a routine that is performed in a series of four measure phrases (example: 16 walking steps, change to 16 jumping steps, etc.), that uses a run, jump, and hop, and shows a change of direction." | Phrases, p. 563 <br> Locomotor skills, pp. 43, 579 | Repeat 3. | Design your own lesson. | Design your own lesson. |
| **Part 2: Skill Development** *(20 to 35 minutes)* | *Individual activities:* <br> 1. Ask children to select an individual rope, find a space, and practice the two-foot basic, alternate step, and one other rope skipping skill. <br> 2. "Make up a routine using eight counts (2 measures) for each step." Repeat with musical accompaniment. <br> 3. "Place the rope on the floor and in a straight line. Design a sequence moving back and forth over your rope." Repeat with a 4/4 musical accompaniment. <br> 4. "Repeat above using the same locomotor skill for two measures (8 counts)." <br> 5. Shifting to a new locomotor skill. <br> *Partner activities:* <br> 6. Repeat 3 to 5 with partners matching movements. <br> 7. Explain you are going to play the same music. "This time, make up your own partner sequence showing a rope skipping step, a twirling action of the rope, and a change in direction." | Matching movements, p. 566 | Repeat 3 to 5. | | |

| Content | Teaching Strategies | References | Lesson 6a | 6b | 6c |
|---|---|---|---|---|---|
| Matching movements to musical phrases | *Group activities:*<br>The basic format of this part of the lesson may be used for the next two or three lessons, modifying challenges and musical accompaniment where desired.<br>8. Divide the class into three groups and assign the following task(s), then play the same 2/4 musical accompaniment for all three challenges.<br>Group no. 1: "Make up a sequence of jumping movements performed in sets of three measure phrases."<br>Group no. 2: "Develop your own routine showing two different jumping movements, a pause, a change of direction, and a change in level."<br>Group no. 3: "Design your own rope skipping routine." | Groups, p. 567 | Rotate groups and repeat challenges. | | |

**Part 3: Closure**
*(1 to 2 minutes)*

Phrases — Ask children what they enjoyed and disliked in this unit. Also, ask for suggestions for the next rhythmic unit.

# Dance Activities
## Developmental Level III
## Unit 2: Creative Folk Dance

---

**Expected Learning Outcomes**

**Psychomotor Skills**

1. Ability to perform locomotor and nonlocomotor movements in time to even and uneven musical accompaniment
2. Ability to move in different directions and pathways
3. Ability to move through a variety of movement designs as a single performer or with two or more performers
4. Ability to dance in and through a variety of dance formations

**Cognitive and Affective Knowledge and Skills**

1. Understanding of the elements of folk dance
2. Appreciation of the feelings and sensitivities of others
3. Appreciation of the individual differences of other students
4. Ability to plan complex dance sequences involving the five elements of folk dance

Evaluative Techniques: See chapter 9 for observational methods and evaluative tools to assess folk dance concepts and skills.

**Level** III  **Unit 2:** Creative Folk Dance
**Lesson 1.** Steps
**Main Theme** Moving to even and uneven rhythm
**Subthemes** Change of speed; Change of level
**Equipment** Individual ropes, recorder, tapes, or records

**Additional Lessons** If students in your class have been taught a series of rhythmic lessons, additional lessons may not be necessary. However, if the class is lacking in the type of rhythmic experience, one or two more lessons stressing steps may be indicated.

| Content | Teaching Strategies | References | Lesson 1a | 1b | 1c |
|---|---|---|---|---|---|
| **Entry Activity** | Place individual ropes in containers. Free play with individual ropes to music. | | Repeat previous. | Repeat previous. | Repeat previous. |
| **Part 1: Introductory Activities** *(5 to 8 minutes)* <br><br> Traveling—to even rhythm <br> Change of tempo | Ask children to put equipment away and find a space. Explain you are going to play a tape (record) and the class is to move according to your directions. Select a good popular tune (4/4 meter) or a march and play a few measures before you give the following commands. <br> 1. "Listen for the beat and begin walking in any direction." <br> 2. As children are walking, add "change to hopping, change to running, change to jumping." Continue pattern. <br> 3. "Make up your own routine of three steps, changing from one to the other every four beats." | 4/4 rhythm, p. 562 Elements of folk dance steps, p. 579 Lesson, p. 581 | Repeat 2 and 3 with new music. | Repeat 2 and 3 with new music. | Design your own lesson. |
| **Part 2: Theme Development** *(20 to 35 minutes)* <br><br> Traveling—to even rhythm, to uneven rhythm <br> Change of level <br> Nonlocomotor movements— clapping, twisting, shaking | *Partner activities:* <br> (Use task cards if desired.) <br> 1. "Make up a matching sequence with your partner that includes a run, hop, jump, and two changes of level." Allow a few minutes for children to develop their sequence, then play the same 4/4 musical accompaniment used above. <br> 2. "Design a routine standing side by side and include a skip, slide, and gallop." Use 2/4 musical accompaniment. <br> 3. "Develop a matching routine that includes a run, hop, clap, and slap." Use 4/4 musical accompaniment. | Task cards, p. 569 Steps, p. 579 | Repeat 2 with new music. | Repeat 3 with new music. | |
| | *Group activities:* <br> Arrange class into groups of four and present the following challenges. <br> 1. "Make up a matching routine that includes a walk, run, hop, and change of level." Allow time for practice before playing the above 4/4 musical accompaniment. <br> 2. Repeat the challenge adding shaking, twisting, or clapping to the challenge. <br> 3. Without music, "Make up a marching routine that includes a run, jump, hop, skip, and slide." Use 2/4 musical accompaniment. <br> 4. Explain you are going to play a "new" record and they can develop their own routine to match the music. (Teacher selects a 2/4 or 4/4 musical accompaniment, but do not tell children the meter.) | | Repeat 4 with new music. | Repeat 4 with new music. | |
| **Part 3: Closure** *(1 to 2 minutes)* <br><br> Steps | Review how the four locomotor skills (walk, run, hop, and jump) use an even rhythm. Play a waltz and illustrate how this even rhythm is also used with these steps. | | | | |

**Level** III  **Unit 2:** Creative Folk Dance
**Lesson 2.** Directional Movement
**Main Theme** Directional movement
**Subthemes** Moving to even and uneven rhythm; Change of speed
**Equipment** Individual ropes, recorder, tapes, or records

**Additional Lessons** With the addition of the second element of folk dance, the potential variety of individual, partner, or group routines is significantly increased. The following outline will provide a guideline for teachers wishing to complete one or more additional lessons before progressing to lesson 3.

| Content | Teaching Strategies | References | Lesson 2a | 2b | 2c |
|---|---|---|---|---|---|
| **Entry Activity** | Place individual and long ropes in containers. Free practice with long or short ropes to music. | | Repeat previous. | Repeat previous. | Repeat previous. |
| **Part 1: Introductory Activities** *(5 to 6 minutes)*<br><br>Directional movements<br>Steps<br>Tempo | Equipment away and find a space.<br>1. "Listen to the 4/4 music we played yesterday (or in the previous lesson), then walk for four counts, change to a run for four counts, to a hop, to a jump."<br>2. Repeat above sequence and change direction with each new step.<br>3. Repeat 2 with the teacher increasing the tempo of the music.<br>4. Repeat 2 adding a change in level to the challenge.<br>5. Design additional challenges stressing forward, backward, sideward, and diagonal directions. | Directional movements, p. 580<br>Steps, p. 579<br>Lesson, p. 581 | Repeat 1 to 3. | Repeat 1 to 3 with new music. | Design your own lesson. |
| **Part 2: Theme Development** *(20 to 35 minutes)*<br><br>Directional movements<br>Steps<br>Level | *Partner activities:*<br>Arrange the class into new sets of partners (different from lesson 1) and present the following tasks.<br>1. Repeat 2 above with partners standing side by side. Use new 4/4 musical accompaniment.<br>2. "Make up a matching sequence that includes a run, hop, two changes of direction, clap, and shake." Use previous 4/4 musical accompaniment.<br>3. "Begin with one standing behind the other. Create a sequence that includes a skip, slide, moving sideways and diagonally, and a change in level." Use a new 2/4 musical accompaniment.<br><br>*Group activities:*<br>1. "See if you can make up a routine that includes one locomotor skill performed to an even musical accompaniment and three changes of direction." Use above 4/4 musical accompaniment (in groups of three).<br>2. In groups of three, repeat 3 of partner activities using the same musical accompaniment.<br>3. In groups of four, repeat 3 of partner activities using the same musical accompaniment.<br>4. Allow children in groups of three or four to write out their own task cards emphasizing directional movements and one or more other elements. Children also like to bring their own musical accompaniment to complement their dance composition. | | Repeat 2 and 3.<br><br><br><br><br><br><br><br><br><br><br><br>Repeat 2 and 3 in new groups of three. | Repeat 2 and 3 with new music.<br><br><br><br><br><br><br><br><br><br><br>Repeat 2 and 3 in groups of four with new music. | |
| **Part 3: Closure** *(1 to 2 minutes)*<br><br>Directional movements | Review different directional movements. | | | | |

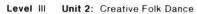

**Level** III    **Unit 2:** Creative Folk Dance
**Lesson 3.** Pathways
**Main Theme** Pathways of movement
**Subthemes** Steps; Directional movements
**Equipment** Individual ropes, recorder, tapes, or records

**Additional Lessons** This third element of pathways provides further variety for children, thus it may indicate the desirability of developing one or two additional lessons stressing pathways before progressing to lesson 4. Develop supplementary lessons according to the format shown in lesson 3.

| Content | Teaching Strategies | References | Lesson 3a | 3b | 3c |
|---|---|---|---|---|---|
| **Entry Activity** | Place individual ropes and hoops in containers. Free play with equipment to music. | | Repeat previous. | Change equipment and repeat. | Change equipment and repeat. |
| **Part 1: Introductory Activities** (5 to 6 minutes) | Equipment away and find a space. *Without music.* | Pathways, p. 580 | Repeat 1 to 3. | Repeat 1 to 3 with new music. | Design your own lesson. |
| | 1. "Travel anywhere in the playing area and show three changes of direction." | | | | |
| Pathways | 2. "Continue traveling and add three changes in the type of locomotor movements." | | | | |
| Directional movements | 3. "Run straight ahead, change to traveling in a curved pathway, then to a | | | | |
| Steps | zigzag movement pattern." | | | | |
| **Part 2: Theme Development** (20 to 35 minutes) | *Partner activities:* | Curved and zigzag pathways, p. 580 | Repeat 2 and 3. | Repeat 2 and 3 with new music. | |
| | 1. "Make up a matching routine that includes a walk, run, jump, and hop, moving in a curved and zigzag pathway." Use 4/4 musical accompaniment. | | | | |
| Pathways | 2. "Develop a sequence with your partner that has a skip and slide, a change in direction, and two changes in pathways of movement." Use a 2/4 musical accompaniment. | | | | |
| Directional movements | | | | | |
| Steps | 3. "Tie two individual ropes together, then make a straight, curved, or zigzag pattern with the rope on the floor. Now, develop a follow-the-leader routine involving locomotor movements and twisting and shaking." Play 4/4 music as they are developing their routines. | | | | |
| | *Group activities:* | | Repeat 1 and 2. | Repeat 1 to 3 with new music. | |
| | Arrange class into groups of three to five. Allow children to choose the size and the constitution of each respective group. Present the following challenges to the class. | | | | |
| | 1. "The music will be a musical accompaniment with an uneven rhythm. Listen to the music, then make up a routine starting in a cross-legged position, then include a shaking movement, a skip or slide, and two pathways of movement." | | | | |
| | 2. Repeat 1 and add "moving forward and backward." | | | | |
| | 3. Allow children to design challenges for the class. | | | | |
| **Part 3: Closure** (1 to 2 minutes) | | | | | |
| Pathways | Review different types of pathways of movement. | | | | |

**Level** III    **Unit 2:** Creative Folk Dance
**Lesson 4.** Relationships
**Main Theme** Dancing positions and movement designs
**Subthemes** Steps; Directional movements; Pathways
**Equipment** Individual ropes, hoops, beanbags, recorder, tapes, or records.

**Additional Lessons** One or two more lessons are clearly indicated here to introduce other folk dance positions and a few other movement designs. These additional lessons should emphasize contacting a partner in a variety of dance positions.

| Content | Teaching Strategies | References | Lesson 4a | 4b | 4c |
|---|---|---|---|---|---|
| **Entry Activity** | Place individual ropes, hoops, and beanbags in containers. Free practice with equipment to music. | | Repeat previous. | Change equipment and repeat. | Repeat previous. |
| **Part 1: Introductory Activities** (4 to 5 minutes)<br><br>Pathways<br>Steps<br>Directional movements | Equipment away and find a space. Without music:<br>1. "Travel around playing area showing a change in steps, pathways, and direction."<br>2. "Travel in curved and zigzag pathways and show a change in level as you travel." | | Repeat previous. | Change equipment and repeat. | Repeat previous. |
| **Part 2: Theme Development** (20 to 35 minutes)<br><br>Dance position<br>Movement designs<br>Steps<br>Directional movement<br>Pathways | *Partner activities:*<br>*Note:* Students should have progressed to a point where arranging in partners would normally mean a boy and a girl, rather than both of the same sex. Since dance positions such as promenade and closed or open positions require partners to be touching each other, a relaxed atmosphere is extremely important. The following challenges encourage this type of atmosphere and appreciation of each partner's role in the dance pattern.<br>1. "Make up a routine with your partner traveling side by side, using a run, jump, and hop, and two changes of direction."<br>2. "Design a sequence that involves a skip and slide step, turning your partner using one and two hands, and passing your partner without touching."<br>3. Repeat 2 with a 4/4 musical accompaniment.<br>4. Demonstrate three folk dance positions. Next, pose the challenge, "Make up a routine that includes a walk, hop and run, and two dance positions." Add directional movements and pathways as indicated. Use familiar 4/4 musical accompaniment.<br>5. "Create a sequence with your partner that has a walk, hop and jump, meeting and parting, and one partner turning the other." Use same music as in 4.<br><br>*Group activities:*<br>Arrange class into groups of four by saying, "Join up with the nearest pair and find a new space."<br>1. Teach each other the routine developed in 5 above.<br>2. Demonstrate starring and weaving and another dance position. Ask groups of four to incorporate starring and weaving into a new routine that also includes a skip and a slide step.<br>3. Allow each group of four to design their own dance to a 4/4 musical accompaniment. Allow children to hear the music as they develop their own sequence of movements. | Dance position, p. 572<br>Movement designs, pp. 574, 581<br><br><br><br>Starring and weaving, p. 577 | Repeat 4 with a new dance position.<br><br><br><br><br><br>Repeat 3. | | |
| **Part 3: Closure** (1 to 2 minutes)<br><br>Relationships | Review different types of dance positions. | | | | |

220

**Level** III  **Unit 2:** Creative Folk Dance
**Lesson 5.** Formations
**Main Theme** Formations
**Subthemes** Steps; Directional movements; Pathways; Shapes
**Equipment** Variety of small equipment, record player, tapes, records

**Additional Lessons** Children should be able to create a dance involving all the basic elements in a very short time period and usually with a lot of enjoyment. Additional lessons should involve groups of six or eight performers to allow children an opportunity to create more intricate dance formations, shapes, and pathways of movement.

| Content | Teaching Strategies | References | Lesson 5a | 5b | 5c |
|---|---|---|---|---|---|
| **Entry Activity** | Place individual ropes, hoops, beanbags, and braids in containers. Free practice with equipment to music. | | Repeat previous. | Repeat previous. | Repeat previous. |
| **Part 1: Introductory Activities** (3 to 5 minutes)<br><br>Steps<br><br>Pathways | Equipment away and find a space.<br>1. "Travel, using a run and a leap and show a change of direction, pathway, level, and speed."<br>2. Repeat 1 with a brisk march (4/4 meter).<br>3. Play a current popular tune and ask the class to develop their own routine to the musical accompaniment. | | Repeat 3. | Design your own lesson. | Design your own lesson. |
| **Part 2: Theme Development** (20 to 35 minutes)<br><br>Steps<br>Directional movement<br>Pathways<br>Dance positions<br>Movement designs<br>Formations | *Partner activities:*<br>*Note:* Prior to beginning this lesson, students should understand the basic dance positions and movement designs that are part of the folk and square dances of this age group. Additional emphasis should also be given these skills during this lesson. Proficiency and ease of performance of these skills provide a strong base for children to dance with each other in a natural and informal manner. The following challenges will reinforce this, as well as emphasize using a variety of dance formations.<br>1. Use the music from 3. "Make up a dance sequence with your partner that includes a shoulder-waist dance position, turning your partner, and two changes of direction."<br>2. Repeat, adding levels, near and far, and/or other elements of dance. | Pathways, p. 580<br>Dance positions, p. 572 | Repeat 1 and 2. | | |
| | *Group activities:*<br>Arrange class into groups of four by joining up pairs from above or creating an entirely new group of four children.<br>1. "Using a walking step, make up a dance that is performed from a square formation, then changes to a circle, and finally to a line formation." Allow a few minutes for practice, then play a 4/4 musical accompaniment.<br>2. "Develop a dance from a line formation and show a skip and slide, a weave, and swinging another performer."<br>3. Develop a set of task cards for 2/4 or 4/4 musical accompaniments and allow groups to choose their own card.<br>4. Permit groups of four to develop their own dances. | Formations, p. 581 | Repeat 1 in groups of six. | | |
| **Part 3: Closure** (1 to 2 minutes)<br><br>Formations | Review different types of dance formations. | | | | |

# Dance Activities
## Developmental Level III
## Unit 3: Folk Dance

### Expected Learning Outcomes

**Psychomotor Skills**

1. Ability to perform tinikling, schottische, polka, two-step, and waltz step in time to musical accompaniment
2. Ability to perform a variety of folk dances with ease and with a quality of movement

**Cognitive and Affective Knowledge and Skills**

1. Understanding of the steps and movement patterns of a variety of folk dances
2. Appreciation of the cultural heritage of folk dances
3. Appreciation of the feelings and sensitivities of other children
4. Ability to modify folk dance activities or create new versions of traditional dances

Evaluative Techniques: See chapter 9 for observational methods and evaluative tools to assess folk dance concepts and skills.

**Level** III  **Unit 3:** Folk Dance
**Lesson 1.** Tinikling Step
**Main Theme** Tinikling step
**Subthemes** Directions; Shapes
**Equipment** Tinikling poles, recorder, and music

**Additional Lessons** Two or more lessons are required to introduce the various tinikling steps. The following outline will illustrate how to add each new step.

| Content | Teaching Strategies | References | Lesson 1a | 1b | 1c |
|---|---|---|---|---|---|
| **Entry Activity** | Place individual ropes, hoops, and beanbags in the containers. Free practice with equipment to music. | | Repeat previous. | Repeat previous. | Repeat previous. |
| **Part 1: Introductory Activities** (6 to 8 minutes)<br><br>Steps—walk, run, hop<br>Directional movements<br>Dance positions<br>Movement designs | Equipment away and find a space.<br>1. Without music: "Travel anywhere about the playing area changing direction and speed."<br>2. "Begin walking three steps forward, change direction and run three steps, change direction and hop three steps." Continue pattern of walk, run, and hop.<br>3. Repeat 2 with tinikling music (3/4 even meter). | Teaching folk dance, p. 577<br>Tinikling music, p. 610 | Repeat 2 and 3. | Repeat 3. | Repeat 3. |
| **Part 2: Dance Development** (20 to 35 minutes)<br><br>Tinikling steps—side stepping, straddle stepping, forward and back step<br>Directional movements | *Individual activities:*<br>The tinikling step is performed to a 3/4 even waltz meter with a distinct strike, tap, tap rhythm throughout the dance. The performer steps on each of the three beats in each measure.<br>1. Without music, demonstrate side step. Follow immediately with demonstration of side stepping to musical accompaniment played at normal dance tempo.<br>2. Individual practice of side stepping step in own space. Follow with music played at slightly slower tempo. After a little practice, gradually increase the tempo. | Tinikling steps, p. 608 | Repeat side step; introduce straddle step. | Repeat side and straddle steps; introduce forward and back. | Introduce matching routines including two different steps, change of direction, and near and far. |
| | *Group activities:*<br>Arrange class into groups of three or four. The size of group will depend upon the number and length of tinikling poles.<br>1. Without music, demonstrate side stepping to rhythm and movement of tinikling poles. Follow with musical accompaniment.<br>2. Individual practice without, then with, musical accompaniment. Rotate pole tappers with dancers after each practice sequence.<br>3. With music, repeat side stepping and try to add a change in hand position, foot action, or directional movement. | Tinikling steps, p. 608 | Repeat above in groups of four. | Repeat above in groups of four. | Repeat above in groups of four. |
| **Part 3: Closure** (1 to 2 minutes)<br><br>Tinikling step | Discuss the cultural background of this dance: Philippine folk dance depicting the movements of the long-legged, long-necked tinikling bird, similar in appearance to the flamingo. | | | | |

**Level III  Unit 3:** Folk Dance
**Lesson 2.** Schottische Step
**Main Theme** Schottische step
**Subthemes** Tinikling step; Pathways; Relationships
**Equipment** Recorder and music, tinikling poles

**Additional Lessons** Once the basic schottische step has been learned, gradually introduce turns and other directional movements as illustrated below.

| Content | Teaching Strategies | References | Lesson 2a | 2b | 2c |
|---|---|---|---|---|---|
| **Entry Activity** | Place tinikling poles and blocks in instructional area. Turn music on for free practice of tinikling steps. | | Repeat previous. | Repeat previous. | Repeat previous. |
| **Part 1: Introductory Activities** (*5 to 6 minutes*) | Equipment away and find a space. | | Repeat 1 and 3. | Repeat 1 to 3. | Repeat 4. |
| | 1. "Make up a sequence of tinikling steps in time to musical accompaniment." | | | | |
| | 2. Add a change of direction and level to the previous challenge. | | | | |
| Tinikling step | 3. Add a clap, slap, twist, or change in speed to previous challenge. | | | | |
| Directional movements | 4. Allow children to make up their own sequences. | | | | |
| **Part 2: Dance Development** (*20 to 35 minutes*) | *Individual activities:* The schottische step is a combination of three brisk walking steps followed by a hop. This step is normally performed with a 4/4 meter. | Schottische step, p. 573 | Repeat 4 adding ladies' turn. | Repeat 4 adding both turn. | Repeat 4 adding Wring the Dishrag. |
| Schottische steps | 1. Without music, demonstrate the basic schottische step (step, step, step, hop). Follow immediately with a demonstration to musical accompaniment. | | | | |
| Pathways—curved, zigzag, straight | 2. Individual practice in own space. Follow with musical accompaniment played at a slightly slower tempo. Within a few moments, gradually increase tempo to normal dance speed. | | | | |
| Dance positions | 3. "See if you can schottische around the instructional area and change pathways when I call out a new pattern . . . curved, zigzag, straight," etc. | | | | |
| | *Partner activities:* | | | | |
| | 1. In couple position, make up a sequence using the schottische step and trace out two pathways of movement. Play music as soon as the couples begin to plan their sequence. | | | | |
| | 2. Repeat above adding "include two other dance positions in your sequence." | | | | |
| | *Group activities:* Arrange class into a double circle with partners facing counterclockwise. | Schottische dance, p. 601 | Repeat 1 introducing ladies' turn. Repeat 2. | Repeat 2 introducing both turn. Repeat 2. | Repeat 2 introducing Wring the Dishrag. Repeat 2. |
| | 1. Without music, perform schottische step for six measures. Repeat with music for remainder of record. | | | | |
| | 2. Arrange class into groups of four. "Can you make up your own schottische dance with four dancers?" After a few minutes, select one or two successful groups to demonstrate to the rest of the class. Have other groups try a new dance. | | | | |
| | 3. Select one or two group dances and see if they can be performed by "fours" in a large circle similar to the original schottische dance. | | | | |
| **Part 3: Closure** (*1 to 2 minutes*) | | | | | |
| Schottische step | Discuss and illustrate different dance positions that couples can use when dancing the schottische step. | | | | |

**Level** III  **Unit 3:** Folk Dance
**Lesson 3.** Two-Step
**Main Theme** Two-Step
**Subthemes** Schottische step; Shapes; Directions
**Equipment** Recorder and music

**Additional Lessons** Additional lessons should include a variety of traditional schottisches and two-step dances as well as an opportunity to improvise or modify these dances by the children.

| Content | Teaching Strategies | References | Lesson 3a | 3b | 3c |
|---|---|---|---|---|---|
| **Entry Activity** | Play a new schottische dance tune. As children arrive, ask them to get into groups of four and practice the schottische dance steps. | | Repeat previous. | Repeat previous. | Repeat previous. |
| **Part 1: Introductory Activities** <br> *(4 to 5 minutes)* <br><br> Schottische step | As soon as everyone is ready, ask class to quickly form a double circle. Repeat one or two schottische dances performed in previous lesson. | | Repeat 1. | Repeat 1. | Design your own lesson. |
| **Part 2: Dance Development** <br> *(20 to 35 minutes)* <br><br> Two step <br> Directional movements <br> Dance positions <br> Formations | *Individual activities:* <br> The two-step is a combination of a step, close, step, pause with the lead foot changing on each new measure. <br> 1. Without music, demonstrate the basic two-step in a forward direction. Follow immediately with a demonstration to musical accompaniment. <br> 2. Individual practice in own space. Follow with musical accompaniment played at a slower tempo. Within a few moments increase tempo to normal dance speed. <br> 3. "See if you can move forward, then backward, sideways, diagonally," etc. <br><br> *Partner activities:* <br> 1. "Begin in an open dance position and practice moving forward, backward, and sideways. Wait a few minutes, then play the accompanying music. <br> 2. Repeat above in closed and open dance positions. <br><br> *Group activities:* <br> The two-step is similar to the schottische step in that both require boys and girls to join hands to perform the dance movements. A few subtle "directions" and "arrangements" will not only contribute to an improvement in skill development but will also provide an opportunity for boys and girls to experience a variety of positive interpersonal relationships. Arrange class in a double circle formation with girls forming the inside circle and facing counterclockwise. Boys on outer circle facing clockwise. <br> 1. "When music begins, walk forward until the music stops. As soon as it stops, turn and face your new partner." From this point, play music and allow children to dance the two-step. Let each couple choose their own dance position or call out the position before the dance begins. <br> 2. "When the music stops, exchange partners with the nearest couple." Repeat dance with same music. <br> 3. Change musical accompaniment and continue dancing. <br> 4. Arrange class into groups of four. "Can you make up your own dance that includes a two-step, a square formation, and two changes of direction?" <br> 5. Repeat, changing the requirements of the dance. <br> *Note:* Allow groups to demonstrate their dances to the class. | Two-Step, p. 574 <br> Dance positions, p. 574 <br><br><br><br><br><br><br><br><br><br><br><br> Oklahoma Mixer, p. 607 | Repeat 1. <br><br><br><br><br><br><br><br><br><br><br><br> Repeat 4. | Repeat 1 and 2. <br><br><br><br><br><br><br><br><br><br><br><br> Repeat 4 and 5. | |

| Content | Teaching Strategies | References | | | |
|---|---|---|---|---|---|
| | | | Lesson 3a | 3b | 3c |

**Part 3: Closure**
*(1 to 2 minutes)*

Two-Step — Discuss and illustrate different directions that can be performed with the two-step.

**Level III    Unit 3:** Folk Dance
**Lesson 4.** Polka Step
**Main Theme** Polka step
**Subthemes** Two-step; Tinikling step
**Equipment** Tinikling poles, record player, and music

**Additional Lessons** Additional lessons should stress dances involving the polka step. Check references for new polka dances. Each supplementary lesson should also include a tinikling, schottische, or two-step dance. At this stage children will enjoy variety in each dance lesson.

| Content | Teaching Strategies | References | Lesson 4a | 4b | 4c |
|---|---|---|---|---|---|
| **Entry Activity** | Arrange tinikling equipment throughout the instructional area. Ask children to form groups of three or four and practice their tinikling skills. Play a familiar tinikling tune. | | Repeat previous. | Repeat previous. | Practice schottische in partners. |
| **Part 1: Introductory Activities** (4 to 5 minutes)  Tinikling step | As soon as everyone is ready, ask class to arrange themselves into groups of four with four poles. "Make up your own tinikling dance involving four poles." Equipment away and move on to part 2. | Tinikling, p. 608 | Repeat 1. | Design your own lesson. | Design your own lesson. |
| **Part 2: Dance Development** (20 to 35 minutes)  Polka step  Slide step  Directional movements | *Individual activities:*  The polka step is a combination of a step, close, step, hop, with the lead foot changing on each new measure. This step is usually performed in a sideways direction created by an alternating series of body turns. The polka can also be performed in a forward or backward direction.  1. Without music, have children begin facing the center, then take short sliding steps around the area. At any time and on the hopping phase of the slide, turn to face the outside. Continue changing, sliding, and changing direction.  2. Without music, demonstrate the basic polka step in a sideways direction. Follow immediately with a 2/4 musical accompaniment.  3. Individual practice moving around the instructional area. Add music after a few minutes of practice.  4. Brief demonstration of the polka step forward and backward.  5. Individual practice forward and backward, with musical accompaniment.  *Partner activities:*  In partners, "Try the polka step in a facing and a closed dance position." Allow time for practice before turning on the music.  *Group activities:* circle with girls on boys' right sides.  1. Demonstrate basic steps and movements of Heel-Toe Polka.  2. Have class walk through steps and movements.  3. Dance Heel-Toe Polka to musical accompaniment.  4. Ask class to suggest modifications or variations. Or, divide class into two separate groups and ask each to modify the dance and later to demonstrate their new version to the other group.  5. Arrange class into groups of four or five children. Ask groups to make up their own dance including a polka step and one or more dance elements. | Polka step, p. 574  Facing and closed dance positions, p. 575  Heel-Toe Polka, p. 607 | Repeat 2 to 3.  Repeat 3 and 5. | | |
| **Part 3: Closure** (1 to 2 minutes)  Polka step | Discuss the similarities and differences between the polka and the two-step. | | | | |

**Level** III    **Unit 3:** Folk Dance
**Lesson 5.** Waltz Step
**Main Theme** Waltz step
**Subthemes** Schottische step; Polka step
**Equipment** Record player and music

**Additional Lessons** At the end of the lesson children should be reasonably competent in performing the four main combined steps used in the upper elementary dance program. Additional lessons should stress the waltz step but also include other steps and dances to provide variety.

| Content | Teaching Strategies | References | Lesson 5a | 5b | 5c |
|---|---|---|---|---|---|
| **Entry Activity** | Ask children to practice the schottische step with a partner as soon as they enter the instructional area. Turn on music and give assistance where necessary. | | Repeat previous. | Practice tinikling steps. | Practice waltz step. |
| **Part 1: Introductory Activities** *(4 to 5 minutes)*<br><br>Polka step<br>Directional movements | As soon as everyone is present, ask the class to keep the same partners but change music to a polka record.<br>1. "Polka with your partner using a facing or closed dance position."<br>2. Repeat polka step and add "moving forward, backward, and sideways." | | Repeat 1 and 2. | Design your own lesson. | Design your own lesson. |
| **Part 2: Dance Development** *(20 to 35 minutes)*<br><br>Waltz step—waltz walk, waltz balance, waltz step<br>Dance positions<br>Directional movements | *Individual activities:*<br>The waltz step is a series of three walking steps with the weight changing to alternate feet on each beat (step, step, close).<br>1. Without music, demonstrate and practice the waltz walk. (Take a step forward on left foot, followed by step forward and right, then left foot closes to right foot (step, step, step). Individual practice walking forward, then backward, adding a change of direction where space permits. Later with music.<br>2. Repeat procedure of 1 with the waltz balance (step forward on left foot, then step in place on left foot; step forward, step in place, step in place).<br>3. Repeat procedure of 1 with the waltz step (step forward and left with a slightly longer step, step, sideward with right foot, step, and close left to right foot).<br><br>*Partner activities:*<br>1. In partners: "Make up a dance sequence that includes a waltz walk and a waltz step."<br>2. Add "two changes of direction" to the above challenge.<br>3. Add a "change in dance position" to the above challenge.<br><br>*Group activities:*<br>Arrange class in a double circle formation with boys in the center and facing the girls on the outside circle.<br>1. Without music, demonstrate the Rye Waltz.<br>2. Repeat above with music.<br>3. Ask class to suggest modifications or variations. Or, divide class into two separate groups and allow each group to create their own variations of this dance. Later, have each group demonstrate their own dance version to the other. | Waltz step, p. 573<br>Dance positions, p. 574<br><br><br><br><br><br><br><br><br><br><br><br><br><br><br><br><br><br><br>Rye Waltz, p. 607<br>Supplementary dances, p. 609 | Repeat 1 to 3.<br><br><br><br><br><br><br><br><br><br><br><br><br><br><br><br><br><br><br><br>Norwegian Mountain March, p. 604 | | |
| **Part 3: Closure** *(1 to 2 minutes)*<br><br>Waltz step | Ask children to suggest ideas for the next folk dance unit. | | | | |

# Dance Activities
## Developmental Level III
## Unit 4: Creative Dance

### Expected Learning Outcomes

**Psychomotor Skills**

1. Traveling in different speeds, directions, and levels
2. Moving with variations in strong and light movement
3. Ability to perform a variety of creative movement responses to different stimuli (sounds, poetry, film, etc.)
4. Ability to perform a variety of individual, partner, and group creative dance activities

**Cognitive and Affective Knowledge and Skills**

1. Ability to plan a variety of relatively complex movement responses to a variety of different stimuli
2. Ability to work and share ideas with two or more children
3. Appreciation of the creative talents and limitations of other children
4. Understanding and appreciation of the feelings and sensitivities of others

Evaluative Techniques: See chapter 9 for observational methods and evaluative tools to assess creative dance concepts and skills.

**Level III Unit 4:** Creative Dance
**Lesson 1.** Turning and Stopping
**Main Theme** Turning and stopping
**Subthemes** Quick and slow; Shapes; Relationships
**Equipment** Variety of small equipment, tambourine, recorder, and music

**Additional Lessons** In most cases it is wise to plan the next two supplementary lessons with quite a bit of detail. After lesson 1b, more freedom can be given to each part of the lesson.

| Content | Teaching Strategies | References | Lesson 1a | 1b | 1c |
|---|---|---|---|---|---|
| **Entry Activity** | Place a variety of small equipment in the containers. Free practice with equipment to music. | | Repeat previous. | Repeat previous. | Repeat previous. |
| **Part 1: Introductory Activities** *(5 to 6 minutes)*<br><br>Traveling—in different directions<br>Speed—quick and slow<br>Shape—twisted | Equipment away and find a space. Use a tambourine and vary the speed of shaking throughout the following challenges. Explain that you want everyone to move in time to your shaking and "freeze" into a twisted shape when you bang twice on the tambourine.<br>1. "Run, change direction and speed." Tap twice.<br>*Note:* Introduce words such as scurry sideways, dash to the corners, and others such as flee, skate, spring.<br>2. "Run, and when I bang the tambourine, leap in the air and make a twisted shape." Continue the shaking and banging rhythm of your tambourine. | Vocabulary for creative dance, p. 615<br>Teaching strategies, p. 614 | Repeat 1 and 2. | Repeat 2, changing shapes each time you bang tambourine. | Design your own lesson. |
| **Part 2: Theme Development** *(20 to 35 minutes)*<br><br>Traveling—turning, stopping<br>Relationships—match, following<br>Shapes<br>Change of speed | *Individual activities:*<br>Ask class to move to their own space. Discuss turning and stopping and make up a list of synonyms for each word. For example: turning—spin, whip, whirl; stopping—freeze, hold, settle.<br>1. Without musical accompaniment, "Make up a sequence (or use the word dance) that moves from a spin to a freeze to a spin." Allow time for practice, then have the class move to your shaking and double tapping of the tambourines. | Vocabulary, p. 615 | | | |
| | *Partner activities:*<br>1. Have each partner teach the other a sequence. Follow this by having partners create a new dance either mirroring or following the other. Once learned, select one or two for demonstrations.<br>2. Select a musical accompaniment. Explain you are going to let the music play while each pair creates a dance showing turning and stopping, quick and slow, and variations in shape. Allow sufficient time for practice. Stress should be toward quality of movement rather than variety for its own sake. | | Repeat 1. Find new partners and repeat 2. | Repeat 1 with a new partner. | |
| | *Group activities:*<br>Most of the partner activities from above should now be expanded to groups of three or more children.<br>1. Ask one set of partners to join with another set close by. "Show each other your sequence, then decide if you can incorporate each into one larger dance or design an entirely new dance."<br>2. Play a new musical accompaniment and ask groups of four to make up their own dance. | | Repeat 1 and 2. | Repeat 2—develop a new dance. | |
| **Part 3: Closure** *(1 to 3 minutes)*<br><br>Sequence building | Ask children to explain how each set of partners developed their own sequence. | | | | |

**Level** III    **Unit 4:** Creative Dance
**Lesson 2.** Speed and Effort
**Main Theme** Combining quick and slow with strong and light
**Subthemes** Pounce and creep; Shapes; Relationships
**Equipment** Individual ropes, drum, and a variety of percussion instruments

**Additional Lessons** As children become more competent and interested in developing their own dances, more time should be devoted to group activities. Wherever possible, allow children to create their own dances stressing the main theme and optionally selecting one or more subthemes.

| Content | Teaching Strategies | References | Lesson 2a | 2b | 2c |
|---|---|---|---|---|---|
| **Entry Activity** | Place individual ropes in the containers. Ask class to practice skipping to music. | | Repeat previous. | Repeat previous. | Repeat previous. |
| **Part 1: Introductory Activities** *(4 to 5 minutes)* <br><br> Traveling—different directions <br> Speed—quick and slow <br> Effort—strong and light | Leave the rope on the floor in any pattern you like. Use a drum for the musical accompaniment. <br> 1. "Run and leap over any rope." Continue pattern. <br> 2. "Keep in time as I beat the drum and run and dodge around the ropes." Vary the tempo of the drum beat from very fast to extremely slow. <br> 3. Repeat 2 adding, "Move quickly and lightly as I beat the drum with a light and rapid tempo; move slowly and sustained with a heavy and sustained beating." | Tempo, p. 563 | Repeat 1 to 3. | Repeat 1 to 3 using tambourine. | Design your own lesson. |
| **Part 2: Theme Development** *(20 to 35 minutes)* <br><br> Traveling—in different ways <br> Speed—quick and slow <br> Effort—strong and light | *Individual activities:* <br> Put equipment away and find a space. Discuss the meaning of the words pounce and creep. Pounce should express a very strong, powerful, and quick movement such as "the leap of the lion onto its prey" or "the sudden and strong swooping and clawing action of an attacking eagle." Creeping on the other hand should depict a slow, quiet, sneaky type of movement. <br> 1. "How can you show a pounce type action?" Watch for children moving from feet to hands or from hands to hands. Allow time for demonstrations. <br> 2. "Show me a slow, sneaky, creeping action." Select one to demonstrate. <br> 3. "Design a sequence that has a creep, pounce, and roll." Allow time for practice, then say you will beat the drum quickly: one strong and heavy beat followed by quick beats. "Match your sequence to the drumming action." <br><br> *Partner activities:* <br> 1. "Join up with a partner and find a new space." Explain they can move together or in another way. Show how two predators can work together in creeping toward and pouncing upon their prey. <br> 2. Repeat the above dance to the same drum accompaniment. <br> 3. Ask partners to make up a dance that clearly shows creeping and pouncing. | Strength of movement, p. 615 <br> Vocabulary, p. 615 | Repeat 1. | Repeat 3. | |

231

| Content | Teaching Strategies | References | Lesson 2a | 2b | 2c |
|---|---|---|---|---|---|
| | *Group activities:*<br>Arrange the class into groups of four children. List words under four headings. Write down two or three words under each heading, asking the class to suggest other words. Then, pose the following challenge.<br>1. "In your group of four, select one word from each column, then put the words together to make up your dance." Give each group one percussion instrument and explain they must make up their own musical accompaniment. | Homemade percussion instruments, Appendix B, p. 636 | Repeat 1 in new groups of four. | Repeat 1 in groups of three. | |

| *Quick* | *Slow* | *Strong* | *Light* |
|---|---|---|---|
| shake | creep | flop | flick |
| quiver | slither | plunk | float |
| wiggle | | | glide |

*Note:* Allow sufficient time for group demonstrations. Also, encourage the class to comment on each dance, pointing out positive aspects as well as constructive criticism or suggestions to improve the dance.

## Part 3: Closure
*(1 to 2 minutes)*

Effort
Discuss and illustrate strong and light movements with individual parts of the body.

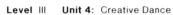

**Level** III **Unit 4:** Creative Dance
**Lesson 3.** Levels
**Main Theme** Shifting levels of movement
**Subthemes** Pathways; Shapes
**Equipment** Hoops, recorder, and music

**Additional Lessons** If additional lessons are desired, follow the suggested procedure described below.

| Content | Teaching Strategies | References | Lesson 3a | 3b | 3c |
|---|---|---|---|---|---|
| **Entry Activity** | Place hoops in containers. Free practice with the hoops to music. | | Repeat previous. | Repeat previous. | Repeat previous. |
| **Part 1: Introductory Activities** (*4 to 5 minutes*) <br><br> Traveling—run, hop, skip <br> Level <br> Speed—quick and slow | Ask children to place the hoops on the floor. <br> 1. "Begin running around as many hoops as possible. As soon as you circle the first hoop, change to a skip. Circle the second hoop, changing to a hop." Continue pattern. <br> 2. Repeat 1, adding a change in level with each change in locomotor skill. <br> 3. Repeat 2, adding a change in speed with each change in locomotor skill. <br> *Note:* If desired, use a musical accompaniment for each of the above challenges. | Levels, pp. 39, 615 | Repeat 1 to 3 using individual ropes. | Repeat 1 to 5 using wands. | Design your own lesson. |
| **Part 2: Theme Development** (*20 to 35 minutes*) <br><br> Traveling <br> Levels—high, medium, low <br> Pathways <br> Shapes | *Individual activities:* <br> Ask children to pick up a hoop and find a space. <br> 1. To emphasize shape, pathway, and level, pose the following challenge. "Design a sequence of changing the level of your hoop as you trace out three different pathways." <br> 2. Review meaning of phrases. Let children listen to music, then ask them to adjust their sequences to the phrases of the musical accompaniment. After a few minutes, select two different children for demonstrations. Let each child explain his or her sequence and the length of each phrase. <br><br> *Partner activities:* <br> 1. "Develop a dance in which you are both in contact with one hoop throughout your dance. The dance should continue with level as a main theme. "Add other subthemes as you desire. Put hoops away!" <br> 2. "Make up a sequence with your partner that includes shape, level, and pathway." <br> 3. Design your own dance with levels as the central theme. <br><br> *Group activities:* <br> Arrange class into groups of five children. Design a series of tasks such as the three examples provided below. <br> *Note:* The challenges on each card are different; however, the musical accompaniment is the same for all tasks. Pass out or allow children to select their own task cards. <br> Task no. 1: "In your group of five, design a dance using five hoops and show levels and shapes." <br> Task no. 2: "From the list of words provided below, select three or four and design a dance around these words." | Phrases, p. 563 <br> Pathways, pp. 39, 580, 615 <br> Shapes, pp. 37, 615 | Repeat 1 and 2 using individual ropes. <br><br><br><br><br><br><br><br><br><br><br><br><br> Rotate groups and repeat. | Repeat 1 and 2 using wands. <br><br><br><br><br><br><br><br><br><br><br><br><br> Rotate groups and repeat. | |

| *Pathways* | *Levels* | *Shapes* |
|---|---|---|
| curved | high | knarled |
| zigzag | control | arrowlike |
| straight | deep | bent |

233

| Content | Teaching Strategies | References | Lesson 3a | 3b | 3c |
|---|---|---|---|---|---|
| | Task no. 3: "Make up a dance that has a main theme of levels and a strong supporting theme of pathways." | | | | |
| | *Note:* Allow time to discuss the musical accompaniment and how they can build their movements to complement the music. Continue playing the music as they practice their dance sequences. Also, provide time for each group to perform their dance. | | | | |
| **Part 3: Closure**<br>*(1 to 2 minutes)* | | | | | |
| Levels | Ask children to suggest new words for high, medium, and low. | | | | |

**Level** III   **Unit 4:** Creative Dance
**Lesson 4.** Meeting and Merging
**Main Theme** Meeting, merging, and clashing
**Subthemes** Quick and slow; Strong and light
**Equipment** Individual ropes, variety of small equipment, variety of percussion instruments

Additional Lessons Continue to follow the previous suggestions if one or more additional lessons are desired.

| Content | Teaching Strategies | References | Lesson 4a | 4b | 4c |
|---|---|---|---|---|---|
| **Entry Activity** | Place individual ropes in the containers. Free practice with ropes to music. | | Repeat previous. | Design your own lesson. | Design your own lesson. |
| **Part 1: Introductory Activities**<br>*(3 to 5 minutes)*<br><br>Traveling | Equipment away and find a space.<br>   1.  Play a shadow game.<br>   2.  Repeat game changing locomotor skill—only hopping, sliding, etc. | Shadow game (p. 35 of this guide) | Repeat 1 and 2. | | |
| **Part 2: Theme Development**<br>*(20 to 35 minutes)*<br><br>Traveling<br>Shapes<br>Speed—quick and slow<br>Effort—strong and light | *Individual activities:*<br>Ask children to find a space and sit down. Discuss developing phrases involving approach, dodging, freezing, and fleeing. For example: run, run, run, freeze, run, run, run, freeze; or forward, forward, forward, stop, backward, backward, backward, freeze.<br>   1.  "Make up a sequence involving three of the following words: approach, clash, merge, retreat, spin, flee, freeze, avoid, and together."<br>   2.  "Add an expressing gesture of the hands and face as you perform the previous sequence." | Phrases, p. 563<br>Words, p. 615<br>Strength, pp. 175, 615<br>Relationships, pp. 41, 581 | Repeat 1 and 2. | | |
| | *Partner activities:*<br>In partners, "Make up a sequence that begins joined together, separate from each other, return, clash, and spin away." | | Repeat 1 to 4. | | |
| | *Group activities:*<br>Arrange class into groups of three.<br>   1.  One of the three performers uses a percussion instrument to provide the musical accompaniment for the partner activity above. Rotate each performer and repeat the same dance sequence.<br>   2.  Select three new words and develop a new dance with one playing the percussion instrument and all performing the dance. In this case the person playing the instrument is also part of the dance.<br>   3.  Allow each group to use hoops, ropes, or wands and develop a new dance emphasizing clashing and retreating.<br>   4.  Rearrange class by having one group of three join up with another group of three. Make up a dance that shows each group of three remaining as a separate group within the new larger group of six. The dance must stress groups meeting, merging, and separating. | Homemade percussion instruments, Appendix B, p. 636 | | | |
| **Part 3: Closure**<br>*(1 to 2 minutes)*<br><br>Meeting and merging | Discuss how each group developed their musical accompaniment for their dance. | | | | |

**Level III  Unit 4:** Creative Dance
**Lesson 5.** Poetry and Movement
**Main Theme** Expressing words and feelings
**Subthemes** Quick and slow; Strong and light
**Equipment** Tambourine, drums

**Additional Lessons** The last challenge of group activities will require one additional lesson. If interest persists, try one or two additional poems in lessons 5b and c.

| Content | Teaching Strategies | References | Lesson 5a | 5b | 5c |
|---|---|---|---|---|---|
| | *Note:* Poems are an excellent stimulus for creative dance activities. However, reading a poem line by line and requiring the class to individually and in concert with others provide specific interpretations of the poet's thoughts is not a productive and creative exercise. During class time, such as within a language arts lesson, discuss the meaning and mood of the poem. From this point, select action words used in previous lessons to express some of the thoughts or moods of the poem. Another approach is to select words from the poem or moods of the poem, or to select words from the poem that could be expressed through creative movements performed alone, with another performer, or as part of a large group dance. The poem "Witches" by Linden Miracles is selected to illustrate how it is used as a major stimulus in a creative dance lesson. | | Design your own lesson. | Design your own lesson. | Design your own lesson. |
| | Some of the most movement stimulating words selected from the poem should be:<br>slinking      soaring      flittering      streaming<br>suddenly    zooming     swooping    fading | | | | |
| **Part 1: Introductory Activities**<br>*(3 to 5 minutes)*<br><br>Traveling<br>Speed—quick and slow | Equipment away and find a space.<br>1. Travel anywhere and express "zooming, suddenly, and slinking." Watch for a few moments, then select one or two for demonstrations. Repeat pattern.<br>2. Add "soaring" to the challenge. | | | | |
| **Part 2: Theme Development**<br>*(20 to 35 minutes)*<br><br>Shapes<br>Traveling<br>Effort<br>Speed<br>Relationships | *Individual activities:*<br>Ask children to find a new space. Discuss the grotesque features of a witch—facial features, strange posture, knarled hands, deformities, etc.<br>1. "Make a twisted and knarled witchlike shape. Now, creep toward your victim (slinking), then slither away." Use tambourine or drum for appropriate musical accompaniment.<br>2. "Run, leap, and make a grotesque shape and facial expression, land, and repeat sequence." Use a drum or tambourine.<br>3. "Make up a sequence expressing slinking, crackling, fading; or soaring, flittering, streaming."<br><br>*Partner activities:*<br>1. Develop a double witch dance showing matching shapes, traveling, and scaring the intended victim.<br>2. Design other challenges for partner-type dances. This includes encouraging partners to create their own challenges.<br><br>*Group activities:*<br>Arrange the class into groups of four, five, or six children.<br>1. Ask each group to select four action words from the poem and develop these into a dance sequence.<br>2. Give each group a new poem (do this during class time) and ask them to express the mood of the poem through dance, or to select certain action words and repeat the procedure of 1. | Words, p. 615 | | | |
| **Part 3: Closure**<br><br>Stimuli | Ask children what they enjoyed and disliked about this unit. Ask for suggestions for future creative dance units. | | | | |